DESIGNING PARADISE

THE ALLURE OF THE HAWAIIAN RESORT

DESIGNING

Paradise

THE ALLURE *of the* HAWAIIAN RESORT

DON J. HIBBARD

photographs by AUGIE SALBOSA

PRINCETON ARCHITECTURAL PRESS

Published by

PRINCETON ARCHITECTURAL PRESS

37 East Seventh Street

New York, New York 10003

For a free catalog of books, call 1.800.722.6657.

Visit our web site at www.papress.com.

EDITING: Linda Lee

ACQUISITIONS EDITING: Mark Lamster

DESIGN: Sara E. Stemen

SPECIAL THANKS TO: Nettie Aljian, Dorothy Ball, Nicola Bednarek,
Janet Behning, Becca Casbon, Penny (Yuen Pik) Chu, Pete Fitzpatrick,
Russell Fernandez, Jan Haux, Clare Jacobson, John King, Nancy Eklund Later,
Katharine Myers, Lauren Nelson, Scott Tennent, Jennifer Thompson,
Paul Wagner, Joseph Weston, and Deb Wood of Princeton Architectural Press
—Kevin C. Lippert, publisher

IMAGE CREDITS: All contemporary images courtesy of Augie Salbosa. All historic
images courtesy of Hawaii State Archives except as noted. National Atlas of the
United States (base map), viii; Bishop Museum, 17; Hawaii Visitors Bureau and
Convention Center, 85, 152 left; Mauna Kea Beach Hotel, 102, 105; Private collection,
6, 28, 29, 37, 42 bottom left, 47 top, 48, 53, 56, 58 top right, 58 bottom right, 61 top
left, 61 right, 66, 67 bottom, 68, 72–74, 81, 82, 84, 88, 90–93, 98, 113, 117, 124, 152
right, 153; Ossipoff, Snyder & Rowland Architects, Inc., 75; Wimberly, Allison, Tong,
& Goo, 54, 71, 78, 79, 94, 96, 97; Ginger Winger, 42 top right, 42 bottom right.

LIBRARY OF CONGRESS CATALOGING-IN-PUBLICATION DATA

Hibbard, Don.

    Designing paradise : the allure of the Hawaiian resort / Don J. Hibbard ;
photographs by Augie Salbosa.

    p. cm.

Includes bibliographical references and index.

ISBN 1-56898-574-6 (hardcover : alk. paper)

    1. Resort architecture—Hawaii. 2. Architecture—Hawaii—20th century.
3. Tourism—Hawaii—History. I. Salbosa, Augie. II. Title.

NA7820.H53 2006

728'.509969—dc22   2005030579

"From dreams the islands grow to realities, then fade to dreams again."

MABEL CLARE CRAFT, FROM *HAWAII NEI*, 1899

This book is dedicated to the lovely lady by the lake.

CONTENTS

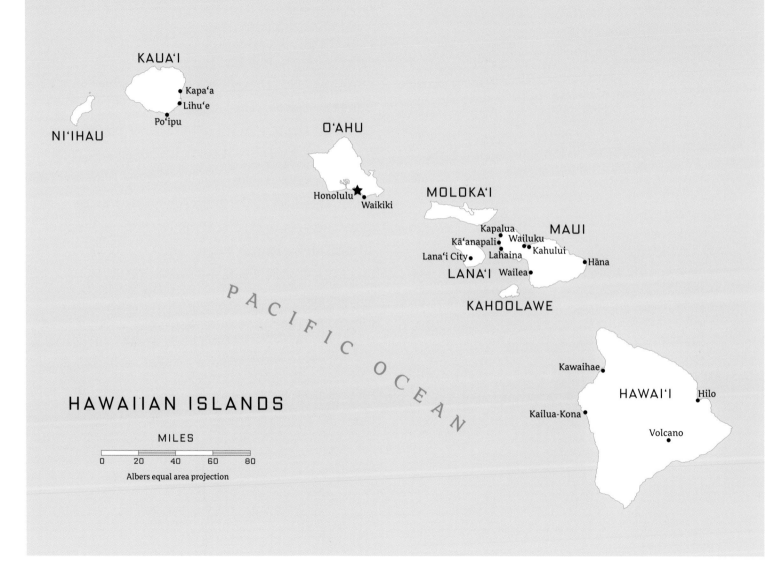

KAUA'I

Kapa'a
Lihu'e
Po'ipu

NI'IHAU

O'AHU

Honolulu
Waikiki

MOLOKA'I

Kapalua
Wailuku
MAUI
Kā'anapali
Kahului
Lana'i City
Lahaina
Hāna
Wailea
LANA'I

KAHOOLAWE

Kawaihae
HAWAI'I
Hilo

PACIFIC OCEAN

HAWAIIAN ISLANDS

Kailua-Kona

Volcano

MILES

0   20   40   60   80

Albers equal area projection

INTRODUCTION

"THE HAWAIIAN ISLANDS define paradise," opens the section "Tourism in Hawaii" in *Ke Kumu, Strategic Directions for Hawaii's Visitor Industry* (2002). This seemingly simple statement acknowledges as fact an image that two hundred years of traveler accounts and advertising have ingrained in the universal mind. Throughout the years, promoters of Hawai'i have promised prospective visitors nothing less than the best life has to offer—paradise. Based largely on the islands' having perhaps the least variable temperate climate on the globe, this utopian assurance has been affirmed by exhilarating descriptions and views of abundant and exotic flora, splendid beaches, and stunning blue skies and waters. Offering a vivid contrast to harsher, more extreme climes to the north and the south, such depictions have been augmented through personifications of a warm hospitality embodied by the spirit of aloha and the lei, as well as the sensuality of the hula and bathing beauties. Couple this with a blissful separation from all the continents and their bustle of activity—as well as extraordinary notions of surfing and benign volcanoes—and a sense of paradise readily emerges.

It is no coincidence that Hawai'i and the vision of paradise are so deeply entwined. Brought to the attention of the West at a time when the philosophy of the Enlightenment was catalyzing such events as the American and French revolutions, the Hawaiian Islands stepped upon the international stage in an era preoccupied by visions of a better world. Rather than be content with enduring life in expectation of a glorious afterlife, humanity strove to improve its experience in the here and now. For the nineteenth century, these tiny, remote islands in the Pacific Ocean romantically held out the hope that a surcease to sorrow might be possible in this lifetime. They offer the same for the twenty-first century; for despite the great strides made in the past few hundred years, the epiphany of heaven on earth has yet to materialize. Hawai'i's resorts continue to embody a mythos, and for many, they are as near as a person can get to attaining the age-old dream of paradise.

The beauty, charm, friendliness, simplicity, and comfort of Hawai'i serve as the lure that has called and recalled countless millions to its shores and caused a multitude to sing its praises. Such is the essence of life in the islands. Such beneficence is real, and although many of its aspects may be elusive and even intangible, they can be expressed architecturally. At their best, the islands' resorts are like a kiss, or to use the words of the author Tom Robbins, they are "a concretized expression of an emotional state," an affirmation of utopia, a heaven momentarily accessed for those with the economic means. An early 1990s matchbook cover for the Four Seasons Maui at Wailea well articulated this mindset. The cover rhetorically inquired, "Why travel so many hours and spend so much money to be in Hawai'i?" The inside responded, "Because you deserve it." Taking this thought one short step further, one pundit noted, "Hawai'i is not a state of mind, but a state of grace."

It is this state of grace that the finest resort hotels of Hawai'i embody. Culturally rich in their own right and sights to behold, these architecturally magnificent scripted spaces portray the convictions of society. By encapsulating special holiday experiences, they translate psychic sensations into forms their guests can readily recall. Their adroit designs celebrate the graciousness of Hawai'i through their glorious, free-flowing relationship between indoor and outdoor, augmented by sumptuously landscaped grounds.

This book chronicles the history of visitor accommodations in the Hawaiian Islands, from the modest taverns of the nineteenth century to the majestic hotel designs to follow, and the forces and motivations that shaped their formation. It describes and explains, and in the process articulates the background and context for these remarkably stunning developments. The nuts and bolts of intricate technologies and layouts necessary to make a hotel operate smoothly, although fascinating, are ignored. Instead, the volume looks at the images conveyed by the hotels, the beauty they extol.

The opening chapters briefly trace the development of hotels and the travel industry in Hawai'i. They offer a glimpse at the considerably different circumstances with which travelers of yore were confronted when encountering the islands. They reveal the changes that have transpired in the past one hundred and fifty years in travel and disclose the foundations and slowly emerging consciousness leading to the development of Hawai'i's highly successful travel industry. From this base, the book focuses primarily on the development of resort hotels over the past forty-five years, especially on the neighbor islands of Kaua'i, Maui, Lāna'i, and Hawai'i.

With over 660 hotels currently operating in Hawai'i, this excursion chooses to scrutinize only those buildings and projects that have contributed in a major way to Hawai'i's pioneering and leading role in the development of tropical destination resorts and to those that have made enduring statements through their architecture. It looks at the crème de la crème that has emerged in an era of democratized travel, when the ability to journey to distant places no longer denotes a life of leisure and affluence. The hotels presented separate themselves from the norm by their emphasis on a more refined travel experience. These are the nicest of the nice. Through these hotels, the book recounts the story of tourism in Hawai'i and allows the reader to look at Hawai'i's best hotel design to garner not only a sense of the beauty but also the evolution of tropical resort-hotel concepts.

Hawai'i is a mecca for the travel industry. Travel industry professionals flock to Hawai'i, for here they can observe not only what succeeds, but also what does not. The success of Hawai'i as a travel destination has allowed Honolulu design and planning firms to be important players in the globalization of the tourism industry. Thanks to the experiences garnered at home, these architects and planners have transcended the tiny islands' shores to leave a mark upon the world.

THE JOURNEY LEADING to the book you now casually hold in your hands has fortunately been a smooth one, thanks to the assistance of many friendly people. It commenced with a series of vaguely related, not quite serendipitous, but certainly fortuitous, events. Work on another book, *The Buildings of Hawai'i*, an as-yet-not-published architectural guidebook destined to be a part of the Society of Architectural Historians' fifty-plus volume compendium, *The Buildings of the United States*, was an initial catalyst. Site visits and research led to the realization that over the past four decades, resort hotel development has produced the most impressive and compelling modern architecture to emerge in the islands. A session on resort architecture at the Society of Architectural Historians Annual Meeting in 2003, chaired by Margaret Supplee Smith, provided an opportunity to coalesce such nascent thoughts. It also brought forth intimations of the pioneering role the islands have played in the development of modern resort planning and architecture. I profusely thank Peggy for not only providing an initial venue for my ideas, but also serving as a promoter between myself and Mark Lamster of Princeton Architectural Press. Her continued encouragement and support throughout the development, researching, and writing of the book has been indispensable. Peggy, *mahalo nui loa* for your supreme confidence, patient listening, and sage advice.

The editors at Princeton Architectural Press are also due a LARGE thank you. Mark Lamster started the ball rolling, and Linda Lee saw the project to completion, all the while dreaming of surfing magnificent waves without a wetsuit. Mark, thank you for your support of the project and convincing others of its worthiness; Linda, thank you for your diligent patience, grand command of the English language, facile avoidance of pitfalls, and magical transcendence of the impossible. You are a true worker of miracles. Also a bouquet of appreciation is extended to Sara Stemen for her enraptured encapsulation of a design beauty comparable to *le beau ideal* of paradise. Most of all, a warm thank you to Kevin Lippert for his willingness to leap beyond continental confines to explore a relatively unknown realm and work with a distant author.

I also appreciate the time a number of people working directly in the fields of design, planning, and development took to talk with me. Their insights and clarity of vision have contributed to making this work a much better book. *Mahalo nui loa* to Ray Cain of Belt Collins; Kevin Chun of Watanabe Chun Iopa Takaki; Previn Desai of CDS International; Don Goo of Wimberly Allison Tong & Goo (WATG); Syd Snyder of Ossipoff, Snyder & Rowland Architects, Inc.; Francis Oda of Group 70 International; Ron Lindgren, Larry Stricker, and Michael McCabe, from the offices of Edward Killingsworth; John Hill of Hill Glazier Architects; and Jeff Mongan of the Athens Group.

A project of this magnitude could not have been accomplished without the aid of numerous helping hands. To all those too numerable to mention, who assisted with their time and energy, thank you. Special *mahalo* is extended to those whose help exceeded their job requirements and whose graciousness and kindness greatly enhanced the project: Kiyoko Kimura and Dennis Morinaga with Diamond Resort; Richard Albrecht, Donna Kimura, and Violet Terawaki with Hualālai and the Four Seasons Resort Hualālai at Historic Ka'ūpūlehu; Mark Simon and Chantelle Sorensen with the Four Seasons Maui at Wailea; Dorian Keyes King at the NaPua Gallery; Neesha Lahiri with the Grand Wailea Resort; Claire Morris Dobie with the Hyatt Regency Kauai; Kalani Nakoa and Patty Key with the Hyatt Regency Maui; Bunny Look and Joyce Matsumoto with the Halekulani Hotel; Maria Cazaux and John Ewing with the Kahala Mandarin Oriental, Hawai'i; Candy Aluli, Bernie Caalim, and Cassandra Cockett with the Kapalua Bay Hotel; Laurence Mountcastle and Jessie Crusat with Kona Village Resort; Elizabeth Fitzgerald, Jeong Ku Hwang, and Laure Hitzig with Lanai-Resorts; Catherine Tarleton and Aven Wright-McIntosh with the Mauna Kea Beach Hotel; Susan Bredo with Mauna Lani Resort; Dean Kawamura of WATG; David Stringer and Blanche Allen of Stringer Architects; Catherine Clover of Hill Glazier Architects; Susan Shaner, Louella Kurkjian, Marlene Paahao, Deborah Lee, Victoria Nihi, Jason Achiu, and the rest of the splendid staff at the Hawai'i State Archives; Deanne DuPont and Charles Myers of the Bishop Museum; Gloria Luat and other helpful staff at the Hawai'i State Public Library; Michelle Palmer at the Department of Business, Economic Development and Tourism Library; Barbara Dunn with the Hawaiian Historical Society; Sandra Fukushima with the Hawai'i Visitors and Convention Bureau; Pearl Imada Iboshi with the Department of Business, Economic Development and Tourism; and Jennifer Lau with Pacific Travel Planners. Thanks also goes out to Moani Hibbard and Thomas Vana for the maps for the book. A final *mahalo* to Clifford Inn, Tonia Moy, Nathan Napoka, J. M. Neil, Elithe Kahn, Cara Mullio, Jennifer Volland, and Ginger Winger for sharing words of wisdom, encouragement, and great images.

Nineteenth-century Visitors

chapter 1

HAWAI'I IS THE most isolated place on earth, further away from any major land body or port of call than any other spot in the world. The vast Pacific Ocean, covering one-third of the planet's surface, separated Hawai'i from the rest of humanity for eons. Thus, the island chain was one of the last areas on earth to be inhabited, and also one of the last to fall under the gaze of Europe. The giant expanse of ocean and the bliss of near worldwide anonymity, when coupled with a paucity of exploitable natural resources, assured that relatively few nineteenth-century travelers reached Hawai'i's shores. Indeed, more visitors arrive in one month today than came to the islands throughout the entire nineteenth century. Those who braved the seventy million square miles of the Pacific to seek out these tiny specks of land were the rare exception.

During the first two-thirds of the 1800s, most of the islands' visitors were "business travelers" usually associated with fur, sandalwood, or whaling. Over 80 percent of these arrivals came from the United States. For most, Hawai'i was not a destination but rather a way station, fulfilling the role of a commercial cloverleaf on

opposite *Royal Hawaiian Hotel, Honolulu, O'ahu, 1872, circular lānai added to the facade in 1899*

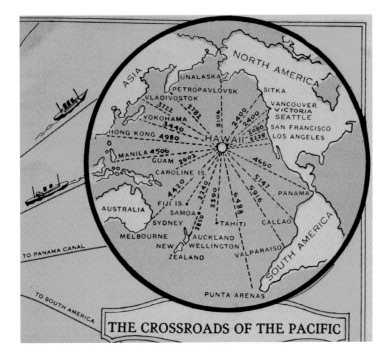

Map from The Story of Hawaii, *Hawaii Tourist Bureau brochure, 1925*

an interstate highway. People came to obtain provisions and find momentary rest before continuing to their journey's ultimate end. They had minimal expectations for accommodations, and for at least the first half century, their needs appear to have been adequately met by taverns.

Taverns differed greatly from the modern hotel. They typically centered around the bar room, a large space that occupied most of the ground floor. This main room not only convivially dispensed spirits but also served as a reception area and usually the dining hall. Operating almost exclusively to provide meals and beverages to the resident community and seafaring men, overnight accommodation was often a remote secondary function, with private accommodations an especially rare commodity. Sleeping rooms, frequently adjoining the bar room or located on the second floor, had no locks, and each housed a myriad of guests who were frequently unfamiliar with one another. The beds were sufficiently large to sleep more than one person, and patrons sometimes found themselves sleeping next to strangers. There were no bathing facilities or indoor plumbing. Linen was not changed daily, or between guests. Meals were served at set times, with set menus, family style.

Hawai'i's reliance on taverns was not uncommon for the time and followed a western tradition that dated back at least to the middle ages. Similar establishments could be found throughout Europe as well as in the U.S., as hotels only began to emerge on the eastern U.S. seaboard starting in 1829 with the opening of the Tremont House in Boston.[1] Honolulu's taverns sometimes called themselves "hotels," but they bore little resemblance to their Boston, New York, or Philadelphia namesakes.

The earliest known taverns in Hawai'i were primarily operated by non-Hawaiians and were frequently private residences converted into boardinghouses. The majority was found in Honolulu, the principal port in the islands. One of the first documented was run by the industrious Spaniard Don Francisco de Paula Marin. He had built a stone house for King Kamehameha in 1810 and a year later also constructed a two-story, coral house for himself (where the highrise apartment Marin Tower now stands). On this property, he and, in turn, his son presided over a boardinghouse, which, during the next two decades, would be referred to as "Manini's Hotel" or the "Oahu Hotel."[2]

Joseph Navarro operated another early inn in Honolulu, Oʻahu, which was open by 1814. Located on the *mauka*[3] side (direction toward the mountains) of Merchant Street between Fort and Nuʻuanu, it remained in business until 1825, when its innkeeper was banished from the Kingdom of Hawaiʻi[4] for shooting at Captain Sistare, who had run off with Navarro's wife. This establishment may well have been a thatched building, as Christian missionaries, on their arrival to Honolulu in 1820, were initially "sheltered in three native-built houses," one of which belonged to Navarro.[5] The utilization of vernacular thatched accommodations, often detached from the main building, remained in practice in Honolulu at least into the 1840s. Chester Lyman, a Yale University scientist, noted in 1847: "Captain Thompson yesterday was thrown from a horse & broke one of his ribs. Is now confined to a thatch house connected with the Mansion House hotel. Was intoxicated at the time."[6]

Anthony Allen, a former slave and mariner who landed in Hawaiʻi during 1810 or 1811, also operated an early tavern in a thatched building.[7] His homestead and farm, situated between downtown Honolulu and Waikīkī, was comprised of approximately a dozen mud-covered, thatched buildings. He, his Hawaiian wife, and their three children lived in this compound that included a blacksmith shop, bar room, bowling alley, and "a kind of boardinghouse for seamen."[8]

A fourth tavern, the Warren House, was established by William "Major" Warren around 1816. It initially stood near the harbor and then moved to the *mauka* side of Hotel Street, between Fort and Nuʻuanu, near where Bethel Street now runs. Prior to Hotel Street receiving its name in 1850, this thoroughfare was noted by the presence of the Warren House. Most likely a thatched structure when it initially opened, this establishment was soon housed in a more substantial wood frame building. By 1825 the Warren House was a popular gathering place in Honolulu. It frequently accommodated public meetings and was famous for its turkey dinners. Its founder, "a gentleman with a smiling visage, a rotund figure, a disposition like a sunbeam, and a heart as big as the island of Hawaii," departed the kingdom in 1838, relocating to Monterey, California, where he opened another inn. The Warren House retained his name and continued in business under different proprietors until 1844, when it was acquired by a Chinese *hui* (a group formed by pooling money for an economic venture), HUNGWA, who changed the name to Canton Hotel. It advertised a billiard room and bowling alley, as well as "superior Chinese cooks." They even offered to deliver meals to Honolulu homes.[9]

In addition to these foreign-owned establishments, Boki, the governor of the island of Oʻahu, entered the hospitality industry in 1827, when he opened the Blonde. This tavern was named after the ship that had brought the remains of King Kamehameha II (Liholiho) and Queen Kalama back to Hawaiʻi after they had died of measles in London. Boki had accompanied the monarchs on that fateful journey and had acquired some familiarity with British accommodations, as the royal party had lodged at the then fashionable Osborne's Caledonian Hotel in Adelphi. The structure housing the Blonde was an American prefabricated, two-story wood-frame building, "with a garret above, and a balcony opening

Hotel Street from Nuʻuanu Avenue, Honolulu, Oʻahu, ca. 1890. The Warren House was destined to be one of the longer-lived, albeit secondary, hotel buildings in the city. It operated as a hotel under several names including the Canton Hotel and Eureka Hotel and Restaurant until 1878, when it was converted into Horn's Confectionery and Bakery, whose sidewalk overhang may be glimpsed beyond the white horse and wagon. It was demolished in 1909.

from the second story," built for Kamehameha I's widow, Kaʻahu-manu, in 1824.[10]

Boki's opening of the Blonde was more than a Hawaiian venturing into the economic realm of American enterprise. In a period of major transition when old ways were being discarded for new, when the American Protestant mission was reaching an apex in its influence over Hawaiʻi's ruling class, Boki and Liliha, his wife, stand out as the preeminent *aliʻi* (the ruling nobility) questioning the ways of the American missionaries and the changes they wrought to Hawaiian society. Just as the tavern with its alcoholic beverages was

an antimissionary icon, the opening of the Blonde may be viewed as a reaction against the missionary presence. Indeed, the activities at the Blonde were not approved by the missionaries, and according to the missionary-educated Hawaiian historian Samuel Kamakau, Boki's saloon, "became a place where noisy swine gathered. Drunkenness and licentious indulgence became common at night, and the people gathered in these places for hula and filthy dances. The foreigners came to these resorts to find women, and Kaʻahu-manu and the missionaries were discussed there."[11]

Following the disappearance of Boki at sea during an expedition to the New Hebrides in 1830, the Blonde was briefly operated by Liliha; the Englishman Joseph Booth managed it from 1833 to 1848. Booth "was famous for his large hospitality to all sailors visiting the port, and the 'Blonde' was a favorite resort because of the genial characteristics of its host. From the tall flagstaff at the corner of the street floated the flag of Merrie England, and no more patriotic representative of his country lived in town."[12]

These pioneer enterprises primarily catered to seafaring men and the occasional traveler who might find their way to Hawaiʻi's shores as well as local residents. Commencing in 1819, ships of the Pacific whaling fleet began to stop in the Hawaiian Islands. Their presence reached its peak between 1843 and 1867, when between 331 and 754 ships dropped anchor annually in Hawaiian waters and accounted for a majority of the islands' visitors. As more whaling ships visited Honolulu the number of visitor accommodations increased with over thirty establishments advertising themselves in the Honolulu newspapers as hotels between 1825 and 1869.

Many of the whaling-period establishments, although using the fashionable appellation "hotel," were bars that would have been condemned by Kamakau and the promissionary segment of

Honolulu's society. In 1844, the church affiliated-publication the *Friend* mentioned the city had

three hotels all of which charged around one dollar a day for boarding or six dollars a week to regular boarders. The *mansion house*, is the best building of the three and appears to be under the best management. They all want [to provide] accommodation [for] transient visitors, of whom there are more than could be expected in a part of the world so remote—especially the case during the spring and fall when whalers frequent the port.[13]

The Mansion House, which opened in 1842, was operated by Captain and Mrs. J. O. Carter. Located on the *makai* side (direction toward the ocean) of Beretania Street between Union Street and Garden Lane, approximately where Bishop Street now runs, the single-story hotel was originally their private residence. Gorham D. Gilman, who was a merchant in Honolulu from 1842 to 1848, recalled,

Captain and Mrs. J. O. Carter were known to all Honolulu by the kindliness of their manner, the warmth of their friendship, and enjoyed the respect and affection of the community in general. They were both of them of fine figure and somewhat large proportions, and although Captain Carter was perhaps one of the heaviest-weight men in town, he was one of the most graceful on the dancing floor. . . . No more hospitable dwelling was in the place [Honolulu]; no more kindly reception given to the wayfarer, and it was home indeed to many a traveler, and especially to the captains of the ships which visited the port."[14]

In 1847, the *Friend* recorded the presence of four hotels in Honolulu, offering board at four-to-seven dollars a week, and

John Hayter, lithograph of painting of Boki and Liliha, 1824. While in London, King Kamehameha II and Queen Kalama arrayed themselves in European apparel for their portraits, but Boki and Liliha opted to wear the traditional attire of Hawaiian aliʻi.

"sleeping apartments, which in general are not attached to the hotels, are extra charge. Room hire and rents in general are expensive, the former from $4 to $12 per month."[15] Over the next few years, more hotels appeared, few that transcended being mere liquor saloons. First Lieutenant Skogman, the astronomer on the Swedish man-of-war *Eugenie*, found during his 1852 visit, "four moderately good hotels . . . located in the city."[16] In all likelihood, he was referring to the French, Commercial, Globe, and National hotels,[17] all of which the lithographer Paul Emmert highlighted in his set of six lithographs of Honolulu in 1853. Similarly, the editor of the *Hawaiian Annual*, Thomas Thrum, who arrived in Honolulu in 1853, remarked that the French, Globe, and Commercial were "better class hotels."[18]

With their ready supply of provisions, these four establishments not only catered to the whaling ships' officers and crews but also served as public gathering places for business and pleasure. Here, the residents of Honolulu could intermingle with the outside world, and vice versa. In their public rooms, matters of business and government were decided: Kings Kamehameha III, IV, and V were said to have frequented the halls of the Commercial. In addition, holiday banquets, "grand balls," and private dinner parties figured prominently in the buzz of activity. On the demolition of the Commercial Hotel in 1903, the *Pacific Commercial Advertiser* recalled,

> From the first the place sprung into popularity. The business men of the city, who had gathered at the smaller Mansion House before the new place opened, congregated there for their evening chat. There was as much business done perhaps in its rooms as downtown during the day and the good livers among the business men of that day were always ready to make up dinner parties and enjoy the feasts which were spread there.

The billiard rooms and buffet [saloon] were always filled with patrons and the people were willing to get up games at all hours. It was the custom of a quartet of whaling captains to purchase a barrel of bottles of beer, roll the barrel into the bowling alley and there roll ten pins until the question of who should pay the chit was settled. There was little money in small pieces in those days, and when a crowd of sailors started out for one of their kind of good times, it was to throw a slug of gold on a bar and stand up to the counter until they had consumed the liquor that be purchased by the piece.[19]

In addition to the bars and dining rooms, many of these early hotels invariably included at least one billiard table for one of

opposite, left, top and bottom *French Hotel, Honolulu, Oʻahu, 1830s. The single-story adobe building at Hotel and Union streets originally housed Dr. Rooke's medical office, with a two-story wood frame residence behind it, fronting on Fort Street. In 1848, the residence was taken over by Pierre le Gueval and Hippolite Psalmon, who opened the aptly named French Hotel. Victor Chanerel took over the entire parcel in 1850, expanding the French Hotel to include both buildings. In 1862, the kingdom acquired this parcel. After 1874, and the completion of Aliʻiolani Hale, it was used by "sundry tenants in various mechanical pursuits" until its demolition in 1914. At the time of its removal it was one of two surviving adobe buildings in the city, a remarkable statement on Honolulu's "progress," as only sixty years earlier, over half the western-style buildings in town were of adobe.*

opposite, right, top and bottom *Commercial Hotel, Honolulu, Oʻahu, 1845. This two-story adobe building, with its encircling verandahs, was situated near the* mauka, Diamond Head *corner of Nuʻuanu Avenue and Beretania Street. Initially the residence of Henry Macfarlane, in 1846 he opened it as a hotel. The ground floor had a cafe and dining room, while sleeping quarters, a billiard room, and "a buffet for refreshments"—most likely a saloon—were upstairs. It was Honolulu's earliest known hotel to advertise hot and cold water for baths and showers. In 1850, a hot bath cost one dollar and a cold one fifty cents. It was here that gas lighting was introduced to the islands in 1858. It operated as the saloon and hotel until 1903 when the building was torn down.*

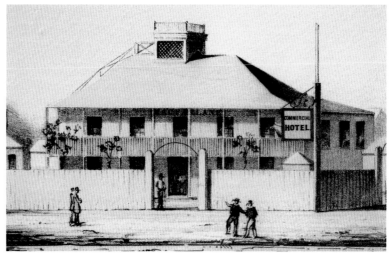

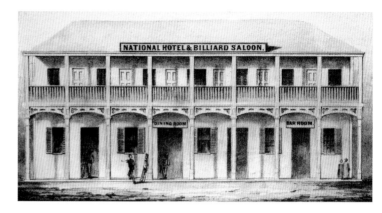

above left *Globe Hotel, Honolulu, Oʻahu, 1830s. Situated on the* mauka *side of King Street between Fort and Bethel streets, the hotel was originally built as a two-story coral-block residence for the American Consul, John C. Jones, Jr., and his wife, Hannah Davis Jones. Converted into a hotel following Mrs. Jones's death in 1847, it later became a boarding house and was demolished in 1897.*

above right *National Hotel, also known as International Hotel, Honolulu, Oʻahu, 1847. The hotel was considered, in the years immediately preceding the opening of the Hawaiian Hotel, to be Honolulu's premier hostelry. Sitting on a one acre lot, bounded by Hotel Street and Nuʻuanu Avenue, and what would later be Bethel Street, the two-story, coral-block building featured a fifty-foot sidewalk, which ran from Hotel Street to the building. Its Chinese granite pavers, having been laid in December 1877, were the earliest known use of that material for that purpose in Hawaiʻi and were "the talk of the town." The complex was heavily damaged by the 1886 Chinatown fire, and the coral building ultimately was demolished with the construction of Bethel Street.*

the most popular games of the period. Somewhat incredibly, in a city almost destitute of furniture, two billiard tables could be found in Honolulu by 1825, one of which was at Navarro's Inn. Henceforth, the game remained a recreational mainstay at Honolulu hotels and taverns throughout the nineteenth and early twentieth centuries, with many establishments having a separate billiard room "for all who are inclined to while away an hour in the delightful and healthy exercise of Billiard playing."[20]

Some hotels also served as bowling alleys and dance houses. The latter, featuring "hulahula" dancers, were introduced into the kingdom around 1852 when the "proprietors of two of our public houses, in order to make their establishments more frequented, instituted nightly dances of native women, dressed exceedingly lewd, which attracted crowds of seamen." The Marshall of the Kingdom, the staid William Parke, shortly arrested and successfully prosecuted the proprietors for operating a common nuisance. Marshall Parke, a strong advocate of New England morality, found the dance houses to be "the great source and indeed the primary cause of fornication and adultery that disgraced the city." At the end of 1856, the issue again reached public attention, when the Liberty Hall and National Hotel reinstituted these shows with dancers less provocatively attired. Upon the opening of a third dance house at the Globe Hotel in November 1856, a correspondent submitted a letter dripping with irony to the *Pacific Commercial Advertiser*:

> The citizens of Honolulu are deserving of much credit for their liberality in furnishing places of "innocent" amusement, for the hardy mariners and others, who make this place their winter quarters. I refer to the elegant "dance houses," or "hulahulas" which are nightly open, *free of charge*, to all who please to visit them, where the sailor or citizen can pass the night in the "mazy dance" with the chaste Island maidens, or make appointments to "meet me by moonlight alone." Such houses are certainly a great public convenience. Heretofore their number has been rather limited; the common sailor was brought too much in contact with his superiors; but that difficulty has been happily obviated by our enterprising host of the Globe, who last Monday evening threw open his splendid saloons for the more special accommodation of the officers and gentry; and several other public spirited citizens are about to follow his example. No fear of losing the whaling trade as long as such inducements are held out. To be sure, some narrow minded old fogies may say such things are immoral, and not tolerated in any civilized community, and that the statutes declare they shall not be tolerated here, but they are behind the spirit of the age, or too old to enjoy a-Hulahula.[21]

The proprietors of the three dance houses, two Englishmen and a French citizen, were arrested by Marshall Parke and convicted in police court in 1856. However, the proprietor of the National Hotel appealed his verdict to the Hawai'i Supreme Court, and under the terms of an 1846 treaty between Hawai'i and Great Britain, he was tried and acquitted by a specially selected jury of British subjects, much to the consternation of the church-affiliated community, including Henry M. Whitney, the editor of the *Pacific Commercial Advertiser*, a missionary descendant. In an editorial, the newspaper acknowledged that public dancing houses existed in every seaport of the world; however,

> no one will presume to say that they are reputable places of resort. [In other seaports around the world] the communities are so large that there is a broad line of division between reputable and disreputable places of resort for amusement. Here the case is different. It is a small community and all classes are brought more or less in contact with each other and consequently have some influence on each other's character.

Labeling the female dancers as "the lowest and vilest" class of abandoned women, and fearing the corruption of the young men of Honolulu, the editor advocated the suppression of such public exhibitions.[22]

The *Polynesian*, edited by Charles Gordon Hopkins, a British subject who had served on the 1857 jury, set forth a more broad-minded position. The editor recognized prostitution as an activity beyond the ability of governments to stop: "Of all the countries in the world we know of none where prostitution is less likely to be suppressed than here. Remember the constant influx of strangers. Remember the traditional feeling that to deny certain advances is a species of inhospitality."

One editorial contributor, who signed himself, "A Juror," explained that the dancers were not a separate class who could be labeled "prostitutes" or "strumpets."

There is, to say the least, no such distinction as is pretended or implied between the class of native women who assemble at the dance houses, and the native women generally speaking . . . they are the public . . . Shall we declare the whole female population a nuisance? It is much to be feared that there exists here some of the Anglo-Saxon race with the selfish, unsympathising, over-bearing natures, only too characteristic of it, who, in their anxiety to establish a *cordon sanitaire* around the pure morality of their own sons or their own brothers, would hardly hesitate to return even this verdict.[23]

Since at least the mid-1820s the hula, the traditional dance form of Hawai'i, had been soundly denounced from the missionary pulpit as "heathen" and "lascivious." King Kamehameha I's widow, Ka'ahumanu, an early convert to Christianity and an ardent supporter of the Christian missionaries, issued an edict banning the public performance of the dance in 1830. The decree was difficult to enforce, especially in areas removed from the missionary centers, and Ka'ahumanu's death in 1832 further compounded compliance problems. In an effort to control public performances, a law was passed in 1851 requiring any person who set up or promoted any "Public Shows, Theatrical, Equestrian, or other exhibitions of any description, to which admission is obtainable on the payment of money," to obtain a license. The hotel owners circumvented this law by not charging an admission fee for the hula shows, gaining profits in the sale of alcohol. By setting hula on such a commercial stage, they unconsciously moved the dance a step away from its traditional cultural context and placed it within a new western one. The hula's new dancehall shows continued the western fascination with the sexual aspects of the dance, but rather than condemn the performance as purulent, the hotel owners commodified it to delight visitors from afar.[24]

TRAVELING OUTSIDE O'AHU

Taverns and hotels, as well as their diverse activities, were not limited to Honolulu. Edmund Butler briefly operated a tavern in Lahaina, Maui, as early as 1819. However, the governor of Maui, the strict Christian Hoapili, curbed the sale of liquor on that island. As a result, only the most righteous sea captains stopped at Lahaina, and it was not until after the governor's death in 1840, that the whaling fleet began frequenting this port on a large scale. A general loosening of public morals, and the availability of white potatoes on Maui, lured a number of whalers away from Honolulu, resulting in the appearance of several institutions serving as hotels in Lahaina, including the Commercial, Universal, American, and Hawaiian. They catered primarily to the entertainment of seamen, causing the American traveler George Washington Bates, a staunch supporter of the missionary efforts to bring "civilization" to Hawai'i, to disdainfully note in 1854 that

there are no licensed taverns in this sea-port, but, what is infinitely worse, there are a number of licensed victualing houses. The very appearance of these dens is enough to create within a man a disgust of his race—enough to make a savage sick. They are kept entirely by a few low foreigners. During the spring and fall seasons, when the whaling fleets are here to recruit, there are no fewer than twelve of these Plutos in full blast. And these hot-beds of vice are termed "Houses of Refreshment!" and "Sailors' Homes!"[25]

With the decline in whaling, these establishments first disappeared from Lahaina, later to vanish almost entirely from Honolulu. As early as 1866, Phebe Finnigan, a correspondent for the *Pacific Commercial Advertiser*, noted the abandonment of Lahaina by the whalers and the subsequent absence of hotels, beer shops, and restaurants.[26] Eight years later, the American journalist and author, Charles Nordhoff, who wrote for the *New York Post* and later the *New York Herald* reported,

> It is one of the embarrassing incidents of travel on these Islands that there are no hotels or inns outside of Honolulu and Hilo. Whether he will or no [*sic*] the traveler must accept the hospitality of the residents, and this is so general and boundless that it would impose a burdensome obligation, were it not offered in such a kindly and graceful way as to beguile you into the belief that you are conferring as well as receiving a favor.[27]

Despite its lack of overnight accommodations, Lahaina remained the gateway to Maui throughout the nineteenth and early twentieth centuries, thanks to its anchorage. Eventually, in October 1901, the Lahaina Hotel opened its doors. Within several years, manager George Freeland changed its name to the Pioneer Hotel, thereby associating his endeavor through nomenclature with the Pioneer Sugar Company in Lahaina, a name the hotel still carries today. It outlasted the inspiration for its appellation, as Pioneer Sugar closed in 1999. Initially, this establishment appeared to have been comparable in many ways with nineteenth-century taverns; for as late as 1916, noted American writer Katharine Fullerton Gerould made the following comments about the hotel and town:

> No one, I might almost say, stops in Lahaina except on business—of which the neighboring sugar plantations create a certain amount. So it is not odd that in the Pioneer Hotel meals should be served at unsophisticated hours, and that the public rooms should consist chiefly of a bar. It is not uncomfortable to

Pioneer Inn, Lahaina, Maui, 1901

> sit on the upper verandah outside one's room and watch the sanpans, and the water breaking on the reef. But it is impossible to think of Lahaina as a place to stay in, even as headquarters for the wanderer. Except for business, there is nothing to keep any one there.[28]

Like Maui, Kaua'i was also destitute of visitor accommodations for much of the nineteenth century. After the abduction of Kaua'i's ruling chief, Kaumuali'i, to Honolulu in 1823, Deborah Kapule, his wife, opened her residence in Wailua to visitors. Referred to as Deborah's Inn, this *ali'i* entertained foreign visitors in her large house for over twenty years. George Washington Bates, who traveled to Kauai in 1853, mournfully noted the demise of this well-known center of hospitality. In Wailua, "everything was going rapidly to decay," as Kapule had gone to live on the other side of the island.[29]

The only other serious attempt of establishing a nineteenth-century visitor resort on Kauai involved the large English-style private residence of Thomas Brown, also in Wailua. Brown had moved to Kaua'i from England in 1845 to improve his declining health and had established a dairy farm and coffee plantation on six hundred acres of land. In 1847, Chester Lyman had met the Brown family while exploring the islands. He noted that Brown "lives at present in a grass house, till he can put up a frame one."[30] Within the next year or two, he built a baronial mansion, at least by Hawai'i standards, with timbers imported from England, the first western building in East Kaua'i. Brown and his family departed Hawai'i for New York in 1852, and on July 9, 1853 an advertisement in the *Polynesian* proclaimed,

TO INVALIDS, TOURISTS AND PARTIES
IN SEARCH OF THE PICTURESQUE
Those who seek for refreshing and invigorating relaxation, in a delightfully salubrious climate, of remarkably equal temperature, will find their desires realized at THE MANSION OF WAILUA FALLS . . . This spacious and commodious mansion, which was originally built by an English Gentleman as his private residence . . . has been constructed on the best principles of ventilation, is surrounded with a fine verandah, 12 feet wide and has every requisite accommodation. The apartments and chambers are lofty, commodious and airy, and are furnished with every convenience. The site is admirably selected on a table land, overlooking the river, which equals in beauty the celebrated highlands of the Hudson, and is surrounded with every variety of mountain, forest, plain and woodland scenery, in which is a magnificent waterfall of about 200 feet high, in the vicinity of the house.[31]

The new owners, in addition to carrying on Brown's dairy business, hoped to capitalize on the appeal of the Romantic movement's enshrining of nature as embodied in the Hudson River School of painters and on the success of Niagara Falls, which had established itself as a natural wonder and a tourist magnet in the early 1830s. Too far ahead of its time and too far removed from a viable client base, the endeavor was unsuccessful, and the property continued as a dairy farm. In 1855, its manager, Duncan McBryde, a Scottish immigrant who would later serve as a judge and acquire large land holdings in the Kalāheo area, advertised that the Wailua Falls has "always been justly regarded as a great attraction to strangers," and few places "can combine so many circumstances to please the eye, gratify the taste, promote the comfort and invigorate the health of the stranger." He was prepared to accommodate eight-to-ten boarders "at moderate rates" in the "spacious and airy" mansion;[32] however, the advertisement failed to attract the desired clientele, and no further efforts were made to develop Wailua Falls Mansion as a resort. Shortly before 1880, King Kalākaua was sufficiently impressed with the dwelling to have it dismantled and taken to Kapa'a where he intended to assemble it as a country residence. However, this plan never reached fruition as delays intervened and planks were lost.

WHILE WAILUA FALLS did not succeed as a nineteenth-century visitor attraction, the island of Hawai'i, also known as the Big Island, was more fortunate in its natural bounty: the Kīlauea volcano needed little advertising to attract visitors. As a result, what later came to be known as the Volcano House became the first hotel in the islands to cater successfully to "respectable visitors," that is, sightseers going to see Kīlauea rather than seamen in search of wine, women, and song. The party of missionary William Ellis was the first-known group of foreigners to view the great volcano, having made the trek in August 1823.

> We at length came to the edge of the great crater, where a spectacle, sublime and even appalling, presented itself before us—
> "We stopped, and trembled."
> Astonishment and awe for some moments rendered us mute, and, like statues, we stood fixed to the spot, with our eyes riveted on the abyss below. . . . After the first feelings of astonishment had subsided, we remained a considerable time contemplating a scene, which it is impossible to describe, and which filled us with wonder and admiration at the almost overwhelming manifestation it affords of the power of that dread Being who created the world, and who has declared that by fire he will one day destroy it.[33]

Volcano House, Volcano National Park, island of Hawai'i , 1866

A succession of foreigners followed Ellis' party in making the journey to the rim of the turbulence. As a result, various Hawaiians built a succession of thatched houses, essentially temporary shelters, between 1824 and 1846 for visitor use. These structures were unattended and free of charge. In 1846, Benjamin Pitman, a Hilo sugar planter, constructed a larger and better thatch house to which he gave the name "Volcano House." It measured about 14' x 18' or 20', and was "a low thatched house. One end of it was open. Running the length of the hut was a framework of poles covered by ferns and overlaid with mats."[34] Like its predecessors, it was built for the convenience of travelers, and there was no proprietor or price to pay.

It was not until 1866 that the Volcano House became a commercial enterprise and Hawai'i's first successful resort. Operated by Julius C. Richardson, George Jones, and J. C. King, their new build- ing was a combination of Hawaiian-thatch and western wood-frame construction, with the former dominating. The rustic lodging represented a marked departure for Hawai'i's hospitality industry; it was, "erected expressly for the comfort of travelers"[35] visiting Hawai'i's most outstanding natural attraction. Over four hundred visitors had journeyed to the molten inferno in 1865, and in hopes of attracting a thousand guests in 1866, the partners advertised in the Honolulu newspapers:

> This establishment is now open for the reception of
> VISITORS TO THE VOLCANO!
> Who may rely on finding
> COMFORTABLE ROOMS, A GOOD TABLE
> AND PROMPT ATTENDANCE[36]

Volcano House, 1877

The *Hawaiian Gazette* described the building as, "a neat little cottage with four bedrooms, a large parlor and dining room. The number of persons who can be provided with beds and shelter during the night is twenty."[37] Mark Twain stayed here in 1866 and remarked, "the surprise of finding a good hotel at such an outlandish spot startled me considerably more than the volcano did."[38] Dr. Samuel Kneeland of Boston echoed Twain's appreciation of the lodging, when recalling his 1872 visit:

[We reached] the Volcano House at sunset. Tired as we were, we looked upon this grass house as a delightful haven of rest.... One does not know until he travels in these out-of-the-way places, how little it takes to make one comfortable, and how much of what is considered indispensable for civilized life is really unnecessary luxury. One of the great lessons taught by travelling is to be content and even happy with a little; grumbling not only sours one's own temper, but irritates those who are not to blame for not supplying impossibilities."[39]

Isabella Bird, one of the most popular nineteenth-century female travel writers, visited Kīlauea a year later, and further elaborated on the Volcano House's charm:

This inn is a unique and interesting place. Its existence is strikingly precarious, for the whole region is a state of perpetual throb from earthquakes, and the sights and sounds are gruesome and awful both day and night.... The inn is a grass and bamboo house, very beautifully constructed without nails. It is a longish building with a steep roof, divided inside by partitions which run up to the height of the walls. There is no ceiling. The joists which run across are concealed by wreaths of evergreens, from among which peep out here and there stars on a blue background. The door opens from the verandah into a centre room with a large open brick fire place, in which a wood fire is constantly burning, for at this altitude the temperature is cool. Some chairs, two lounges, small tables, and some books and pictures on the walls give a look of comfort, and there is the reality of comfort in perfection. Our sleeping-place, a neat room with a matted floor opens from this, and on the other side there is a similar room, and a small eating-room with a grass cookhouse beyond. . . . The charge is five dollars a day, but everything except the potatoes and *ohelos* has to be brought twenty to thirty miles on mule's back. It is a very pretty, picturesque house both within and without. . . . It is altogether a most magical building in the heart of a formidable volcanic wilderness.[40]

By 1877, George Jones bought out his partners and rebuilt the "magical building" completely of wood. Its framing was hewn on site from local timbers *ʻōhia* and *naio* while its doors, windows, and other building materials had to be transported from the landing at Keauhou by horseback and two-wheeled cart. In many ways the new building, like its thatched predecessor, resembled in form the earliest style of American frontier taverns, as illustrated in A. B. Hulbert's *Pioneer Roads and Experiences of Travelers*.[41] The new Volcano House was a

top right *Volcano House, 1891. The two-story turreted building was constructed for the Volcano House Company by George Warren. The earlier 1877 building was moved and remodeled.*

bottom right *Volcano House, 1941. George Lycurgus acquired the Volcano House in 1904, and his family operated the hotel until 1921 when the Inter-Island Steamship Company gained ownership. Lycurgus reacquired the hotel during the early 1930s. A February 6, 1940 fire destroyed the 1891 building, leaving only the lava-rock columns that supported the front lānai standing. Rebuilt, the present Volcano House opened on November 8, 1941.*

single-story structure, 35' x 110', with a lateral running gable roof and a wide, pent-roofed verandah running the length of the facade. It contained six private guestrooms, each capable of holding three persons, a parlor, and a dining room. The parlor had several sofas, a large melodeon, and its now-famous fireplace whose hospitable fire has burned continuously ever since its first ignition in 1877.[42] In 1886, the Wilder Steamship Line purchased the Volcano House and advertised biweekly steamship service from Honolulu to the island of Hawai'i for the cost of fifty dollars, which included steamer rates, horse, guide, and an overnight stay at the Volcano House.

THE NEW CLIENTELE

The increased popularity of the Volcano House signaled a change in the type of visitors who were arriving in Hawai'i during the last half of the nineteenth century. These new travelers included within their midst writers, artists, scientists, and adventurers. They came to discover Hawai'i, its culture, traditions, and landscape, and arrived with a desire to know and understand the islands firsthand through the senses.

A few visitors of this type had come earlier to Hawai'i, but improved steamship service to the islands greatly increased their numbers by greatly decreasing their time at sea. The coal powered steamers took about nine days to go from San Francisco to Hawai'i, as compared to an unpredictable sailing voyage usually lasting twenty to thirty days; however, the islands still remained a long ocean journey from anywhere. People who came here craved a firsthand experience; yet at the same time, the citizenry of Hawai'i recognized many of these travelers also expected a certain level of comfort upon their arrival. In 1865, demand for a first-class hotel in Honolulu mounted; and the *Pacific Commercial Advertiser* announced a public meeting to discuss the need for such a hotel:

Any observing person will see the growing need of a hotel for the accommodation of parties visiting here from San Francisco particularly. Our packets come crowded, and as has often been the case, the parties have to remain on board a day or two until a place has been found in some private family for their accommodation.[43]

Perhaps in response to this public perturbation, the American House opened on March 1, 1866, joining the small ensemble of surviving whaling-era hotels in Honolulu. The new establishment, situated at King and Maunakea streets, more closely approximated a hotel than a tavern. The *Friend* rejoiced: "We are glad to learn that a hotel is to be opened this day far more worthy of the name than anything which has before existed in Honolulu."[44] The *Hawaiian Gazette* concurred and found that the proprietor, Kirchoff, had "fitted [it] up in excellent style with every appliance for the comfort and convenience of guests. It is undoubtedly by far the best arranged hotel ever seen in Honolulu, and under the careful, neat and liberal management of the proprietor will unquestionably deserve and receive the patronage of the public."[45] Several months later, Mark Twain, expressed similar sentiments when noting, "I did not expect to find as comfortable a hotel as the American, with its large, airy, well-furnished rooms, distinguished by perfect neatness and cleanliness, its cool commodious verandas, its excellent table, its ample front yard, carpeted with grass and adorned with shrubbery, *et cetera*—and so I was agreeably disappointed."[46] The hotel, although lasting until the 1890s, apparently did not live up to its initial promise as public outcries for a first-class hotel continued to mount in Honolulu, as trans-Pacific steamships increasingly appeared in the port.

The Australian Steam Navigation Company's initiation of steamer service between Australia and San Francisco by way of

Hawai'i, prompted the Hawaiian government to undertake the construction of a major hotel in December 1870. Recalling the 170 passengers who arrived on the *Wonga Wonga* from Sydney in May 1870 and were unable to find suitable accommodations, the monarchy believed the public interest required a new hotel. However, the government recognized that "the enterprise would be too large, in view of all the circumstances, for any private persons to undertake,"[47] and the crown moved to fill this void. On learning of the government's intentions, the *Pacific Commercial Advertiser* announced,

> For a number of years past, our community has had periodical spells of moderate excitement on the subject of building a hotel in Honolulu, which so far have all ended in talk. But as our means of communication with other parts of the world are multiplying rapidly, owing to our central-ocean position, the absolute necessity of a good hotel for the accommodation of our transient visitors has become an acknowledged fact. But what is wanted, is some one to take the lead in the matter, and carry out to a satisfactory completion the desires of the public. In our small community we have no individual men who can devote their time or means to such a project; and to the multitude of counselors, there would, in this instance, very probably result a confusion that would kill the enterprise. Consequently the Government, taking the cue from the often expressed tenor of public opinion, steps forward and proposes a plan by which the desired result can be obtained very speedily, and in a manner which to us appears to be quite feasible. While the community itself will be the owner of the hotel, and will have a voice in the plan of its erection and management, the immediate work will be in the hands of the Government . . . We cannot doubt but that

Although the British Cormorant, *the first steamship to dock in Honolulu, arrived in 1846, the following two decades remained the age of sail in Hawai'i, with steamers only sporadically appearing in Honolulu harbor. Regularly scheduled round-trip steamer passenger service between Honolulu and San Francisco was established in 1883, when the Oceanic Steamship Company placed the* Mariposa *and* Alameda *on the San Francisco-Honolulu route. Each could carry around one hundred passengers.*

> our citizens will avail themselves promptly of this opportunity to provide our city with a commodious, elegant and well-conducted hotel. The plan proposed is plain, fair and practicable.[48]

In February 1871, a meeting of government officials and persons willing to subscribe money to the endeavor convened. A committee, comprised of the Minister of the Interior, F. W. Hutchinson, and subscribers L. L. Torbet and C. H. Lewers, was selected to procure a site and undertake other preliminaries. This committee was denied even an obsequious role, as the Minister of Finance, John Mott-Smith, and the Minister of Foreign Affairs, C. C. Harris, usurped

control of the project and expeditiously proceeded according to their own desires. By May 1871, the block bounded by Beretania, Hotel, Alakea, Richards streets was procured as the hotel site, although many in the business community preferred a site between the harbor and King Street, in closer proximity to the retail center of the city. A design that ignored the community suggestion of including stores on the first floor to help defray construction costs, was selected, and ground was broken during the second week of May, all without consultation with the subscribers or the original committee of three. Such single-minded actions raised the ire of government critics, especially when the anticipated $42,500 price tag more than doubled, and the anticipated two-story building emerged as three stories.

The Hawaiian Hotel was a substantial building for the islands, and as noted in *The Hawaiian Guidebook for 1875*, "probably no building in Honolulu was ever built more faithfully than this hotel, whose every part was constructed with a view to strength and permanence."[49] It was one of several reinforced-concrete buildings of the period sponsored by the government—the earliest use of the material in public buildings in what is now the U.S. The technology, which involved the on-site manufacture of blocks of concrete individually reinforced with rebar, was introduced to Hawai'i by the British masonry contractor J. G. Osborne, who erected the Honolulu post office in 1871. Other buildings in the city to employ the new material included Ali'iolani Hale and the no longer extant Dillingham and Castle & Cooke buildings.

Osborne prepared the plans and elevation for the new hotel, and C. H. Lewers, Honolulu's leading supplier of building materials, directed and oversaw its construction. The forty-two-room, 120-by-90-foot hotel featured lānai on each of its three stories on both the *makai* and *mauka* sides; its English slate roof was capped by a prominent widows walk, which afforded views of the city, mountains, and

top *Hawaiian Hotel (later known as the Royal Hawaiian Hotel), dining room*
bottom *Hawaiian Hotel, side lānai*
opposite *Hawaiian Hotel. According to Isabella Bird, "The hotel was lately built by government at a cost of $120,000, a sum which forms a considerable part of that token of an advanced civilization, a National Debt."*

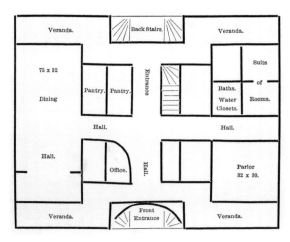

Hawaiian Hotel, floor plan

Hawaiian Hotel, side lānai. Charles Warren Stoddard, in a 1894 letter, noted "You wonder how we kill time in the tropics, dear boy? We never kill it; we never get quite enough of it, and murder were out of the question. Time with us flows softly and swiftly, like a river, and we drift with it. . . . We may not have made any visible effort; we certainly have not hurried ourselves, but you will find upon investigation that we have accomplished fully as much as you would were you here with your high pressure engine at full blast."

harbor. At the reception desk, "a courteous attendant is always waiting to supply [the guest's] wants, answer his questions, and aid in making him comfortable and at home." The parlor opened onto the lānai through large French doors. The billiard room on the ground floor featured three Strahle & Company tables, made in San Francisco of choice California laurel oak: "No better tables are made in any part of the world, and the proprietor has spared and will spare no expense to render this part of the establishment a popular resort to the lovers of the game." Strahle & Company's quality woodwork had earlier been recognized when it was selected in 1869 to provide the ceremonial tie into which the Trans-Continental Railroad's golden spike was driven.[50]

The guestrooms on the top floor had French doors to access the verandahs. Each floor had bathrooms with both hot-and-cold running water and water closets. In addition, hot-and-cold baths were available from sunrise to midnight, "for the convenience of those who wish to enjoy this most healthful and pleasant recreation." Female attendants were available to assist ladies and children with their baths.[51]

The beds were of "the best of hair mattresses and linen" and, more importantly, had bed springs. The latter was an 1831 invention, which in 1871 was still a handmade item and very much a rarity—most Americans and Hawaiians were still sleeping on the old-style corded beds or those made of slats. Every room was connected with the office via a Will & Frink Annunciator, allowing guests at the push of a button to request ice water, the bellboy, or some other service.[52] In use ever since the opening of Boston's Tremont Hotel in 1829, annunciators remained state-of-the-art hotel communication devices up through World War I, several decades after the 1894 introduction of in-room telephones. Such modern accommodations placed Hawai'i on equal footing with other tourist venues, or as Henry M. Whitney noted, "Tourists in pursuit of health or the most delightful tropical climate and scenery; men of business as well as men of leisure, can have no excuse for delaying their visits to this historic group or passing by the port for lack of suitable accommodations."[53]

American traveler Charles Nordhoff in 1874 declared the Hawaiian to be

> a surprisingly excellent hotel, which was built at a cost of $120,000, and is owned by the government. You will find it a large building, affording all the conveniences of a first-class hotel in any part of the world . . . you might imagine yourself in San Francisco, were it not that you drive in under the shade of cocoa-nut, tamarind, guava, and algeroba trees, and find all the doors and windows open in midwinter; and ladies and children in white sitting on the piazzas.[54]

The presence of ladies and children in white reaffirmed that the Hawaiian Hotel certainly was not an establishment that intended to cater to seamen on leave from their maritime pursuits.

Isabella Bird, further amplified the merits of Honolulu's premier hotel, having visited it only a year after its opening:

> This is the perfection of an hotel. Hospitality seems to take possession of and appropriate one as soon as one enters its never closed door, which is on the lower verandah. Everywhere only pleasant objects meet the eye. One can sit all day on the back verandah watching the play of light and color on the mountains and the deep blue green of the Nuuanu valley, where showers, sunshine, and rainbows make perpetual variety . . . There are no female domestics. The host is a German, the manager an American, the steward a Hawaiian, and the servants are all Chinamen in spotless white linen, with pigtails coiled round their heads, and an air of superabundant good-nature. They know very little English, and make most absurd mistakes, but they are cordial, smiling, and obliging, and look cool and clean. The hotel seems the great public resort of Honolulu, the centre of stir—club-house, exchange, and drawing-room in one. Its wide corridors and verandahs are lively with English and American naval uniforms, several planters' families are here for the season; and with health seekers from California, resident boarders, whaling captains, tourists from the British Pacific Colonies, and a stream of townspeople always percolating through the corridors and verandahs, it seems as lively and free-and-easy as a place can be, pervaded by the kindliness and bonhomie which form important items in my first impressions of the islands. . . . I dislike health resorts, and abhor this kind of life, but for those who like both, I cannot imagine a more fascinating residence.[55]

The Hawaiian Hotel was indeed first class, however, the flow of visitors was insufficient to fill the hotel until the late 1880s, when, fortunately, occupancy rates improved.[56] Allen Herbert operated the hotel from 1872 until 1882, and then a succession of managers followed, each, in turn, optimistically bidding on the government's lease. Over the years, the hotel expanded somewhat, and by 1885, twenty guest cottages stood on the four-acre grounds. The Hawaiian, or Royal Hawaiian as it was renamed in the 1880s, would reign supreme for over thirty years, operating as a hotel until 1917 and as a YMCA until its demolition in 1927.

2

Hawai'i as a Tourist Destination

FOLLOWING THE DECLINE of whaling, Hawai'i experienced a precipitous drop in foreign visitors as the number of adventurous, experience-seeking travelers constituted but a trickle compared to the earlier inundation of whalers. Whereas the fifty years between 1820 and 1870 saw approximately 400,000 visitors arrive on Hawai'i's shores, the ensuing fifty years witnessed less than 200,000 travelers partaking of the islands' charms. Throughout the last three decades of the nineteenth century, an average of approximately 2,200 tourists arrived on an annual basis.[1] It was not until after Hawai'i's annexation as a territory of the United States in 1899, that this small but steady flow of visitors increased dramatically. Hawai'i's new political status provided a sense of stability that both the provisional government, formed after the overthrow of Queen Lili'uokalani in 1893, and subsequently the republic had lacked. However, the shift from independent nation to a U.S. colony was but one of several factors that coalesced in increased visitor numbers. Other significant developments included an increased pool of perspective clientele, a conscious promotion of Hawai'i as a

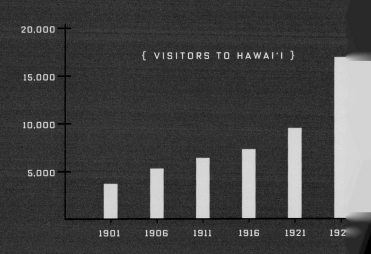

{ VISITORS TO HAWAI'I }

20,000

15,000

10,000

5,000

1901   1906   1911   1916   1921   192

opposite *Royal Hawaiian Hotel, Waikīkī, O'ahu, 1927. During the 1920s, visitor stayed in Hawai'i an average of four to six weeks. They either rented cars for $50 week ($125 with driver), or brought their own vehicles and chauffeurs with the*

above and opposite *A. S. MacLeod, illustrations from* The Story of Hawaii, *a booklet published by the Hawai'i Tourist Bureau (HTB), July 1925*

visitor destination by both the private and public sectors, and improved transportation opportunities.

National newspaper coverage of the overthrow of the monarchy and the ensuing debate over the U.S. annexation of the independent Pacific nation embedded a hitherto relatively unknown, remote island chain into the minds of Americans, a greater number of whom now resided on the West Coast, in relatively close proximity to Hawai'i. Between 1870 and 1900, the population of California, Oregon, and Washington almost quadrupled, from 675,135 to a staggering 2,416,692. By 1930, this number would again almost multiply fourfold, reaching 8,194,433, a sufficiently large demographic upon which Hawai'i's visitor industry readily could draw. While a handful

of these people would travel to Hawai'i on business, the vast majority was attracted to the islands because of the renowned health-instilling climate, hospitality, and titillating exoticism.

The reputation of Hawai'i's magical magnificence had been proclaimed for over one hundred years, melding with the accounts of other Pacific isles to form an idyllic South Seas collage. Eighteenth-century explorers' reports presented the first vivid images. Later, these were modified, embellished, and expanded through numerous nineteenth-century travelers' accounts. From the first contact by Europeans, the exotic islands of the Pacific were described in utopian terms, not only as lands of warmth and incredible natural beauty but also of freedom and delight. These islands were a tropic paradise peopled by the Enlightenment's noble savage, where the constraints and demands of civilization were beneficently set aside. The islands knew "no other god but love; every day is consecrated to it, the whole island is its temple, all the women its idols, all the men its worshippers."[2] As for the fair maidens of Hawai'i, Captain James Cook informed the world, "no women I have ever met with were more ready to bestow their favours, indeed it appeared to me that they came [to the ship] with no other view." Less than one hundred years later, Hawai'i became known as a place where Mark Twain "moved in the midst of a summer calm as tranquil as dawn in the Garden of Eden," where a twenty-five-year-old, East Coast-bred, Una Hunt Drage felt "hoydenish" playing croquet without gloves in 1901, and where people partook in moon-lit dips in the ocean. In the words of Isabella Bird, "I felt as if in this fairy-land anything might be expected."[3]

The romantic image of Hawai'i as the "Paradise of the Pacific"[4] easily wove its way into the global consciousness, and was made doubly attractive by laudatory accounts of a safe, missionary-inspired, civilized society. Hawai'i seemed to offer the best of two worlds, a home to an exotic, "primitive" culture, yet also a place offering all the comforts and security of modern living. Reiterated in travelog after travelog, such visions could not fail to instill desires and curiosities, for as J. D. Spreckels noted in the *Overland Monthly*, "There is but one Pacific Ocean, but one Hawaiian group, to sail for a week over the clear and calm waters of the one and to luxuriate in the tropical beauty of the other are pleasures not to be duplicated the world over."[5]

In addition to literary word of mouth, people in Hawai'i began to consciously promote the islands' charms in the last quarter of the nineteenth century. Henry M. Whitney, the editor of the *Hawaiian Gazette*, published *The Hawaiian Guide Book for Travelers* in 1875, revised as *The Tourists' Guide Through the Hawaiian Islands* in 1890. In January 1888, a magazine aptly entitled *Paradise of the Pacific* began monthly publication. "Devoted to Hawaiian Tourist Travel Interests," the magazine extolled the beauty of the islands and provided travel information. It was distributed for free, relying upon advertising, later augmented by government subsidies, for its revenues. Aimed at "the inquiring and traveling public," the publishers provided copies to steamship companies, plantations, "various centers of 'tourist' travel," and six hundred public libraries across the mainland.[6]

In August 17, 1892, the short-lived, privately sponsored Hawaiian Bureau of Information was formed to collect, compile, and disseminate "correct" information about Hawai'i to foreign nations. This organization strove to "encourage the establishment of hotels, sanitariums and other resorts in the Hawaiian Islands for the entertainment of tourists, the care of invalids and others seeking recreation and health."[7] Its activities included contacting various tourist agencies, publishing the brochure "Hawaii the Paradise of the Pacific and Inferno of the World," and organizing Hawai'i's exhibit at the 1893 World's Columbian Exposition in Chicago. The

latter included hula dancers in grass skirts and a cyclorama of Kīlauea volcano.

Among other things, the new publicity emphasized the inviting, health-promoting Pacific Ocean as one of Hawai'i's principal lures. In the closing decades of the nineteenth century, promoters of Hawai'i as a visitor destination adopted the health-oriented rhetoric of mainland hot springs and ocean resorts, and began to proclaim the islands' restorative climate and the benefits of sea bathing. Such enticing palaver had been commonly employed by the East Coast hot springs from at least the latter years of the eighteenth century. The appeal of better health, coupled with the "promise" of amorous encounters, had successfully promoted such mineral hot springs as Saratoga, New York, and White Sulphur Springs in West Virginia from the 1820s to the turn of the century. During the 1840s and 1850s, the restorative qualities of water, previously confined to hot springs, were expanded to encompass the ocean, and such seaside resorts as Cape May, Long Branch, Newport, and, later, Atlantic City gained popularity as venues for "the great cure-all."

The advent of improved steamship travel encouraged people interested in first-hand natural and cultural experiences to travel and also opened the health market to Hawai'i. It was illogical to induce the infirm to board a sailing ship and arduously traverse the ocean for twenty-to-thirty days in order to restore their health. Though the Hawaiian Hotel anticipated a health-conscious clientele, it was not until after John D. and Adolph Spreckels's Oceanic Steamship Company's establishment of regularly scheduled, seven-to-nine day cruises between Honolulu and San Francisco in 1883, that proximity to the ocean began to figure into Hawai'i's hotel equation. Several beachfront houses in Waikīkī were converted into hotels; the earliest known was the Park Beach, the most famous was Sans Souci, where Robert Louis Stevenson convalesced in 1893. In addition, the downtown Royal Hawaiian Hotel (formerly the Hawaiian Hotel) erected an elaborate bathhouse on the beach for its guests in the 1890s, with four rooms for those adventurous few who might wish to stay a night.

None of Waikīkī's nineteenth-century beachfront hotels survived more than eighteen months. The lure of the sea, however, did not die, and following the annexation of the islands, the seventy-five-room Moana Hotel opened its doors in 1901. It was one of three major turn-of-the-century hotels to be constructed on O'ahu and part of an enormous building binge propelled by the optimism generated by

top right *Park Beach Hotel, Waikīkī, O'ahu, 1888. Previously the residence of George W. Macfarlane, the Park Beach is the earliest known beachfront hotel at Waikīkī. Sitting at the Kapi'olani Park end of the beach, it closed in less than ten months.*
bottom right *Waikiki Villa, Waikīkī, O'ahu, 1889, originally opened as a bathhouse. When Hamilton Johnson took over the management of the downtown Hawaiian Hotel in 1891, he made the bathhouse available to patrons of that hostelry; it became known as the Hawaiian Annex. The present Royal Hawaiian Hotel stands at this location today.*

Hawai'i's new territorial status. Between 1899 and 1903, much of downtown Honolulu was rebuilt, following the Beaux-Arts vision of "City Beautiful," and its hotel accommodations kept pace.

As the improvements in transportation promoted the construction of hotels, the explosion in hotel construction in turn expanded transportation opportunities to the islands. In 1898, only two passenger steamers plied the waves between California and Honolulu, the Oceanic Steamship Company's *Alameda* and *Mariposa* each making a round trip about once a month, each ship holding about one hundred passengers. By 1901, two or three steamers arrived each week from San Francisco, as the Spreckels brothers had added the *Sierra*, *Sonoma*, and *Ventura*, each with a capacity for over four hundred passengers, to their Pacific routes (in 1900), and the *Australia* and *Zealandia* also began stopping regularly in Hawai'i on their Sydney to San Francisco or Vancouver journeys. Also in 1901 Captain William Matson augmented his fleet of sailing vessels with the steamer *Enterprise*, the first oil-fueled steamship in the Pacific. He continued to acquire steamships, which carried freight and passengers to Hawai'i, and by 1917, Matson offered weekly passenger steamer service between San Francisco and Honolulu.[8] Thus, with new, readily available trans-Pacific steamers, a new territorial status, and an American population that was increasingly aware of the islands' alluring beauty, Hawai'i was poised for a major expansion in its tourist trade.

THE NEW HOTELS OF THE TURN OF THE CENTURY

By far the grandest manifestation of Hawai'i's new circumstances was the six-story, downtown hotel, the Alexander Young, with its three hundred guestrooms and suites. Completed in 1903, at a cost of two million dollars, it was the largest building in Hawai'i and remained Hawai'i's tallest building until the completion of the

top *Alexander Young Hotel, Honolulu, O'ahu, 1903, was Honolulu's premier hotel during the first quarter of the twentieth century.*
bottom *Alexander Young Hotel, second-floor lobby*

Aloha Tower in 1926. The *Pacific Commercial Advertiser*, on the hotel's opening, joyously, and fairly accurately, boasted,

> San Francisco, with its 400,000 people, has only one caravansary as good and is priding itself on the prospect of one more. Across the bay, Oakland, with 100,000 people, has nothing to compare with it. East through Nevada, Utah, Colorado, Kansas and so on to the western limits of Chicago, no hotel of equal cost and splendor can be found. Between Chicago and Honolulu is a distance of 4,000 miles and a population of over thirty millions of people, yet but one hotel can be found in all the region which equals in size, modern fittings and general attractiveness the hotel which bears the name of Alexander Young.[9]

Designed by Oakland architect George W. Percy (1847–1900), the building had twenty-four-inch-thick walls faced with sandstone from Calussa, California. The Renaissance-revival-style hotel's main body stood four stories and terminated with a roof garden, evocative of, though more climatically appropriate than, the famed gardens of New York's Waldorf-Astoria and Chicago's Palmer House. The building's wings, with their Corinthian columns, towered a full six stories above Bishop Street. With marble wainscoted walls, plaster ceilings, lushly carpeted or mosaic floors, and granite entry columns from Alexander Young's homeland, Scotland, the hotel radiated opulence. Indeed, the magazine *Paradise of the Pacific* reported in 1903 that visitors to Honolulu justifiably mistook the building for the royal palace.

Complementing its palatial appearance, the hotel offered an array of up-to-date conveniences. Not only did it have its own artesian water supply, an electric generator, and a refrigeration unit capable of producing two-and-one-half tons of ice a day, but also

above *Alexander Young Hotel, roof garden*
opposite *Mabel Clare Craft, in 1899, serenely espoused, "It is a geographical blessing that one cannot reach Hawai'i by rail. To arrive there with soot in the eyes and dust in the garments, tired and travel-stained, with the throb of the rails sounding in the ears, would be like appearing before royalty in old clothes. But to slip smoothly down through six days of delicious rest and languor is fit preparation for entering into the presence of this queen of the sundown sea."*

twenty-two elevators and telephones in every guestroom connected not only to the front desk but the whole of Honolulu. The Alexander Young offered sixty-one rooms and suites with private baths and another sixty-seven with shared baths. Augmenting the food and entertainment on the resplendent roof garden, two dining rooms were on the sixth floors, and a bar and billiard room in the basement. Its two second-floor parlors were modeled after those in the White House, further emphasizing Hawai'i's new association with the United States.

In an era of grand gestures and ambitious undertakings, when more was more and bigger was better, this building stood as an awesomely outrageous act. Honolulu, with its population of approximately 40,000 and a visitor count of less than 4,000, could not support the hotel, and it was not until the 1920s that this venture showed a profit. To compensate for the losses incurred by the hotel, Alexander Young purchased his two major competitors, the Moana Hotel in Waikīkī in 1907 and the downtown Royal Hawaiian Hotel in 1909; the profits from these two hotels would help cover costs of the Alexander Young.

The Moana Hotel, at the time of its opening in 1901 was declared, "the costliest and most elaborate hotel building in the Hawaiian Islands."[10] It and the Alexander Young, though both adhering to a classical architectural tradition, were designed for different audiences. The Palladio-inspired, elegant, dignified, and majestic Alexander Young was the major landmark and social hub of the city. Its formality addressed the needs of people coming to Honolulu for government, business, or military purposes, while its roof garden, dining rooms, and cafe catered to the social life of both travelers and Honolulu's residents. In contrast to the imposing solidity of its downtown compatriot, the Moana was less substantial in terms of materials and massing, more playful and light hearted in design, and explicitly addressed Hawai'i's tropical climate. It was designed exclusively to serve a clientele intent on leisure and tourism. Oliver G. Traphagan (1854–1932), Honolulu's preeminent architect, who left a successful career in Duluth, Minnesota, to relocate in Hawai'i for his daughter's health, considered the six-story Colonial-style building to be "designed for Honolulu alone. It was difficult to adhere to any strict method of architecture for such a climate and there is no hotel on the face of the earth which is similar in outline."[11] Its broad oceanfront lānai

comported to mainland resort hotels, but the openness of the building explicitly reflected its adjustment to the local climate. Its second- and fourth-story balconies and fifth-floor "observatory lanai" provided ample opportunity for interaction with Hawai'i's delightful blue skies and tropical balm, as did its dining room, which was "open to every breeze which might float in from ocean or from the valleys."[12] Thoroughly modern, it had its own electrical and cold storage plants; each of its seventy-five rooms had a bath and telephone. Private room phones were just coming of age, as the Hotel Netherland in New York was the first hotel to offer this amenity in 1894. Even New York's Waldorf-Astoria was still bereft of a switchboard and room phones in 1901.

Whereas the Alexander Young and the Moana hotels served the traditional function of providing accommodations for those visiting Waikīkī or Honolulu, O'ahu's third new hotel of the period, the Haleiwa Hotel was conceived as a destination unto itself. Opening twenty months before the Moana, on August 5, 1899, it was commissioned by Benjamin Dillingham, the owner of the Oahu Railway & Land Company. The railway's primary purpose was to open the lands west of Honolulu and on O'ahu's north shore for sugar cultivation by providing a means to transport the sugar to Honolulu harbor. However, Dillingham hoped to encourage passenger travel as well, and his new hotel was a means to this end. To entice passengers to take the "scenic," three-hour, fifty-six-mile rail journey from Honolulu to Hale'iwa, Dillingham decided to develop deluxe accommodations placed within a delightful setting as a near-end-of-line attraction. Leasing forty acres of land along the ocean and the Anahulu stream from Bishop Estate, the railroad magnate employed Traphagan to design his hotel.

As at the Moana Hotel, the architect employed a colonial style, masterfully combining a sense of majesty and informality

Moana Hotel, Waikīkī, Oʻahu, 1901. "Moana, known far and wide among the Polynesians and to every race in the Pacific Ocean as the 'broad expanse of the ocean,' was a fit cognomen for the magnificent hostelry which was dedicated as a resting place for the tourists of the wide, wide world who visit the Paradise of the Pacific."

clockwise from top left *Moana Hotel, view from Waikīkī beach; view from its pier. The three-hundred-foot pier was torn down in 1930, the victim of poor maintenance. The hotel's two concrete wings were added in 1918; a gala evening during the 1920s; banyan courtyard where the popular radio program "Hawaii Calls" commenced broadcasting live Hawaiian music to the mainland on July 3, 1935 and attracted millions of listeners over the next forty years. The melodious moments inspired many to come see the islands firsthand.*

into this retreat from urban Honolulu. He softened the two-story building's lines by rounding its ends and wrapping an expansive lānai around it. A one-and-a-half-story, semicircular portico with imposing Ionic columns made a strong entry statement while continuing the curvilinear flow of the building. Shingled roofs dominated the massing, which was broken up by several spacious second-story balconies. A rustic bridge with Adirondack railings and thatch-roofed portals quaintly conveyed guests from the railway terminal, over the Anahulu stream, to the hotel and provided a picturesque "Kodak moment" to the newly emerging population of amateur photographers, who began clicking in earnest following the introduction of the Brownie camera in 1900.

The hotel's fourteen guestrooms each had a private bath, hot-and-cold running water, and telephone connection with the front desk. Several guest cottages were located on the property, and one cottage exclusively housed the billiard and pool room. Augmenting this nineteenth-century pastime, the north shore retreat offered a myriad of more vigorous and contemporary recreations including tennis, canoeing, ocean fishing, and golfing. The ocean-front nine-hole golf course, the second to be constructed in the islands, placed the hotel in the forefront of resort innovation—the earliest known resort golf course opened in 1898 at Pinehurst, North Carolina. The Haleiwa Hotel's associated hunting lodge, a log cabin five miles distant in the mountains, was another popular amenity, as well as "a big cemented pool of soft fresh water filled from the wonderful springs on the old Emerson homestead (a part of the

right *Back cover from* The Story of Hawaii, *a booklet published by the HTB, July 1925. The illustration allegorically depicted the tropical cornucopia of Hawai'i with Waikīkī and the Moana Hotel in the foreground.*

above and opposite *Haleiwa Hotel, Haleiwa, Oʻahu, 1899. Promoted as a get-away from the city, the hotel was almost exclusively patronized by Hawaiʻi residents. With the tapering off of this clientele, in part a result of the increasing preference for automobiles over rail travel, the hotel closed in 1928. It reopened in 1931, as the Haleiwa Beach Club, a fairly exclusive private club. In 1939, it briefly re-emerged as a hotel, and during World War II, it was used as an officer's club. Following the war, it fell into disrepair and was torn down in 1952.*

Major Curtis P. Iaukea, Queen Lili'uokalani's former chamberlain, 1883. Major Iaukea was hired as the first manager of the Haleiwa Hotel, and as a result, a number of pieces of furniture from 'Iolani Palace also adorned the hotel.

Let us first resolve that we want tourists and are determined to offer them such inducements as will entice them here; let us then resolve that we want the best of the species, the wealthy, the healthy, and the Bohemian, who has money to spend and will spend it, rather than the weak and hollow-chested invalid; we do not want to make Honolulu a hospital but a recreation ground. We want a class that will know what they require, know when they get it, pay for what is furnished, and insist on having it.[14]

The report recommended supporting the improvement of transportation services with the West Coast and the commencement of a long-term, community-supported advertising campaign "to thoroughly establish Hawaii as the most desirable summer and winter resort extant." To this end, the Honolulu Merchant's Association partnered with the Honolulu Chamber of Commerce to form the Hawaii Promotion Committee (HPC) in 1903, and the territorial legislature immediately appropriated $6,000 for the committee to use for advertising. The business community augmented this government subsidy with contributions of approximately $12,000. Edward M. Boyd was named the HPC secretary, and in October 1903, the organization commenced publishing magazine advertisements and printed pamphlets and a booklet, titled "Beauty Spots of Hawaii." The HPC also established mailing lists by asking banks and county assessors for names and addresses of people in their community sufficiently affluent to travel to Hawai'i and contacted school districts for names of teachers, who would likely have the time during summers and the cultural curiosity to venture to the islands. To further expand its efforts, the HPC established mainland offices in Los Angeles in 1908 and Seattle in 1910. Thanks to the HPC, the venerable Cook Tours, which had provided tours of Europe and the world since 1855, included Hawai'i as one of their itineraries by the winter of 1910–1911.[15]

hotel property)...a drawing card for those who do not take kindly to salt water." This made the Haleiwa Hotel one of the earliest caravansaries in Hawai'i to have a swimming pool. The hotel also generated its own electricity and kept its own garden and chickens for fresh eggs.[13]

WAIKĪKĪ COMES OF AGE

Although the Haleiwa Hotel offered ocean bathing, it could not compete with Waikīkī as a tourist destination. This was due in part to the active promotion of tourism by the Honolulu Merchants' Association, which in 1902 decided to concentrate on attracting a recreation-minded clientele, declaring in its Rothwell-Humburg-Lishman report:

The HPC's goal of making Honolulu a first-class visitor destination was not achieved until 1927, when the new Royal Hawaiian Hotel opened, providing Waikīkī with a hotel of worldwide distinction. However, the building of the new hotel was but one of several, closely related development projects dedicated to enhancing and expanding Hawai'i's visitor industry. The territorial government stepped forward with two critical endeavors, which, in turn, led to private sector capital investments. First and foremost came the construction of the Ala Wai Canal, which profoundly transformed Waikīkī's landscape. By diverting the mountain streams that fed the rice, fish, and duck ponds of the district, the canal converted Waikīkī from a wetland to solid ground. The Ala Wai Canal not only accomplished its purported purpose of eliminating pesky mosquito from the area but also banished wetland agriculture from Waikīkī and literally paved the way for residential and commercial use. With the completion of the canal in 1924, Waikīkī's lovely sand beach and calm, reef-protected ocean waters were augmented with a surrounding environment capable of supporting a visitor destination.

In addition to undertaking the new drainage canal, the territorial government also upgraded Honolulu's visitor reception facilities. Piers 8, 9, and 10 were rebuilt with concrete sheds between 1920 and 1924, and the construction of Aloha Tower followed. The ten-story tower, the tallest building in the islands until 1955, was designed by Arthur Reynolds, and, after some debate, was completed in 1926. A number of citizens feared the tower would detract from the natural beauty of the islands and mar the incoming ship passengers' impressions of the Ko'olau Mountains, which form a backdrop for Honolulu. Despite such objections, the proponents of progress carried the day.

With Aloha Tower moving toward completion, the Matson Navigation Company kept pace with the government's commitment to tourism when it issued a $7.5 million contract for the construction of the 17,000-ton *Malolo* in 1925. This new 650-passenger luxury oceanliner was the fastest ship on the Pacific at the time, plying the waves at a cruising speed of twenty-two knots, or approximately twenty-five miles per hour. Reducing the six-and-a-half day journey down to four-and-a-half days, the ship placed a Hawai'i vacation a tantalizing four days closer to California.

Also in 1925, the Territorial Hotel Company, the owner of the Moana, Honolulu Seaside, and Alexander Young hotels, decided to demolish the Honolulu Seaside in Waikīkī and replace it with the Royal Hawaiian Hotel, a hostelry worthy of the other visitor-oriented improvements. Warren & Wetmore of New York were selected to design the new hotel. The U.S.'s premier hotel architects, the firm had established its reputation through works such as the Ritz-Carlton, Biltmore, Belmont, Vanderbilt, Commodore, Chatham, and Ambassador hotels in New York City, the Broadmoor in Colorado Springs, and a number of Atlantic City hotels. This Beaux-Arts firm, also the designers of Grand Central Station, produced a highly competent, albeit rather straight-forward, Spanish Colonial revival building, accentuated by a 150-foot campanile. A giant of a structure by Hawai'i standards, the hotel almost doubled Waikīkī's room count with its four hundred guestrooms, each with its own bath and balcony. The building's slightly modified H plan invited the trade winds and featured a six-story main body, from which the campanile rose. One of the four-story wings ran parallel with the beach, offering splendid ocean and Diamond Head vistas. The courtyards on the other three sides flowed out onto fifteen acres of lushly planted grounds, the work of landscape architect R. T. Stevens of Santa Barbara, California. The garden's sumptuous collection of tropical exotics was presided over by large monkey pod trees and the palms of the royal Helumoa coconut grove.

Preliminary Announcement
Matson Travel Offerings
HAWAII & SOUTH SEAS

The interior of the hotel was equally splendid, with the walls and ceiling beams of the ballroom and oceanfront gallery hand painted by Guiseppe Gentiluomo of New York, making a "fairyland of birds and plant life drawn from the artist's imagination."[16] Hotel amenities also included a banquet hall, an auditorium with two stages, and a motion picture theater. For outdoor recreation, the hotel offered tennis and badminton courts, lawn bowling, and croquet, in addition to ocean bathing. The Royal Hawaiian Hotel also had its own off-premises golf course, now the Waialae Country Club, which was originally laid out by internationally renowned golf course designer Seth Raynor of New York. In developing the Royal Hawaiian's course Raynor modeled certain holes after celebrated holes from such courses as St. Andrews and North Berwick in Scotland, Biarritz in France, and the National Golf Links of America at Southampton, New York. Between 1915 and 1925, Raynor laid out over one hundred courses across the U.S., including the Dune course at Pebble Beach, California. The course at Wai'alae was his last project, as he died in January 1926, a month after completing the design and departing Hawai'i.[17]

left *E. D. Tenney (1860–1934), the President of Castle & Cooke, was also president of Matson Navigation and also the Territorial Hotel Company, which owned the Moana, Alexander Young, and Royal Hawaiian Hotels.*
below *Royal Hawaiian Hotel, Waikīkī, O'ahu, 1927*

opposite, clockwise from top left *Matson Navigation's* Lurline *enters Honolulu Harbor on its way to Aloha Tower, ca. 1950. After the success of* Malolo, *Matson upgraded its fleet, entering the* Monterey, Mariposa, *and* Lurline *into service in 1931 and 1932. The* Malolo *was renamed the* Matsonia, *and it and the* Lurline *handled the California-Hawai'i route while the* Monterey *and* Mariposa *handled the Honolulu-South Pacific route; The S. S. Malolo's smoking room's dark, paneled walls, fireplace, and classical detailing provided a masculine space in the best men's club tradition; The upper deck staterooms of the S. S. Malolo included an enclosed lānai with sliding doors that accessed the deck; Matson Navigation Company brochure cover, 1935*

Costing over five million dollars to build, the Royal Hawaiian Hotel catered to the rich and near rich. Those who came stayed an average of four to six weeks and frequently brought their own cars and chauffeurs with them. The new hotel redefined the meaning of elegance for Waikīkī and, with the new luxury oceanliner *Malolo*, attracted a new clientele to Hawai'i. As its nickname, "the Pink Palace" signified, it became the home away from home for America's reigning royalty. Such stars of Hollywood's silver screen as Charlie Chaplin, Shirley Temple, Clark Gable, Mary Pickford and Douglas Fairbanks, Carol Lombard and William Powell, Groucho Marx, and Bing Crosby all stayed at the Royal, as did the Rockefellers, Fords, and Roosevelts. Indeed, the affluent now had not only a high-quality ocean liner upon which to travel to the islands, but also a hotel that met their standards. The traveling public responded positively to these improvements: in 1928 Hawai'i's visitor count exceeded 20,000 for the first time, the most people to come to the islands since 1846, the apex of the whaling period.

Reacting to the expectations engendered by the opening of the Royal Hawaiian Hotel and other visitor industry advances, the owners of Waikīkī's principal cottage-style hotels upgraded their properties with architect designed buildings; the Waikiki Tavern, Niumalu, and Halekulani all undertook major construction programs between 1926 and 1931. None could compare with the majesty of the Pink Palace, but with these additions, Waikīkī emerged as Hawai'i's primary visitor destination, containing more than 50 percent of the 2,500 hotel rooms in the territory at the outbreak of World War II.

opposite *Royal Hawaiian Hotel. The coconut trees in the courtyard descended from the royal grove, Helumoa, which a century before numbered over 10,000 trees.*
right *Royal Hawaiian Hotel. All rooms at the hotel had their own lānai or balconies.*

Royal Hawaiian Hotel. The fifteen acres of lushly planted grounds was the work of landscape architect R. T. Stevens of Santa Barbara, California.

HOTELS OUTSIDE O'AHU

Although Waikīkī in O'ahu was the hub of the visitor industry, traveler accommodations existed on the outer islands (later known as "neighbor islands") as well. Hotels had been established in Līhu'e, Kaua'i; Wailuku, Maui; and Hilo, Hawai'i; in the late nineteenth century, when the sugar industry greatly expanded the economic vitality of these islands and created the need to travel there. On Kaua'i, C. W. Spitz opened the Lihue Hotel for business in 1889 on Nawiliwili Road. Renamed the Fair View a year later, it was acquired in 1892 by William Henry Rice. Offering seventy-five guestrooms, it remained the primary hostelry on Kaua'i, serving both business and vacation oriented travelers for almost fifty years.

On the island of Maui, Wailuku began to supplant Lahaina as the island's commercial center, and by 1894, the Wailuku Hotel emerged to serve the increasing number of business travelers to that city. However, the grandest hotel in Wailuku was the Grand Hotel, which opened its doors in 1916. Designed by Honolulu architect J. Holmberg, the building featured a spacious lobby and dining room, as well as broad, wrap-around lānai. In 1920, this property was sold to the Maui Hotel Company, which also operated the Wailuku Hotel and the Pioneer Inn in Lahaina. In 1929, E. J. Walsh and his wife acquired the Grand Hotel, extensively remodeled the interior, and added a new twenty-five-room stucco wing to the hotel. With its sixty-one guestrooms, it was the largest hotel in Maui County until after World War II.

On the island of Hawai'i, the Hilo Hotel started in the 1890s in a thirty-year-old residence on Waiānuenue Avenue. The chief claim to fame of the residence was that King Kalākaua had once lived there. In 1897, a new stick-style hotel, designed by Honolulu architects Ripley & Dickey replaced it. Maui born and M.I.T. educated, C. W. Dickey (1871–1942), the period's premier architect in Hawai'i, had previous

left *Luggage decal for the Grand Hotel, ca. 1930*
below *Grand Hotel, Wailuku, Maui, 1929 addition, changed its name to the Maui Grand in 1938, an appellation it retained until its closure in the early 1960s.*

above *Seaside Hotel brochure, late 1920s. By the 1920s, the hula had been stripped of its bawdy lasciviousness, but not its sensual connotations. The dance's public performance in a hotel environment, which had been so soundly denounced seventy years before had become sufficiently sanitized to be socially acceptable for the delectation of a sophisticated audience of mixed company during this era of the flapper. The dancer's grass skirt, so frequently associated with the hula, derives from the Gilbert Islands, having been introduced to Hawai'i in the 1880s by King Kalākaua when he revitalized the dance form.*

right *Viola Weight and Bert Carlson, "Honolulu Lou," 1931*

hotel-design experience with San Diego's Hotel del Coronado. The *Pacific Commercial Advertiser* applauded the erection of the new Hilo Hotel in its new location, opposite the courthouse, as its predecessor "was limited as to rooms and void of conveniences. The place has been a nightmare to the people of Hilo, for the reason it had a tendency to drive people away, while the new one will be inviting."[18] George Lycurgus (1860–1960), the proprietor of the Volcano House, acquired this property in 1908, and his family operated this establishment until 1969, when the Honolulu firm of C. Brewer purchased it.

Standing in marked contrast to the hotels in Līhu'e, Wailuku, and Hilo, where business travelers figured heavily as the clientele, the Kona Inn at Kailua-Kona on the island of Hawai'i opened in November 1928 with the tourist market specifically in mind. Built by the Inter-Island Steam Navigation Company, a subsidiary of Matson Navigation, the company's secretary-treasurer and main proponent of the project, Stanley C. Kennedy (1890–1968), informed the newspapers:

> We have the Volcano House in the Kilauea locality, and our new hotel in the Kona district on the end of the island makes an ideal [automobile] stopping place, to say nothing of its historical interest.

top *Hilo Hotel, Hilo, island of Hawai'i , 1897. Characterized by its sprawling, wraparound lānai with attenuated columns, it was a Hilo landmark until a more modern structure replaced it in 1956.*
bottom *Halekulani Hotel, Waikīkī, O'ahu, 1931. The Halekulani, originated as the Hau Tree in 1907, in a former beach house of the Lewers family. In 1917, Clifford Kimball acquired the property and renamed it the Halekulani, the House Befitting Heaven, the name grateful Hawaiians had bestowed upon the property when the Lewers family allowed them to store their canoes on the property. An expansion of the hotel commenced in 1926 and culminated in a new main building, designed by C. W. Dickey, opening in 1931.*

clockwise from top left *Kona Inn, Kailua-Kona, island of Hawai'i , 1928, octagonal-shaped lobby; koa-canoe bar, a headboard maintaining a tropic ambiance; lānai for the guestroom wing*

opposite *Kona Inn, 80' x 40' beachfront swimming pool*

Our tourist business is increasing rapidly on Hawaii and having no adequate facilities for handling travelers in that district heretofore, we were compelled to put up this hotel to accommodate our patrons.[19]

For all intents and purposes, the Kona Inn may be considered Hawaiʻi's first outer-island, oceanfront resort hotel. Designed by C. W. Dickey, the hotel featured a turretlike, octagonal lobby and lounge, from which a pair of wings extended along the ocean frontage. One wing housed the kitchen and dining room and the other guestrooms, each with a private bath. Lānai graced the *makai* side, providing every room with an ocean view and refreshing sea breezes, which were further enhanced by a tropic decor. The grounds were landscaped by Hawaiʻi-born landscape architect Catherine Richards.

Numerous skeptics relied upon the hackneyed "Kennedy's Folly," when discussing the project; however, the Kona Inn met with immediate success, and within two years, Dickey prepared plans that doubled the capacity of the hotel. The August 4, 1929, *Honolulu Advertiser* reported, "It is expected that Kona Inn will have a capacity to accommodate even the heaviest weeks of travel. Since its opening, Kona Inn has proved to be a valuable asset to Inter-Island and the addition is a result of the continuous patronage of tourists and local people." The article addressed the early realization that tourism was a means to attract permanent residents and concluded by noting that tourist travel had the potential of enhancing Hawaiʻi's real estate market, as "last week several prominent

Cover of a souvenir booklet, 1943

real estate firms reported tentative sales to tourists who intend building residences here."[20]

Unfortunately, the early success of the Kona Inn was shortly decimated by the onset of the Great Depression and the advent of World War II. These two tumultuous events consigned visions of tourism development to oblivion, and more than two decades elapsed before any major hotels were built in Hawaiʻi. When hotel construction began again, the world that peered out from under the atomic bomb's mushroom cloud was much different from the one that gasped at the crash of the stock market on Black Friday in 1929. For Hawaiʻi's tourist industry, the change was for the good.

opposite *Kona Inn. The Inter-Island Steam Navigation Company originally intended to build the Kona Inn on the site of Huliheʻe Palace. This idea met with sufficient opposition that the Territory of Hawaiʻi purchased the palace and the company erected its new hotel on a four-acre parcel adjoining the former royal residence.*

3 # The Incipient Boom

A TRAVEL-INDUSTRY SUCCESS story beyond anyone's wildest dreams, tourism in Hawai'i following the conclusion of World War II accelerated at an unimaginable and spectacular pace. Certainly, the continued western migration of America's population, placing more people closer to Hawai'i fueled the influx, as did an unprecedented postwar prosperity, which provided Americans with the disposable income and inclination to undertake vacation travel, not only by automobile, but also overseas.[1] Heightened and more sophisticated marketing of the island paradise also played a role, augmented by the numerous veterans who had experienced Hawai'i firsthand during the war. However, the coming of age of affordable passenger air travel and Hawai'i's admission into the United States as the fiftieth state in 1959, more than other reasons, propelled the islands' upward spiral of visitors during the mid-twentieth century.

Prior to the war, leisure travel to Hawai'i was the almost exclusive domain of the affluent, who had the necessary time and the wherewithal to enjoy the pleasures of ocean liners. Though Pan

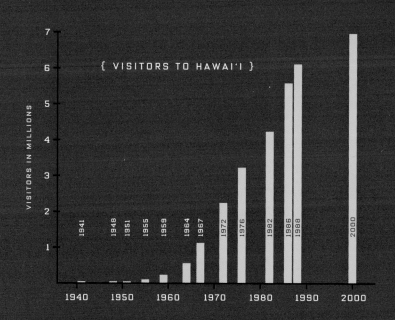

{ VISITORS TO HAWAI'I }

opposite *Waikikian Hotel, Waikīkī, O'ahu, 1956, guest rooms housed in a long two-story building*

right *Pan American World Airways brochure, 1948*
opposite
Pan American Airways Clipper landing in Hawaii, ca. 1937. The journey to Hawai'i suddenly shrunk from days to hours when Pan American Airways inaugurated its passenger service to Honolulu on October 21, 1936.

American Airways introduced passenger air service to Hawai'i in 1936 with its four engine "flying boats"—making the flight from San Francisco to Hawai'i in eighteen to twenty hours depending on the winds—less than three thousand people came to the islands by air prior to World War II due to the high cost, and ocean liners reigned supreme. This abruptly changed in the years immediately following the war as surplus C-54 cargo planes were cheaply acquired and converted by airlines into passenger-carrying DC-4s. In 1947, the Civil Aeronautics Board certified United Airlines whose founder and president, William A. Patterson, had been born and raised in Waipahu on the island of O'ahu, to join PanAm in flying from San Francisco to Honolulu; fourteen months later, it certified Northwest Orient for the Seattle and Portland to Honolulu routes. Between 1946 and 1948 British Commonwealth Pacific Airlines (later acquired by Quantas) and Canadian Pacific Airlines commenced their Vancouver to Sydney routes, with a stop in Honolulu. Philippine Airlines initiated flights between Manila and San Francisco with a Honolulu stop in 1946, and in 1954, Japan Airlines' Tokyo-Honolulu-San Francisco service commenced. The competition led to the development of considerably cheaper coach or economy fares—introduced in late 1952 on United's Hawai'i flights for $125. The number of tourists to Hawai'i rose, and by 1955, 77 percent of all visitors arriving in Honolulu came by airplane, compared to less than one percent in 1941.

Travel time continued to decrease. The DC-4, starting in 1946, made the San Francisco to Hawai'i run in eleven hours and forty-five minutes; in 1950, both United and Pan American began flying Boeing Stratocruisers between California and Hawai'i, with a travel time slightly over nine hours; in 1955, United introduced the fifty-four passenger DC-7, with a seven-and-a-half hour flight time. However, the big breakthrough came on September 6, 1959, when

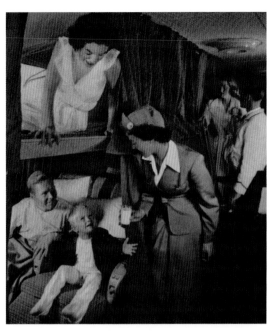

Pan American's Boeing 707 jet aircraft traversed the Pacific in under 5 hours. The coming of jet travel led more visitors to Hawai'i, and by 1963, Honolulu International Airport not only boasted the world's longest runway but handled more flights a day than Washington DC.

On August 14, 1959, only weeks before the first passenger jet set down in the islands, President Dwight D. Eisenhower signed the Hawai'i Statehood Bill into law. Hawai'i was now officially a part of the United States. Although still a remarkably different place than the other forty-nine states, travelers were now assured that life in the islands was sufficiently familiar to be part of the nation. All the comforts of home were now added to Hawai'i's exotic South Seas allure.

The growth in popularity of Hawaii as a vacation destination affected every facet of its culture. Recognizing the economic potential of tourism for the islands, Territorial Governor Ingram M. Stainback in his message to the 1947 legislature proposed that the government match private contributions to the Hawaii Visitors Bureau (HVB) on a dollar for dollar basis, rather than the earlier formula of one government dollar for every two private.[2] The legislature agreed and appropriated $75,000 for the bureau to advertise Hawai'i. In 1949, this amount was elevated to $250,000, with a stipulation that $150,000 be expended on promoting the neighbor

islands of Kaua'i, Maui, and Hawai'i. Government support of the HVB's efforts continued to grow throughout the 1950s, surpassing the million-dollar mark in 1960. Although private contributions increased during the period, they could not keep pace with the enthusiasm of the territorial government, and by the end of the decade, the state was providing three dollars for every one contributed by the industry. Still, Hawai'i's government expenditures lagged behind that of such East Coast competitors as Florida, Bermuda, and the Bahamas.[3]

HOTEL HANA MAUI

The first significant hotel project to emerge in the postwar years was the Hana Ranch Hotel, which officially opened in June 1947 in Maui. San Francisco millionaire, sportsman, businessman, and rancher Paul l. Fagan (1890–1960), the husband of Helen Irwin, the sole heiress to the Hawai'i sugar-generated fortune of William Irwin, purchased the faltering Ka'elekū Sugar Company in Hāna in 1943. Observing the economic and social disruption experienced in the neighboring town of Kīpahulu when its sugar mill suddenly shut down, Fagan acted to avert a similar fate in Hāna. He converted his newly acquired, 10,000-acre plantation into a ranch, providing jobs for many displaced sugar workers. To diversify the community's economic base, he envisioned a resort hotel for Hāna and broached the idea to Matson Navigation, the owners of the Royal Hawaiian and Moana hotels, in August 1945. Unsuccessful in convincing Matson "to make the Valley Island one of the garden spot resorts of the postwar tourist world,"[4] Fagan moved forward on his own, announcing to the *Maui News* that he was "going ahead with plans for the hotel and [a residential] subdivision in order to stabilize the population of Hana. By providing work for local people we can help to achieve our stabilization project."[5]

opposite *The largest, fastest, and most comfortable passenger plane of its day, the Boeing 377 Stratocruiser, with its distinctive bullet nose, may well have been the most luxurious plane ever to fly a commercial route. Though capable of seating 112 passengers, the Stratocruisers on the San Francisco-Honolulu run only accommodated 52, as its main cabin was outfitted with sleeping berths and fully reclining seats. The interiors of the Hawai'i bound planes were specially decorated with lauhala clad walls, trimmed with bamboo and tropical curtains. A byproduct of World War II, the Stratocruiser's lineage, and many of its parts, can be traced back to the B-29 Super Fortress bomber.*

left *Matson Navigation matchbook, 1950s*
below *The* Lurline *arrives in Honolulu harbor, 1950s.*
right Holiday, *1948. The issue dedicated twenty-five pages to the islands and featured Fritz Henele's portrait of Puunani on the cover.*
opposite *With the conclusion of World War II, the visitor industry had to retool. The Royal Hawaiian Hotel underwent a $1,250,000 renovation following its use by the military during the war and did not reopen until January 28, 1947. Matson's primary ocean liners servicing Hawaiʻi, appropriated for wartime purposes, had to be refitted. Aloha Tower did not shed its camouflage until May 1947.*

APRIL 1948 / 50c

HOLIDAY

Work was soon underway on the hotel, which still remains an economic mainstay of Hāna. Seattle landscape architect Butler Sturdevent began transforming a former canefield into a tropical garden for the hotel's grounds, and Honolulu architect Albert Ely Ives (1891–1966) was brought on to design the "simple informal ranch hotel, set in the atmosphere of old, largely unchanged Hawaii."[6] A cottage hotel sitting on twenty acres, the Hana Ranch Hotel's largest building, a single-story, wood-frame structure, housed the office as well as a dining room and offered views of Hāna Bay and Kaʻuiki Hill. Characteristic of its openness, a lānai served not only as the building's entry but also as the reception lobby. Two other lānai provided informal spaces for cocktails and lounging.

Catering to a high-class clientele, the hotel changed its name from the Hana Ranch Hotel to the more sedate Hotel Hana Maui within a year of its opening. Blending a sense of "old Hawaii" with an air of refined sophistication, the up-scale yet casual main building featured lauhala-clad walls adorned with late eighteenth and early nineteenth century lithographic and engraved prints of the islands acquired in Europe by Hawaiian art collector Donald Angus at the request of the Fagans, as well as magnificent 1920s oil paintings by Arman Manookian vividly portraying romantic images of ancient Hawaiʻi from Mrs. Fagan's private collection. Similarly, the library was comprised exclusively of first edition books.[7] The resort offered guests the use of a movie theater, an eighteen-hole pitch-and-putt course, a swimming pool, and riding stables. However, what it offered most was isolation wrapped in a native Hawaiian

top right *Hotel Hana Maui, Hana, Maui, 1948, lobby*
bottom right *Hotel Hana Maui, lānai*
opposite *Hotel Hana Maui, front entry*

Hotel Hana Maui, main building

social environment. Responding to an ever-accelerating globe where privacy is a rare commodity, Fagan based his new resort on Hawai'i's traditional isolation from the world, just at the moment when the islands were becoming easier to access. The Hotel Hana Maui appealed to those nineteenth-century sensibilities expressed by Charles Nordhoff in 1874:

> Society in Honolulu possesses some peculiar features, owing in part to the singularly isolated situation of this little capital, and partly to the composition of the social body. Honolulu is a capital city unconnected with any other place in the world by telegraph... To a New Yorker, who gets his news hot and hot all day and night, and can't go to sleep without first looking in at the Fifth Avenue Hotel to hear the latest item, this will seem deplorable enough; but you have no idea how charming, how pleasant, how satisfactory it is for a busy or overworked man to be thus for a while absolutely isolated from affairs; to feel that for a month at least the world must get on without your interfering hand; and though you may dread beforehand this enforced separation from politics and business, you will find it very pleasant in the actual experience.[8]

Located in lush, but very remote Hāna, the hotel had no telephones or air conditioning and also shunned television's intrusive presence, introduced to Hawai'i in 1953. The hotel was accessed either over a poor, fifty-six mile, near-single lane road, renowned for its 617 twists and turns and 54 bridges and unpaved until 1962, or, after the completion of the airport in November 1950, via a twelve-minute flight from Kahului or an hour plane ride from Honolulu. In order to assure the tranquil environment would work its charms, the resort would not accept reservations for less than four days.

Hotel Hana Maui, dining area with Manookian paintings on the lauhala walls

Fagan was not the only one to recognize the potential for neighbor-island tourism, but achieving this vision was a long, uphill struggle. Hawaiian and Aloha airlines' institution of regularly scheduled inter-island airline services transformed the "outer islands" into the "neighbor islands," and made neighbor-island tourism development a truly realizable possibility.[9] This promise was not fulfilled until the introduction of the package tour to Hawai'i in the 1950s, which included trips to one or more neighbor islands. Appealing especially to groups and conducted tour businesses, the package tour was well received by mainland travel agents who found such offerings highly salable and more profitable

than just booking transportation and a hotel. By 1962, almost two-thirds of the 362,145 travelers staying in Hawai'i visited at least one neighbor island. However, the character of these trips followed a pattern consistently associated with whirlwind sightseeing tours, "three islands in five days." As a result, the neighbor-island hotels saw only a short-term, highly transient clientele. The hotels were designed to furnish sleeping accommodations, meal-and-beverage service, a swimming pool, and usually some form of evening entertainment. There was little need for daytime recreation, as the patrons spent the day sightseeing. The hotel provided shelter for the night, while the traveler visited the island. The Hotel Hana Maui carved out its own niche, standing apart from the typical neighbor-island hotel by defining itself as an exclusive domain unto itself.

KAUA'I'S RESPONSE TO TOURISM

Of all the neighbor islands, Kaua'i, with its verdant, tropical character, superb beaches, and breathtaking mountain scenery, appeared best suited for increased tourism development. Closer to Honolulu than Maui or Hawai'i, it "had the most to offer in the way of tourist attractions."[10] As a result, the Inter-Island Navigation Steamship Company, in January 1946, mere months after the close of World War II, moved to assert its position on Kaua'i in the postwar travel market. Picking up where it had left off in 1929 when it built the Kona Inn, the company purchased the Lihue Hotel, with its 15.3 acres of grounds, from the estate of William Henry Rice and renamed it the Kauai Inn. Inter-Island's president, Stanley C. Kennedy, explained,

This move is in line with the company's previously announced belief that hotel properties must be developed and more modern facilities be maintained for local residents as well as tourists.

opposite *Hotel Hana Maui postcard, 1958*
top *Hotel Hana Maui*
bottom *The Inter-Island Steam Navigation Company's subsidiary, Inter-Island Airways, the predecessor of Hawaiian Airlines, inaugurated regular commercial flights between the four largest islands on November 11, 1929. A fleet of three twin-engine, eight-passenger Sikorsky S-38 amphibious airplanes with open-air seating took three-and-a-half hours to fly from O'ahu to Hilo, with a stop on Maui.*

Hawaiian Airlines

PACIFIC OCEAN

Kauai

Niihau

Oahu

Molokai

Maui

HAWAIIAN ISLANDS

Hawaii

Flight Information

above *Kauai Inn, Nāwiliwili, Kauaʻi, 1948, view of buildings and grounds dating from the 1950s, after its acquisition by Inter-Island Resorts. In 1922, proprietor Rice renamed the Fairview Hotel the Lihue, and operated it under this name until the hotel closed its doors with the U.S. entry into World War II.*

opposite, left *Hawaiian Airlines flight information packet, 1950s. The packet's romanticized paradise imagery reflected the shift in passenger demographics from business to pleasure travelers.*

opposite, right *Lloyd Sexton, postcard depicting Hawaiian Airlines' forty-four-passenger Convair 340, early 1950s. The airline postcard accurately claimed that the Convair "brings inter-island air travel to a new peak of achievement," while the sender of the postcard noted, "Larry loved this little plane—I did also, but oh! My! The way it would take off and landed really gave me the trills—Tis* truely *[sic] lovely lovely here."*

For the outside islands, small, comfortable, moderately priced inns or cottage type hotels are essential. We must start work immediately if the territory is to be in a position to handle visitors two or three years from now when transportation is available.

The scenic beauty of the Garden Island has never been adequately "sold" either to tourists or residents of the territory. With adequate hotel and transportation facilities available a visit to Kauai will be a "must" for everyone.[11]

The *Garden Island* newspaper editor C. J. Fern approached the purchase with cautious optimism in the editorial, "What is Kauai Going to Do About Tourists?": "The attitude of the island in the past toward the tourist has been one of sufferance," as sugar and pineapple anchored the island's way of life. He saw the economic possibilities of the "tourist business" and urged others to meet the new industry's challenges "with cooperation and interest."[12]

Within a few years, other hotels appeared on the island, with the Coco Palms, "the granddaddy of Kauai resorts,"[13] coming to the fore. On January 25, 1953, Island Holidays Ltd., whose membership included Lyle Guslander, the company president, William Newport, William Mullahey, and Grace Buscher, leased the Coco Palms from Veda Hills with an option to buy. This twenty-four-room operation consisted of a family residence converted into a lodge with eight guestrooms and a surplus army barracks reconfigured to hold sixteen rooms with paper-thin walls. Situated on the site of Deborah Kapule's nineteenth-century inn, the hotel was set across the road from a sandy beach in a thirty-five acre grove of two thousand coconut trees, the remains of a former copra plantation started by William Lindeman in 1896. Mullahey, a regional director for Pan American Airlines, who joined the group as a personal investment, informed The *Garden Island* newspaper that Island Holiday intended to expand the hotel and develop a Hawaiian atmosphere, which would not be difficult considering the property's lagoons, coconut grove, and seaside location.[14]

Grace Buscher (1910–2000) was named manager of the hotel, and Island Holidays commenced an ambitious building program developing the property into a cottage-style hotel. By 1956, the Coco Palms was the largest hotel on the neighbor islands, with eighty-two rooms; in that year, Lyle Guslander (1914–1984) demolished ten cottages to construct a twenty-four-unit building, raising its room count to ninety-six. He claimed to be "looking ahead to the rapidly approaching jet-age of commercial transportation. When that strikes in a couple of years Hawaii will be swamped by visitors and we've got to be ready to handle them."[15]

The lure of the hotel was based largely on its atmosphere. Buscher's inimitable hospitality and ingenious management, as well as the hotel's setting and design, made it "the citadel of Polynesia."[16] Although she had no experience with hotel management, Buscher knew well the art of presentation, having previously worked in gourmet food preparation at Harry Good's restaurant in Honolulu and as a wine and food columnist for the *Honolulu Advertiser*. She had a definite flair for marketing ambiance, weaving her enchantment to transform the lagoons on the property into "royal fishponds" and to have celebrity guests replenish the coconut grove with trees that bore their names on bronze plaques. Bing Crosby, the Princess of Japan, Duke Kahanamoku, and others planted coconuts on the grounds. Her greatest inspiration, however, gently exploded upon an unsuspecting world in 1954, when

---

opposite *Coco Palms, Wailua, Kauai, ca. 1965*

she transformed a daily maintenance chore into a vivid tourist memory. With a bartender beating on a drum borrowed from a Buddhist temple and a waiter blowing a conch shell, a gardener jogged along the lagoon swinging a flaming torch to light stationary tiki torches. "The Call to Feast" torch-lighting ceremony was thus born and continued every evening at dusk for almost forty years. This picturesque, close-of-day ritual was featured in the motion picture *Blue Hawaii*, starring Elvis Presley, and immediately imprinted itself on the minds of millions. It has since become standard fare at many resorts in Hawai'i and around the globe, an indispensable part of the Hawaiian resort experience.

The hotel's architecture correlated well with Buscher's machinations. The expansion of the hotel between 1956 and 1965 provided ample opportunity for the manager's imagination to intertwine with that of architect George "Pete" Wimberly.[17] The main building included an enormous arched lobby; its form, but neither its scale nor materials, inspired by ancient Hawaiian canoe sheds. A coral-block floor contrasted with the dark wood and lava rock interior and provided guests with textures of the islands, as did the fishnet chandeliers and imitation tapa on the reception desk. The hotel and its thatch-roofed cottages were adorned with artifacts from across the Pacific, with the guestrooms' imported South Pacific giant-clam-shell bathroom sinks proving to be most memorable. Stone images of the turtle and eel, traditional Hawaiian family gods, caught the eye of visitors before they entered the lobby, as also did a

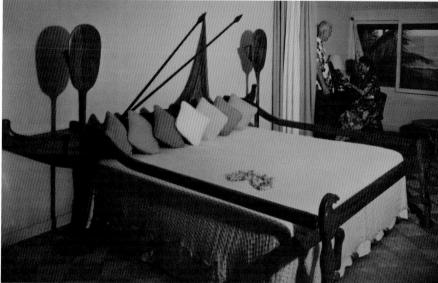

top right *Coco Palms, postcard of bathroom with giant clamshell basin, early 1970s*
bottom right *Coco Palms, postcard of a guest room with koa outrigger bed with paddle lights and fishnet bed spread, 1960s*
opposite *Coco Palms, postcard of the grounds, 1974*

*Coco Palms matchbook,
date unknown*

above *A pilgrimage to the Coco Palms, the Graceland of the Pacific, has become a must for all true Elvis aficionados. Most of the last twenty minutes of* Blue Hawaii *were filmed on the hotel's grounds and its neighboring area. The wedding scene of Elvis and Joan Blackman gliding down the lagoon in an outrigger canoe has inspired many couples to take their vows at the hotel, and the King, himself, honeymooned here with Priscilla following their lavish Las Vegas wedding in 1967.*
right *Coco Palms, postcard of lobby, 1969*

lele, or oracle tower. Carved tiki abounded. Discussing the hotel, Wimberly explained that many of the Hawaiian features were synthetic: "It is a matter of verisimilitude—the appearance of reality—rather than authenticity, but it reflects the spirit of things that are distinctive here."[18] In addition, the grounds featured a wedding chapel that was donated to the hotel by MGM in the mid-1950s after its use in the film *Miss Sadie Thompson*, starring Rita Hayworth.

The Coco Palms made Wailua the center of tourism on Kaua'i for the 1950s, with Po'ipū's four-mile stretch of dry, sunny coastline remaining virtually ignored, except by some local residents who owned cottages along the beach. The conversion of the Prince Kuhio, a three-story condominium apartment, into a hotel in the early 1960s marked the first move toward tourism development in the Po'ipū area. The Waiohai opened in Po'ipū shortly thereafter, in 1961. Called "the Kauai cousin of the Halekulani," it was established by George and Richard Kimball, whose family had previously managed the Haleiwa Hotel for eight years and then operated the Halekulani Hotel in Waikīkī from 1917 on. Designed by one of Honolulu's foremost architects, Vladimir Ossipoff, the Waiohai, with its twenty-four units and understated architecture and decor, epitomized "restrained good taste."[19] It followed a low-key sensibility that "attempted as much as possible to retain Hawaii's charm."[20] The Kimballs felt Kaua'i should not "develop its tourism on a mass basis, but should cater to quality" and hoped the ten-acre beachfront hotel would attract independent travelers who would stay a week or longer. Thus the Kimballs, like Paul Fagan in Hāna, broke

top *Waiohai, Po'ipū, Kaua'i, 1962, cottages with bleached redwood board and batten exterior walls viewed from the beach*
bottom *Waiohai. The Kimball brothers insisted that all rooms at the Waiohai have an ocean view, including the dining room.*

above *Kauai Surf Hotel, Kalapakī Beach, Kauaʻi, 1960. Inter-Island Resorts' ten-story hotel was the first highrise hotel on the neighbor islands and had the first passenger elevator on Kauaʻi. Its construction was a response to the tripling of Kauaʻi's visitor count between 1958 and 1961.*

opposite *The Biltmore, Waikīkī, Oʻahu, 1955. It was the tallest building in Hawaiʻi when completed. Others followed, maintaining Waikīkī as the hub of Hawaiʻi's visitor industry.*

from the neighbor island norm of catering to sightseers on tour, in hopes of attracting a clientele in search of peace and comfort. Though featuring, "a relaxed atmosphere and luxury service,"[21] the hotel only managed to break even, and in July 1964, the Kimballs sold it to Lyle Guslander who added twenty-to-thirty rooms, but retained a similar character.

HIGH RISES IN WAIKĪKĪ

While the Hotel Hana Maui, Coco Palms, and Waiohai embraced the repose of a tropical retreat from civilization, Waikīkī moved in a completely different direction. Commencing with the Islander Hotel in 1945, an explosion of new hotels redefined the district in the decade following World War II. In March 1948, the Site and Location Committee of the HVB recommended that emphasis be placed on hotel development in Waikīkī and projected an additional 200 to 400 rooms would be needed over the next five years.[22] This number proved to be conservative, as between 1948 and 1953 this premier beach's room count increased from approximately 1,100 to 2,000. Thenceforth, the concentration of rooms in this district accelerated rapidly, surpassing 3,000 by 1955 and tripling to almost 9,000 by 1962. Towering seven-to-twelve stories in the air, the Edgewater, Reef, Surfrider, Waikiki Biltmore, and Princess Kaiulani hotels dramatically altered Waikīkī's previously lowrise skyline.

In response to this burst of building, some residents expressed distress; however, the *Paradise of the Pacific* approvingly observed: "We believe the Waikiki beachfront we pictured in our May [1962] issue is lovelier than the same scene as shown in a full-color photo of ten years ago . . . Both lovelier and more exciting."[23] The editors found "the lei of brilliantly-lighted hotels [along Waikīkī beach] a true—and attractive—part of any 1962 [Hawaiʻi] Image." The magazine further declared that if Waikīkī was to remain

above *Waikikian Hotel, Waikīkī, Oʻahu, 1956, guest room*
right *Waikikian Hotel, lobby*
opposite *Waikikian Hotel. An exception to the norm, designed by Wimberly & Cook, this low-rise modern adaptation of Pacific Island forms made "hyperbolic paraboloid" a household word in fifties Honolulu.*

competitive in the global tourism market, visitors would have to be shown, "*why Hawaii is a better point-of-call than Miami, Las Vegas, and Cannes,* . . . not why it is as good as Tahiti." Hawai'i had to be portrayed as "a modern paradise with unmatched facilities," rather than some "sort of mid-Pacific sideshow."[24]

Responding to this vision, the development of Waikīkī intensified. Ever-enlarging hotels, primarily concrete boxes of uninspired design, accommodated an ever-expanding number of people who took advantage of inexpensive roundtrip airfares (under one hundred dollars) to cavort on Hawai'i's famous crescent of sand. Opening on February 19, 1955, the Waikiki Biltmore Hotel earned the distinction of being the territory's tallest building. Scant months later, the Princess Kaiulani Hotel surpassed the Biltmore's height, only, in turn, to be overshadowed by the Hawaiian Village's seventeen-story Diamond Head Tower in 1961 and Foster Tower in 1962. Impelled by statehood, the advent of jet-passenger service to Honolulu, and an ever-growing budget of the HVB, each passing year saw taller and taller buildings appear along the beach. The ensuing years witnessed the construction of the twenty-seven-story Ilikai Apartment/Hotel (1963) and the thirty-story Rainbow Tower (1968). Waikīkī's success as a visitor destination prompted Holiday Inn to build a 650-room hotel, the largest hotel in its chain, in the district in 1970. The following year, the Sheraton Corporation opened the thirty-one-story, 1,904-room Sheraton-Waikiki. Designed by Wimberly, Whisenand, Allison, Tong & Goo of Honolulu, it was, at the time, the largest resort hotel in the world and the fifth largest hotel on the planet. Slightly smaller, but grander hotels followed on the heels of the Sheraton, including the Hawaiian Regent and Hyatt Regency Waikiki, both which delightfully celebrated Hawai'i's unique climate. The former, with its 1,346 rooms, was erected in two phases between 1970 and 1979. Designed by John Tatum in association with Chamberlain &

Associates, it featured a completely open lobby, lush courtyards and a landscaped upper level with a pool and tennis courts. The latter, also the work of Wimberly, Whisenand, Allison, Tong & Goo, completed in 1976, featured twin thirty-nine-story octagonal towers connected by an open-air atrium with a three-story waterfall. This 1,260-room, $150-million hotel was the most expensive construction project undertaken in Hawai'i to that date.[25]

THE ADVENT OF TOURISM PLANNING

In 1959, no one accurately foresaw the incredible growth that Waikīkī and Hawai'i's visitor industry was about to experience in the remaining four decades of the twentieth century. However, a number of people recognized the travel trade would figure prominently in the future economic wellbeing of the islands. In October 1959, the recently formed Hawai'i State Legislature directed the state's planning office to prepare a study on the future of tourism in Hawai'i. Several planners, contracted by the fledgling Hawai'i State Planning Office, articulated the fiftieth state's vision for an expanding visitor industry, and set forth an ambitious statewide tourism development strategy, the first broad-scale tourism planning undertaken in the United States, if not the world.[26] Local planner John Child's September 1960 report, *Structure and Growth Potential of Tourism in Hawaii*, predicted that tourism was about to become Hawai'i's major industry. Child recognized that the advent of jet-passenger service to Hawai'i and statehood were new market forces, two unique events with no real historical precedents from which to project solid numbers, leaving no "dependable means of judging this market potential."[27] However, he went on to make some projections and, to the disbelief of many, suggested 1.5 million tourists would annually come to Hawai'i by 1980, an incredible 446.5 percent increase. These crystal-ball gazers considerably

How do you make a concrete box more alluring? Superimpose a surfer riding a wave in the foreground as on the cover of this 1964 Foster Tower brochure, or, better yet, pose a bikini-clad beauty cavorting in the surf in front of the Outrigger Hotel for a pulchritudinous 1960s postcard image.

left *Elithe Aguiar, Miss Kauai 1963, of Hawaiian, Chinese, Portuguese descent, "one of Hawaii's Golden People," poses at the Kauai Surf Hotel in a 1966 postcard with an equally exotic multicultural sculpture carved for the emerging visitor trade. A popular model in the 1960s, Aguiar also appeared in the Brady Bunch's 1972 trip to Hawai'i , as well as in* Hawaii 5-0 *and* McCloud.

right *Island Holidays brochure, 1967. Moving beyond the Coco Palms, Island Holidays, headed by Myrtle Lee, expanded to the other islands with the Maui Palms and Hotel King Kamehameha. In 1958, the company formed its own travel service, which served as a feeder for the company's hotels.*

missed their mark; in 1980, 4 million tourists flocked to Hawai'i, a staggering increase of more than 1,350 percent.

Child's report noted that Waikīkī was already established as an urban resort, but to accommodate the influx of visitors, the industry would need to expand to the neighbor islands where the tropical Polynesian paradise image could be further nurtured. For the 1950s and the 1960s travel industry, a tropical Polynesian paradise equated itself with beaches, a warm climate, and an exotic, titillating, "primitive" freedom signified by material objects and architectural ornament, now nostalgically referred to as "tiki culture."

The close correlation between the reality of Hawai'i's physical environment and the tourist images of a tropical paradise was a high priority for the tourist trade. Donald Wolbrink, the head of the Honolulu office of nationally known community planner Harland Bartholomew & Associates, observed,

> We are concerned primarily in Hawaii with those tourists and visitors who openly, and in an uninhibited manner, enjoy the more sensuous things in life. They do not clutter up their minds with a camouflage of appearing to seek intellectual betterment. They are not seeking cultural enhancement. They just want to relax and have fun. And they want to do it in a place of great physical beauty.
>
> This is an attractive type of clientele, because such people know what their interests are. And those of us charged with planning and designing their environment can think quite clearly about those interests.[28]

For Hawai'i to continue to attract such a clientele, the paradise image of Hawai'i had to be nurtured and, ultimately, translated into resort design throughout the islands. Projecting a potential build out of Waikīkī to 20,000 hotel rooms, Wolbrink and other planners found "this over-crowding, this high density, this congestion makes it most difficult to maintain the 'paradise' image"[29] and determined the necessity of the development of neighbor-island resorts.

The expansion of tourism to the neighbor islands was more specifically advocated in another 1960 Hawai'i State Planning Office report, *Visitor Destination Areas in Hawaii*. This four-part study was prepared by several consultants, including John Child; Belt, Collins & Associates; Harris, Kerr, Forster & Company; and the Honolulu office of Harland Bartholomew. Placing an emphasis upon the need to develop enhanced neighbor-island venues, the report noted,

> The real growth development of neighbor islands hotel business and facilities will require the development of a different group market [than the package tour]... the vacationer as distinguished from the sightseer. It is in this class of vacationer that the future potential lies [sic] for supporting major hotel development in the neighbor islands.[30]

Part three of the report identified thirteen areas as suitable resort regions that could be "known internationally for their own sake, not as side trips after Waikiki." The report envisioned these destinations to exude the "charm of old Hawaii... [and contain] most of the important conveniences of a modern one-stop tourist resort." The densities of these new tourist destination areas were to be less than Waikīkī and were anticipated to range from five-to-twenty units per acre.[31]

Planning consultant, Walter Collins declared,

top row *Airline brochures emphasized the sun, fun, and beauty aspects of the paradise image. The ancient Hawaiian "sport of kings," surfing—both on boards and in outrigger canoes—was rejuvenated between 1914 and 1920 as a means of marketing Hawai'i and frequently figured in postwar advertising.*

bottom left *Trade Winds Tour brochure, 1958. International Travel Service, formed in 1946 as a travel agency to service outbound Hawai'i residents, established a separate department, Trade Wind Tours, to meet the needs of visitors arriving in the islands. It eventually became the largest tour-and-travel company in Hawai'i and one of the largest travel wholesalers in the nation.*

bottom center *Jimmie MacKenzie's tour company was one of Hawai'i's longer-lived independent escort tour operators. The part-Hawaiian owner invited visitors "to enjoy my islands in the authentic Hawaiian way," and included in his 1967 offerings the "Paradise Discovered" tour, an eleven-day trip around the island chain.*

bottom right *Happiness Tours extolled the freedom of an island vacation with "Do-As-U-Please" tours in 1961.*

[The state planning documents were] a major break-through in resort planning.... I felt we had an enormous opportunity here, not only for development but to achieve something that did not exist anywhere else.... Through [the development of resort destination areas] we have the opportunity for excelling in a highly competitive field.[32]

The plans, although far off the mark concerning tourism's growth and scale, set the general direction for Hawai'i's visitor industry for the next thirty-five years. They guided government decisions concerning zoning and the provision of such public improvements as roads and water systems, airports, and historic attractions necessary to support private resort development.[33]

In 1960, certain areas, such as Kā'anapali on Maui, were already moving forward, others would bide their time, awaiting an appropriate infusion of capital. The remainder of this book is their story.

HVB poster girl Rose Marie Alvaro dances the hula at the United Airlines ticket counter in Los Angeles, accompanied by the music of Ernie Paschoal and his Gray Line Troubadours, 1961. The HVB and the tour companies sponsored entertainers to travel across the mainland to promote Hawai'i.

chapter 4

Hawai'i's First Master-planned Destination Resort

BEFORE THERE WERE the artificial islands off Dubai, or even a Cancun, Laguna Phuket, or Costa do Sauipe, there was Kā'anapali. Although not the world's first master-planned beach resort, it was, for its time, certainly the most ambitious and far-reaching endeavor of its kind. A few efforts had been made during the 1950s to design new seaside towns on the Mediterranean, such as Torre del Mare on Italy's Ligurian coast, by Milan architect Mario Galvagni, in 1959. In Brazil, Pernambuco Beach on Santa Amara island, designed by architect Henrique E. Mindlin, emerged along the shore as a completely new town.[1] However, these developments were overwhelmingly residential in character and primarily focused on community. They were conceptually similar to the master-planned community Reston, Virginia—totally new towns, only with a beach and a hotel as a commercial component.

Kā'anapali, on Maui's leeward coast, presented Hawai'i, and most of the globe, with an infant idea of infinite intensity: a visitor-oriented, completely master-planned destination resort. Rather than build a resort hotel for visitors, American Factors (Amfac)

opposite *Aerial view of Kā'anapali, late 1960s. In 1960 there were only three employees tending the two hundred acres of sugar growing at Kā'anapali. The land's gross income amounted to $18,500. Fifteen years later the resort area employed over two thousand people and earned a gross income of $45 million.*

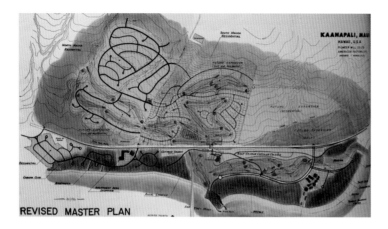

Donald Wolbrink, Kāʻanapali revised master plan, 1962

proposed to construct an entirely self-contained resort city where, "the tourist can stay without ever having to leave the resort."[2]

The idea for such a new destination resort emerged in 1953, when Amfac president, George Sumner, directed Belt, Collins & Associates, a Honolulu planning and engineering firm, to undertake a land-use study and economic analysis for shoreline property owned by Pioneer Mill, a sugar company and subsidiary of Amfac, at Kāʻanapali. As a result of these studies, Pioneer Mill's Board of Directors met at a luau on the beach near Black Rock in 1956, and the sugar company voted to venture into the unknown and develop a fully master-planned visitor-destination resort, a first for the twentieth century. Billed as "a second Waikiki,"[3] Amfac intended to develop its new visitor playground on four hundred acres of scrublands and sugar-cane fields, fronting a magnificent two-and-a-half-mile-long, crescent-shaped beach. Almost twice the size of Waikīkī and receiving less than sixteen inches of rain a year, this sun-soaked

property was owned solely by Pioneer Mill, who found itself in the omnipotent position of master developer: it had complete control over what facilities would be built and how to determine the character of the area. Eschewing the haphazard, unplanned streetscape of Waikīkī, with its multitude of individual property owners each intent on his or her own enterprises, Amfac intended to avoid the shortcomings of Hawaiʻi's world famous beach: Kāʻanapali was to be less dense, with a dozen beautiful beachfront lots, of approximately ten acres each, allocated for hotel use. In addition, residential units, proposed primarily for transient-visitor use, and a shopping center were to be provided, as well as one, and later two, golf courses. Lush, green, open space with designated pockets of activity became the order of the day, and the norm for subsequent oceanfront resort development worldwide.

The project was audacious in many ways. Of all the islands, Maui was the least visited, and usually only for a day trip—although some tours deigned to spend the night. The Pioneer Inn, with all of ten rooms, offered the only visitor accommodations on Maui's sun-drenched western shore; most Maui travelers stayed near Wailuku at the town of Kahului in Island Holidays's sixty-six-room Maui Palms, opened in 1954.

Looking beyond Maui's lackluster record for tourism to invest in a future of its own making, Pioneer Mill hired Donald Wolbrink (1912–1997) to complete the master plan. Wolbrink was born in Ganges, Michigan. Receiving both bachelor's and master's degrees in landscape design from the University of Michigan, he worked for the National Park Service between 1934 and 1941 and, for the first three years of World War II, was employed by the U.S. Army Corps of Engineers in Missouri Valley. From 1944 to 1946, he served on active duty as a Naval officer in Hawaiʻi. Following the war, he joined Harland Bartholomew & Associates, working as a

The Wo Hing Society Hall, Lahaina, Maui, 1913. This was one of a number of buildings restored by the Lahaina Restoration Foundation. The foundation was organized in conjunction with Kā'anapali to transform the sleepy town of Lahaina into a visitor point of interest. Initially envisioned as "a 'little Williamsburg' type of development," it quickly morphed into a mecca for consumption.

field representative in the Midwest. In late 1947, he returned to Hawai'i to open the firm's Honolulu office, the first planning company in Hawai'i. By 1959, he had already established a reputation on the islands, having master planned the National Cemetery of the Pacific at Punchbowl in Honolulu, Honolulu's Wai'alae-Kāhala residential area for Bishop Estate, and Kahului for Alexander & Baldwin. From his imagination sprang Kā'anapali's resort plan replete with hotels sited on spacious, oceanfront grounds, affording views of the Pacific on one side and vistas across the golf course to the verdant West Maui Mountains on the other.

The first step to implement Wolbrink's plan was convincing the government to relocate the coastal highway inland to its present location, giving Pioneer Mill an uninterrupted oceanfront project area. Maui County, at a cost of $120,000, had just extended its highway through Kā'anapali in 1956. Less than a year later, at the request of Amfac, the Maui Board of Supervisors approved the brand new highway's relocation, "for the economic development of Maui."[4] A one million dollar undertaking, the new Honoapi'ilani Highway was completed in 1959; however, work on the new resort did not begin until mid-1960. The initial stirrings of activity included the construction of the infrastructure, featuring all underground electric and telephone lines, and a Robert Trent Jones golf course, the only eighteen-hole course on Maui. As the Wai'alae Country Club was no longer associated with the Royal Hawaiian Hotel, Kā'anapali was the only resort in Hawai'i with its own golf course. It would not be the last. Traditionally considered a leisure activity of the affluent, golf experienced a surge of popularity in the U.S. in the 1950s, with country clubs popping up in communities across the nation. Kā'anapali's developers recognized the value of this trend:

> The cost of the first nine holes—$1 million—is probably an all-time high, and the results promise to justify the investment. Lahaina backers are determined to make this course a mecca for golfers from round the world, a championship course which will bring those who demand the best.[5]

Now all Kā'anapali needed was some hotels.

In 1961, construction commenced on a 212-room, "Polynesian resort" on a prime lot at Kā'anapali leased by Sheraton Hotels, at that time the largest hotel company in the world with fifty-six properties. It was the chain's first neighbor island venture,

Sheraton Maui Hotel pop-out brochure, 1963

although it had already acquired the Royal Hawaiian, Moana, Princess Kaiulani, and Surfrider hotels in Waikīkī. Indeed, the new hotel project, the Sheraton Maui Hotel, brought "to a Neighbor Island for the first time the vast marketing and promotional facilities of a major national hotel chain."[6] Up to this moment, all neighbor-island hotels had been Hawaiʻi owned and operated. The hotel opened on January 23, 1963—a specially chartered United Airlines Mark IV DC-8 Jet Mainliner had brought the Sheraton's first guests to Maui the previous day. The plane's arrival marked the first time a commercial jet airliner flew from the mainland directly to a neighbor island. Schools were closed so everyone could participate in Maui's giant step into the future, and people jammed the airport to see the then-uncommon sight: a jet airliner arriving with visitors enroute to Kāʻanapali. That day, the passengers included such celebrities as Sammy Snead, Bob Hope, and Bing Crosby. Following

its arrival, the plane was placed on public display, the first DC-8 to be viewed on the neighbor islands.

The Sheraton Maui Hotel's distinctive architecture drew even more attention than United's DC-8 as it dramatically strove to match its compelling cliff, beach, and ocean setting. Built on top of and alongside the prominent cliff Puʻu Kekaʻa, the western-most point on Maui, the new Sheraton was labeled, "the hotel built upside down." Guests took a winding drive up the back of the cliff to its top, where they entered the hotel's lobby situated at the cliff's summit. From there, they descended by elevator to their rooms and the magnificent beach below. Built on a fifteen-acre beachfront parcel, thirteen oval-shaped "Polynesian cottages" of modern design, each with six units, augmented the eight-story hotel's capacity.[7]

The hotel's playful circular lobby, open to the sky, was vaguely reminiscent of Edward Durrell Stone's Bay Roc Hotel at Montego Bay, Jamaica, completed in 1953. However, the lobby's lava-rock columns, central pool, and fountain, housing an Edward Brownlee sculpture of the mythical Tahitian canoe of Rata rising from the water, vigorously proclaimed a Polynesian presence and moved it well beyond Stone's simple design. The curved lines of the lobby were echoed in the adjoining lower-level dining room with its evocative whaling-era decor. Beyond the dining room, the Barkentine Bar and Terrace encircled the brow of the cliff, offering panoramic views of the Pacific Ocean, Molokai, and Lānaʻi.

The bold, white concrete main building stunningly contrasted with the black cliff face, while its massing integrated itself with the natural feature. Broad, curvilinear lānaʻi seemed to terrace down the cliff side, and their plantings appeared to make "a series of hanging gardens on the sheer face of the rock."[8] The contour-conforming layout gave every guestroom superb panoramic views from the mountains to the sea.

clockwise from top left *Sheraton Kāʻanapali, Kāʻanapali, Maui, 1963; lānai; Barkentine Bar and Terrace; lobby*

"This is my
HAWAII
You'll never forget the golden days you spend with us."

Elizabeth Logue, a featured star in the Mirisch Corporation's spectacular motion picture of James Michener's monumental novel, "Hawaii"

above *HVB Brochure, 1966. During the 1960s, the HVB regularly chose the wholesome eroticism of Elizabeth Logue to sensually spark Hawai'i's come-hither tropical allure. Beyond her enchanting beauty, the HVB capitalized on her role as Noelani in the movie version of* Hawaii, *James Michener's best-selling novel. Today, the charming siren is best remembered as the ingenue who ran down the beach at the beginning of each episode of* Hawaii 5-0.
right *HVB Brochure, interior pages*

Architectural Record applauded the design as "resort architecture of distinction: spectacular and romantic, yet carried out with taste and a proper degree of restraint. The romantic tropic setting seems to ask for romantic architecture—harsh rectilinearity could hardly provide the careful atmosphere the architects have achieved."[9]

The hotel was designed by Wimberly, Whisenand, Allison & Tong. Receiving the commission from Sheraton was a dream come true for the firm's president, Pete Wimberly. The architect had been entranced by the Pu'u Keka'a cliff for almost a decade, having drawn rough sketches for a hotel as early as 1952. He felt the site "tops them all for uniqueness and beauty, and lends itself to many innovations in design and construction."[10]

Wimberly (1915–1996) was born in Ellensburg, Washington, and came to Hawai'i in 1940, after graduating from the University of Washington's architecture program in 1937 and working for several years in Los Angeles. During World War II, he worked at Pearl Harbor, where he met Howard L. Cook, with whom he went into partnership following the war, forming Wimberly & Cook. At the start of the Sheraton project, during 1962, their firm dissolved as Cook disagreed with Wimberly's desire to expand the business beyond the borders of Hawai'i. The firm was reorganized as Wimberly, Whisenand, Allison & Tong, which later became Wimberly, Allison, Tong, & Goo (WATG). This Hawai'i firm has since garnered an international reputation for its resort designs and in the course of the next forty years received commissions for hospitality and leisure projects across the globe; many of these hotels have been recognized as among the best in the world. WATG has designed more hotels on the lists of the world's finest hotels, as compiled by *Travel & Leisure* and *Condé Nast Traveller*, than any other architectural firm, giving credence to the assertion that the company is "the world's

Sheraton Maui Hotel postcard, 1963

number one hotel, leisure, and entertainment design firm." Their website even includes designs for resorts in outer space.[11]

WATG now operates offices in Newport Beach, Los Angeles, Seattle, Orlando, London, and Singapore. As one Honolulu architect ruefully noted in hindsight, while his colleagues were going to AIA conventions, Wimberly smartly busied himself attending travel-industry conferences, absorbing the needs and language of this new industry, making contacts, and building relationships. He also convinced industry representatives that a resort hotel should have a positive effect not only on its guests but its surroundings, and that the globe's cultural diversity needed to be appreciated and reflected in a resort's architecture. As he explained,

You have to look at the purpose of the hotel from the traveler's viewpoint. On his trip, certainly, he wants to relax, but he also wants to "participate" in a country that is different. He is there to see and in some way understand a different way of life. He probably doesn't have the muscles to sit on the floor, for example, but he still wants to feel that for a little while he is a part of the country he is visiting. His hotel can give him some of that feeling by its design if it draws legitimately upon the local culture.... If we can combine good features from the local culture with such standard creature comforts as good plumbing and air conditioning, then we've got something.[12]

In 1968, Wimberly further predicted in *Architectural Record*:

As hotels which combine modern conveniences, proper operation, and local building practices become more common, increasing numbers of knowledgeable travelers will patronize them at luxury rates, leaving the expediently built stacked boxes to lower cost tour operators.[13]

Hotel buildings would again become architecture.

OTHER EARLY WIMBERLY HOTELS

Prior to the Sheraton Maui, Wimberly & Cook had designed the Coco Palms Hotel on Kaua'i, the Waikikian Hotel in Waikīkī, and the Hotel Bora Bora in Tahiti. All of these employed various types of wood-frame construction in a somewhat modernist manner, while very consciously emoting a sense of place. The Sheraton was the

opposite *Kona Hilton Hotel, Kailua-Kona, island of Hawai'i, 1968, renamed the Royal Kona Resort in 1994*

firm's first venture into articulating the spirit of Hawai'i in concrete; it would not be their last.

The Kona Hilton on the island of Hawai'i followed on the heels of the Sheraton and further elaborated on Wimberly's efforts to embody a Hawaiian sense of place—the romantic tropics—within the multistory context of modern architecture. "A significant landmark on the Kona coast,"[14] the Kona Hilton avoids a rectilinear box appearance with its sleek, swooping profile and oversized lānai. An entity unto itself, situated about a half mile south of the heart of Kailua-Kona on a ten-acre parcel at Pa'akai Point, the hotel's seven-story mass dramatically juts out into the ocean. Its white concrete facade vividly contrasts with the blue sky and black lava rock upon which it is built. The five million dollar hotel stirred the imagination, inciting visitors to explore the distinctiveness that is Hawai'i. Seemingly at every turn, architectural embellishments and applied ornament elicited a sense of Hawai'i with decorative features inspired by Hawaiian and Asian cultures: a large reproduction of a *hōlua* (Hawaiian sled), which originally accentuated the dining room, a chandelier composed of large wooden fish-hook motifs with a cluster of Japanese paper lanterns rendered in modern materials, and the bar area featuring a *kōnane*-stone topped bar and a wine rack wound with the leaves of the ti and 'awa, native plants used in the production of intoxicants by ancient Hawaiians. Traditional Hawaiian musical instruments also adorned the bar area. Terrazzo floors included designs depicting 'iwa birds and sea urchins, both patterns used in Hawaiian tapa, and an extensive use of lava rock joins the hotel to the land. The flowing first-floor public spaces are delightfully open to the outdoors, and offer the immediacy of ocean-shoreline interactions. At every opportunity, the hotel presents its guests with another wonder of Hawai'i, natural or cultural, and does so within an exceptionally modern context.

COMPLETED IN JANUARY 1968, the Kona Hilton, the first major national hotel chain to open on the island of Hawai'i, was viewed as another major step forward in the development of the visitor industry on this island. In a spirit of boosterism, local newspaper headlines proudly declared, "Kona Hilton's 190 Rooms Put Isle Over 2,000 [Room] Mark."[15] The article went on to note that the island of Hawai'i now had forty-one hotels, with eight having over one hundred rooms. Further bolstering the island's optimistic fervor of a tourism future, United and Pan American airlines announced in February 1968 that they would double the number of direct flights between the mainland and the island of Hawai'i's primary airport in Hilo.[16] Even more significant, Hawaiian Airlines convinced United Airlines to start its "common fare" program, allowing United passengers to fly Hawaiian to a neighbor island for no additional charge, as long as they did not stop over in Honolulu. Pan American and Northwest Orient quickly followed with similar programs, bringing the neighbor islands enticingly closer to mainland vacationers.

At its opening, the Kona Hilton was the third largest hotel on the Big Island, with only the Kona Inn, which by now had expanded to 264 rooms, and the Naniloa Hotel in Hilo, with its 205 units, having greater capacities. Within a year, it surpassed these two hotels, when the first of its two six-story tower wings opened, raising its room count to 318. With the opening of the addition, the hotel's

top left *Kona Hilton Hotel. Emulating the slope of Mauna Loa rising from the shore, the Kona Hilton's floor-by-floor setback design, accentuated by sweeping stair towers at each end of the building, provides a distinct silhouette.*

bottom left *Kona Hilton, reception desk. Virtually outdoors, it is fronted by a roofed walkway/lānai.*

opposite *Kona Hilton Hotel, view to the ocean. The chandelier draws upon Japanese lantern and Hawaiian fishhook motifs, and the terrazzo floor's pattern recalls Hawaiian depictions of* iwa *birds on tapa.*

Life, *October 8, 1965. Statehood amplified Hawai'i's presence in the minds of many Americans, thanks to media coverage, which ran the gamut from* Life *magazine's nineteen-page coverage of the "50th State," with its Elizabeth Logue fold-out cover to* Playboy's *August 1961 pictorial tribute, "The Girls of Hawaii: A Paean to the Winsome Wahines of Our Elysian Archipelgo."*

general manager, John McGuigan, told reporters that the hotel's occupancy rate during its first year was a more than anticipated 85 percent, and expressed optimism for the future by turning *Paradise of the Pacific*'s earlier advocacy for a contemporary, upbeat image for Waikīkī on its head by declaring, "the growing trend is to come to the Neighbor Islands. If you're thinking of going to Honolulu, why not just go to Chicago or New York, instead?"[17]

THE SUCCESS OF KĀʻANAPALI

By the time the Kona Hilton opened its doors for business, Kāʻanapali had come into its own, and Maui's tourist industry had sharply expanded. At the end of 1960, only 339 hotel rooms existed on Maui, and by the end of the following year, that number had only advanced to 395 rooms. The opening of Kāʻanapali's Sheraton Maui, as well as the Royal Lahaina Beach Hotel, more than doubled that figure, prompting the veteran Maui newsman Charles Young to describe Maui's tourism development as, "mushroom growth of a startling order."[18]

By 1966, the magazine *Hawaii Business and Industry* claimed that Kāʻanapali was, "beginning to look like a success," with three hotels built and a fourth underway.[19] However, Amfac's 1966 annual rental receipts were a lackluster $600,000 from Kāʻanapali. The company had initially offered extremely low rents, essentially a subsidy to induce development to get the project off the ground, which did not offset expenses. Thus in 1967, the company formed the Property Group under the management of R. Gregg Anderson. This subsidiary moved into the hotel business in 1969 when it purchased Island Holidays from Lyle Guslander. It also constructed the Whalers Village Shopping Center, which opened in December 1970 with "more realistic," i.e. higher, rents. The Property Group also developed, at Kāʻanapali, a second "executive" golf course "for duffers who had been complaining about the difficulties of the Robert Trent Jones 'championship' layout."[20]

However, Kā'anapali's major economic contribution to Amfac's bottom line and resort developments in Hawai'i occurred when the company hired John Carl Warnecke, the architect for the John F. Kennedy Memorial at Arlington Cemetery in Washington, D.C. (1963) and the Hawaii State Capitol in Honolulu (1969), to update the Kā'anapali master plan in 1966. His scope of work not only addressed the resort area, but also encompassed the lands adjoining the resort, as the company came to realize that "the real profit lies in appreciation of value in the 17,000 Amfac acres surrounding the resort."[21] Thus began a new economic perspective on the function of resort-hotel construction, which remains a truism to this day. Hotels would be built only incidentally to provide guests shelter. The resort hotel's primary purpose would be to create value, to catalyze economic appreciation of surrounding lands, which is then reaped in the sale of housing units. To the resort developer in Hawai'i, the occupancy rate of hotels has been almost irrelevant, a concern only for the hotel's management. Indeed, billionaire David Murdock, the head of Castle & Cooke, claimed in 1994 that the two luxury hotels he built on Lāna'i would never generate a profit, even if operated at 100 percent occupancy; profit derived solely from the high-end housing projects built adjoining the golf courses.

In the ensuing years, the model established at Kā'anapali fostered many progeny, both in Hawai'i and around the world. Master-planned destination resorts became readily recognized as a distinct land-use development, and by 1991, planner Glenn Kimura could facilely explain,

We define our resorts as totally planned, high activity environments which function as the destination for the vacationer. A resort is not simply a hotel in isolation. It is usually a self-contained community made up of many facilities including hotels, dining facilities, shopping and entertainment facilities, recreational facilities, and other attractions that are integrated into a naturally beautiful setting.[22]

These new resort developments reshaped the story of tourism in Hawai'i, slowly but surely, promoting an allure for the neighbor islands. In April 1975, Kā'anapali greeted 4,200 State Farm Insurance conventioneers, who made history by being the first major convention held exclusively on a neighbor island, with a visit to Waikīkī as an optional side trip. Up until that time, less than 4 percent of Hawai'i's visitors went solely to an "outer" island. Henceforth, the neighbor islands would no longer be viewed as merely an adjunct to a Waikīkī vacation, and by 1988, 33 percent of the islands' visitors were choosing to stay exclusively on a neighbor island, thanks primarily to the appearance of master-planned destination resorts.[23]

Giving flesh to the ideas laid out in the state's 1960 destination area's plans, Kā'anapali led the way, showing other landowners in Hawai'i that destination resorts were not only possible to develop, but also economically advantageous. Others followed Pioneer Mill's lead, and within thirty years, the distribution of Hawai'i's room count disclosed the dramatic shift that had occurred in the islands' visitor industry. In 1959, Waikīkī accounted for 81 percent of Hawai'i's hotel rooms, by 1990, the neighbor islands' visitor accommodations had risen to become 49 percent of the statewide total. The near fifty-fifty balance has been maintained until this day, the result of a few ideas concisely laid out in black and white in 1960 and made concrete at Kā'anapali.

5

Where God Left Off
THE DIAMOND TIARA OF LAURANCE ROCKEFELLER
AND A POLYNESIAN VILLAGE

AS KĀʻANAPALI WAS getting off the ground in Maui, smaller-scale, but equally ambitious, projects were taking shape on the island of Hawaiʻi's Kona-Kohala coast. This leeward shoreline of the Big Island, although dry and sunny, presented many challenges, and led the Hawaiʻi State Planning Office's 1960 *Visitor Destination Areas* report to project that resort development would cluster only around Kailua-Kona and Kawaihae. The supposition was well founded: no roads or utilities serviced the thirty-five-mile stretch of lava-encrusted lands separating them. Travel between Kailua-Kona and Kawaihae was possible by ocean, or an hour and a half journey by automobile via Waimea. Fresh water was near to nonexistent, resulting in a desertlike moonscape. Indeed, its starkness in 1819 caused Rose de Freycinet who accompanied her husband on a round-the-world scientific voyage to declare, "Nobody can ever have seen a more arid and dreadful aspect than this part of the island of Owighee [Hawaiʻi] that we have before us; there is not a tree, not the smallest part of a plant; one would say that fire had passed over it."[1] Any development in this area would have to

opposite *Mauna Kea Beach Hotel, Kohala coast, island of Hawaiʻi, 1965. As an* Honolulu Advertiser *editorial stated,*

> *The deep impression which lingers after a visit to the new Mauna Kea resort is that of beauty—man-made beauty sensitively blended with real natural beauty. The respect for environment, for the integrity of surroundings is everywhere evident. [It] has provided Hawaii not only with a magnificent place . . . but a reminder that physical development can enhance—rather than mar—its setting.*

Laurance Spelman Rockefeller (right) reviews plans for Mauna Kea Beach Hotel with Robert Trent Jones (center), ca. 1962.

"depend heavily upon enhancement through planting and establishment of a character similar to that of an oasis."[2] The planners envisioned Kailua-Kona as the place most promising for hotel development, as it already had an established town center, which included the Kona Inn. However, any development would have to be undertaken by a variety of landowners, similar to Waikīkī. The planners felt a dramatic major hotel was necessary if Kailua-Kona was to attain pre-eminent resort status. The area needed "the unexpected, startling surprise of a beautiful, large impressive hotel with all the niceties of comfort, elegance, architectural challenge. It calls for a hotel that identifies and establishes itself as a destination goal."[3] The planners hoped such a structure would catalyze the area in a manner similar to what the Royal Hawaiian Hotel had done for

Waikīkī some thirty years earlier. Although Kailua-Kona failed to attract such an ambitious structure, Kawaihae succeeded in doing so with the construction of the Mauna Kea Beach Hotel.

The development of such a magnificent hotel in such a desolate area was no accident. Its beginnings may be traced back to the head of Hawai'i's Department of Economic Development, George Mason's visit to Caneel Bay Plantation, a resort hotel on St. John Island in the Virgin Islands, built by Laurance Rockefeller (1910–2004). Knowing Rockefeller had invested in tropical resort development, Mason went to the Caribbean to learn more details. Following a series of conversations with hotel manager Leslie H. Moore, Jr., he invited Rockefeller to Hawai'i with the hope of inducing him to construct a hotel on the islands. In July 1960, the affluent New Yorker and his family, following a trip to Alaska and at the invitation of Hawai'i's Governor William Quinn, crossed the Pacific to visit the fiftieth state for twelve days. The media reported that he came to undertake an inventory of Hawai'i's recreational resources as part of a nationwide study prepared by the Federal Outdoor Recreation Resources Review Commission, which he chaired. In reality, the primary purpose of the journey was to investigate investment opportunities. While on the islands, Rockefeller toured Kā'anapali, met with state planning officials, and, thanks to a chartered plane donated by Aloha Airlines for the state's use, visited or flew over every potential visitor destination area identified in the state's recent 1960 study. He stayed at the Volcano House, Kona Inn, Coco Palms, and Hotel Hana Maui, where Rockefeller asked its manager, Robert Butterfield, a plethora of questions on the chal-

---

opposite *Mauna Kea Beach Hotel, view from guestroom lānai. As described by* Star Bulletin *columnist Jim Becker: "I am looking off the lanai onto a view that would be rejected by any self-respecting postcard publisher as unbelievable."*

lenges of operating a hotel in a remote island location. The final stop in this special tour was Parker Ranch in Waimea, which included a jaunt down to Kauna'oa Bay, where George Mason, Allston Boyer, and Laurance Rockefeller went for a swim. As hoped, the millionaire was completely fascinated by the setting, captivated by his view of Mauna Kea's snow-covered peak while floating in the warm, blue Pacific.

The third son of John D. Rockefeller, Jr., was favorably impressed, not only by the beauty of the islands, but also by its progressive tourism planning efforts. Recognizing Hawai'i's visitor industry's potential, he informed Governor Quinn in a January 31, 1961 letter that he intended to develop a resort, the Mauna Kea Beach Hotel, on the island of Hawai'i, beside the clear, calm waters of Kauna'oa Bay near Kawaihae. Preliminary plans were soon prepared and clearing and surveying of the site commenced. At the end of May 1961, the millionaire, along with nationally renowned golf course designer Robert Trent Jones and the governor, made a two-day visit to the area, and plans for the new hotel and golf course were solidified.[4]

The decision to invest Rockefeller money into Hawai'i's fastest growing industry was not an impulsive one, as the fifty-one-year-old businessman had already overseen three successful resort hotel projects: Jackson Lake Lodge in Grand Teton National Park, Wyoming (1955), Caneel Bay on St. John Island in the U.S. Virgin Islands (1955), and the Dorado Beach Hotel in Puerto Rico (1958). Rockefeller also had acquired the Estate Good Hope in St. Croix in 1959 and was in the process of developing Little Dix Bay in the British Virgin Islands (1964). Several motivating factors came to play in selecting these development locations. The properties were all pristine sites of exemplary beauty, which the conservation-recreation-minded Rockefeller wished to open to a wider audience and make "available to people who, like [him], want to get back to nature now and then."[5] Indeed, in Wyoming and St. John Island, he donated the natural areas surrounding his hotels to the U.S. to expand the Grand Teton National Park and establish the U.S. Virgin Islands National Park, respectively. This munificent benefactor also considered the enfeebled economic situations of the areas, which he hoped to ameliorate on a long-term basis via his developments. This was especially true of the Dorado hotel project, which supported the Puerto Rican government's Operation Bootstrap program with its objective to expand tourism opportunities beyond San Juan.

Kauna'oa Bay's crescent beach, situated in a secluded corner of the Big Island, was gorgeous but virtually inaccessible except via a dirt road and hiking trail, both over private property. In addition, Kohala's economic mainstay, sugar, was already tottering on its last leg, poised to wreck tsunami-scale socioeconomic havoc in the wake of its demise. It seemed appropriate for Rockefeller to continue his exploration of philanthropic, conservation-oriented capitalism in this circumstance. As in some of his previous projects, his foray into resort development expanded his relationship with the National Park Service: he acquired and donated the neighboring Pu'ukohola heiau, the temple built by Kamehameha the Great at the onset of his campaign to conquer the island chain, to the National Park Service, who made it into a National Historic Site.

Rockefeller selected Belt, Collins & Associates to be the project's site planners and engineers. The president of the firm, planner Walter Collins (1917–1975), had accompanied Rockefeller during his initial exploration of the islands. Collins was a local boy who grew up on Maui. He graduated from Yale University in 1941 with a degree in architecture, followed by a year of postgraduate study in planning. In 1945, after serving in the Navy and on the staff of the San Francisco Planning Commission, Collins returned to Hawai'i to work for Honolulu's City Planning Commission. A year later, he went to Hilo to help with a land-use study and became the county of Hawai'i's first planning director. In 1947, he joined the Territorial Department of Public Works as director of highway planning, and there came to know Robert Belt. In 1950, his uncle, Frank Baldwin, asked him to return to the island of his youth to serve as assistant manager and planner for the Kahului Development Company, overseeing the "Dream City" project with its 1,600 dwellings and shopping center. Upon its completion, the rapidly rising planner returned to Honolulu at the invitation of Robert Belt, to form Belt, Collins & Associates in December 1952.

Robert Belt (1907–1995), a native of Oregon and a civil engineering graduate from Oregon State University, came to Hawai'i in 1931 to work for the U.S. Bureau of Public Roads. For the next decade, he held the position of highway engineer in the Territorial Department of Public Works, and then, during World War II, served in the Navy. Following the war, he returned to the Department of Public Works, which he headed from 1947 until the formation of his partnership with Walter Collins. Their embryonic office armed the vision of a planner with the necessary practical knowledge to implement the envisioned project, adding a new wrinkle to Hawai'i's infant planning community. The nascent company's first planning effort was Pioneer Mill's feasibility study for Kā'anapali. Mauna Kea became their first major destination resort hotel project. The project required not only the construction of the hotel, its grounds, and golf course, but also the drilling of three wells, and the construction of a sewage treatment plant and a segment of what would become the Queen Ka'ahumanu Highway from Kawaihae to the hotel.

Belt, Collins & Associate's work on the Mauna Kea Beach Hotel paved the way for the firm to become one of the preeminent resort planners in the world. Over the next four decades, the company undertook projects in the U.S., Asia, Africa, Europe, India,

Mauna Kea Beach Hotel, the hotel and golf course under construction, ca. 1963

Australia, and across the Pacific. Today they maintain offices not only in Honolulu, but also in Seattle, Singapore, Hong Kong, Bangkok, and Guam.[6]

The construction of the Mauna Kea Beach Hotel proved to be a fairly prodigious logistical operation, as it was located in the middle of nowhere. All the cement for the project was barged to Kawaihae and then trucked to the property; all other materials came by way of Hilo, a good hour-and-a-half to two-hour drive away. A temporary camp was erected to house and feed the approximately five hundred men who worked on the site. The endeavor was the largest construction project on the island of Hawai'i at the time. It opened in July 1965, a year that also witnessed the completion of the

jet runway at Hilo's Lyman Airport, the Volcano National Parks' Chain of Craters Road, the road to Akaka Falls, the road to Puʻuhonua o Hōnaunau, and a highway from Honokaʻa to Waipiʻo. With all these improvements occurring rapidly, the Big Island was developing the venues necessary to support an expanded visitor industry. Ground had been broken not only on the Keāhole Airport outside Kailua-Kona by 1965, but also on the Queen Kaʻahumanu Highway, which would eventually connect the new airport to Rockefeller's new resort. The completion of these two state projects fulfilled commitments made by Governor Quinn to move the Mauna Kea Beach Hotel forward. The design of the latter state project owed a special debt of gratitude to Rockefeller as he insisted the utility poles be located fifteen hundred feet *mauka* of the highway, eliminating their unsightly presence by blending them into the dark lava fields.

The new hotel was initially conceived to follow a cottage format, similar to Rockefeller's previous ventures in wilderness and ocean hospitality and consistent with the Hotel Hana Maui and the Waiohai on Kauai's Poʻipū Beach. Abandoning his initial selection of architect John Carl Warnecke, Rockefeller turned to Skidmore, Owings & Merrill (SOM) of New York. Then considered *the* modern architecture firm of corporate America, SOM's reputation was already firmly established due to projects such as the curtain-walled Lever House in New York (1952). Rockefeller was already familiar and comfortable with the modern idiom, having introduced it to the National Park Service with Gilbert Stanley Underwood's Jackson Lake Lodge in Grand Teton National Park.

Turning a back on the simple cottages of Hāna or the Waiohai, an ultramodern, "moonage" daydream was proposed for the Mauna Kea Beach Hotel. Rockefeller described the structure as a "very radical design, totally unlike any other hotel room I've ever seen,"[7] while Allston Boyer of his staff simply described it as "a

above *Mauna Kea Beach Hotel, garden*
opposite *Mauna Kea Beach Hotel, lobby*

pretty weird looking thing" with a roof that looked like a cereal bowl turned upside down.[8] Designed to avoid air conditioning through the use of natural ventilation, the cottage's main ceiling was open, covered by an overlapping dome, which would allow the breeze to come in from any direction. A full-scale model was built on site; tests proved the natural ventilation system to be inadequate, making the interior unrelentingly hot. The structure was also unsuitable for inclement weather as evidenced by the inundation of water in the model following several storms. From these experiences, a decision was made to provide at least the availability of air conditioning;

this tilted the scales of cost efficiency in favor of a monolithic structure rather than cottages.

Armed with the new direction, SOM proceeded to design a tour de force. A seminal work, the hotel won an American Institute of Architects' Honor Award, making it not only the first building in Hawai'i to achieve such recognition but also one of the first hotels to be so honored.[9] Addressing the tropical environment with modern elan, the Mauna Kea Beach Hotel, according to the AIA judges, possessed, "gracious interiors, the gardens and green spaces capture the flavor of a resort hotel. It is completely suitable for a sub-tropical climate with its restrained detailing and fine spatial sequences in a completely modern idiom."[10]

Edward Charles "Chuck" Bassett (1921–1999) of the San Francisco office of SOM was the primary architect on the project. The building moved hotel architecture into an entirely new realm of delightful, inviting openness, grace of line and space, and a relaxed, serene majesty. *Fortune* magazine, in 1966, recognized it as one of the top ten buildings in the U.S.;[11] a year later, *Esquire* magazine proclaimed the Mauna Kea Beach Hotel to be the finest resort hotel in the world and one of the top three hotels on the planet.

Architectural Review praised it for "the astonishing interpenetration" of indoors and outdoors provided by the courtyards and lobby,[12] with its open, flowing spaces blurring the distinction between inside and outside. With the atrium lobby at the foreground, its doorless entry immediately set the tone and framed views of the horizon-spanning Pacific. The hotel's openness and attention to ocean vistas set the standard for the succeeding generation of beach

top *Mauna Kea Beach Hotel, courtyard*
bottom *Mauna Kea Beach Hotel, outdoor Terrace restaurant overlooking Kauna'oa Bay*

resorts in Hawai'i and throughout the world. Elements such as the outdoor Terrace Restaurant overlooking Kauna'oa Beach; the stepped-back, almost cascading, ocean-facing rooms; the lushly planted grounds and courtyards; the subdued evening lighting; and the over $90,000 worth of Asian and Pacific Island art selected specially for the hotel by Davis Allen of SOM all became signatures of high-end resort fare in the ensuing years. The hotel's understated elegance single handedly set forth the basic design vocabulary for ocean-front luxury globally and continues to influence tropical resort design to this day. Few resort hotels have approached the Mauna Kea Beach Hotel's level of excellence, although all have found a need to respond to it. The timeless beauty of SOM's design, coupled with an outgoing, friendly *kama'āina* (Hawai'i born) staff allows this hotel to remain in the top echelon worldwide as judged by travel publications such as *Condé Nast Traveller*, *Travel & Leisure*, and *Zagat*.[13]

Glowing accolades from the enraptured national press captured the spirit of incredible originality and quality of design that had been set before it in remote Hawai'i. Richard Joseph in *Esquire* declared the Mauna Kea to be

> the greatest resort hotel on earth. It is in fact, a compendium of superlatives.... Nobody but a Rockefeller can spend that sort of money, and nobody but Laurance Rockefeller could have spent it with such superb taste.[14]

Caskie Stinnett, writing for *Holiday* magazine, further elaborated:

> For a long time now I have stubbornly held to the view that anything Laurance S. Rockefeller can do, God can do as well. But my first glance from a plane window at Mauna Kea, the

Mauna Kea Beach Hotel, terrace

Mauna Kea Beach Hotel, third hole of golf course designed by Robert Trent Jones. The course minimized modifications to the natural terrain. His incredible inspiration, the course's signature over-the-ocean third hole has since been emulated at a number of other resorts. Journalist Ben Wood's initial reaction to the audacious design remains the best: "For a quarter of a century, Robert Trent Jones has been trying to build golf courses to ruin the morale of golfers. . . . But until he invented the third hole at Mauna . . . he never completely succeeded in destroying men's confidence." The course opened before the hotel was completed, with Gary Player, Arnold Palmer, and Jack Nicklaus playing four rounds between December 8–11, 1964. The event was filmed and the televised by NBC on successive Saturdays in March 1965.

clockwise from top left *Mauna Kea Beach Hotel. A seventh-century granite Buddha from India serves as a focal point for a stairway accessing a secluded garden; Sunday brunch is as diverse as Hawaii's multiethnic culture, blending taste treats from Asian, Hawaiian, European, and American traditions. Two wooden sculptures, watching over the area adjoining the bar, are ancestral tablets that once resided in a spirit house in the Middle Sepik region of New Guinea.*

resort that Rockefeller created amid the lava rock and desert waste of Hawaii's west coast, caused me a moment's hesitation. If nothing else, one had certainly picked up nicely where the Other had left off.... It is a Godforsaken landscape running from the foot of Mauna Kea [volcano] to the sea, and on this wasteland the Mauna Kea Beach Hotel has been placed, like a diamond tiara in the hair of a pygmy. It is an Olympian thing that has been done, but it has been done simply, gracefully and in a way that makes Mr. Rockefeller seem infinitely remote. The gleaming white four-story hotel nestles in a green oasis of palms and flaming Hawaiian foliage, a half-moon of beach lies in front of the hotel, a three-million-dollar golf course stretches along the sea and extends on volcanic rock out into the ocean, and a swimming pool and cork-turf tennis courts are hidden in the palms. After this, I presumed, Mr. Rockefeller rested.[15]

Leavitt Morris of the *Christian Science Monitor*, expressed a similar astonishment:

I have been asked many times—in a joking manner, of course—when are you going to the moon? "Never," I have replied. But today I must revise that answer on one condition. If Mr. Rockefeller decides to build a hotel on the moon I would want to go there to see it![16]

The hotel remains a joy, well worth at least a journey across the Pacific to experience.

Horace Sutton of the *Saturday Review* was one of three hundred people who attended the opening of the Mauna Kea Beach Hotel in July 1965. He called the hotel "one of the most elaborate playlands ever constructed in the United States" and declared the hotel to be "one of the greatest great houses ever conceived by anyone less than a Pharaoh."[17] Sutton's allusion to the great country houses of the affluent was not coincidental. Rockefeller had indeed, in many ways, taken the word "hotel" back to its French origins when the term referred to large private residences, or mansions. The recreations offered at the Mauna Kea Beach Hotel were those enjoyed by the affluent at their country houses: tennis, swimming, golf, and horseback riding. Here guests could anticipate the quality of life the rich enjoyed at their private retreats. The hotel was their country home in Hawai'i, and Rockefeller their host. The hotel was meant for guests who had "enough inner resources to enjoy an unorganized environment, to appreciate peace, serenity, beauty and reasonable comfort."[18] Costing $43/58 a night for a modified American plan of room and board, some speculated the remote hotel would not fare well. However, its allure was undeniable and during the first several years, it averaged over 90 percent occupancy, and its sumptuous, now world renowned, luncheon buffet attracted more than half its patrons from beyond the hotel guest list.

The motivation behind constructing the Mauna Kea Beach Hotel was to open to visitors the beautiful Kauna'oa Bay with its sparkling white-sand crescent beach and turquoise and indigo waters. However, Rockefeller, perhaps unconsciously, went much further and created, in essence, a total package, a completely human designed environment, using the beach and bay as a foundation. In so doing, he heralded the modern transformation of a resort hotel into a destination unto itself. Indeed, at the time of the hotel's opening, *Paradise of the Pacific* went so far as to claim that Rockefeller "is more responsible than anyone else for the renaissance of the destination resort."[19]

Kona Village Resort brochure, 1960s

Over the next few decades, the total transformation of the landscape would become the norm, undertaken at resort after resort. Following in the footsteps of Kāʻanapali and Mauna Kea, resorts would miraculously emerge along the leeward, lava-encrusted shores of the Big Island; on Maui, Wailea would transform Haleakalā's barren southwest coastline. The site planning precepts laid out at Kāʻanapali and Mauna Kea were further elaborated, and the design lead of the Mauna Kea Beach Hotel would undergo a variety of permutations.

A POLYNESIAN VILLAGE

At the same time Rockefeller was developing his masterwork near Kawaihae, Texas oil man John H. "Johnno" Jackson was quietly undertaking the construction of the Kona Village Resort about twenty-five miles to the south of the Mauna Kea Beach Hotel, at Kaʻūpūlehu. Jackson's resort differed radically from the East Coast millionaire's superbly handled, relaxed modern design by revisiting the thatched tradition of Oceania for its inspiration. The development of Kona Village Resort began in 1961, when Jackson acquired a sixty-five-year lease on sixty-two acres of Bishop Estate property fronting Kahuwai Bay. Like Rockefeller's endeavor, this project was also situated on a pristine, albeit remote, beach. Surrounded on three sides by an 1801 lava flow and covered with *kiawe (Prosopis pallidan)* trees, the property was originally accessible only by boat, presenting challenging construction logistics. All equipment and materials came in at the beach, with Jackson enlisting a World War II surplus LST (Landing Ship Tank) for deliveries. Twenty-five to thirty workers also came daily, first by boat and later by a small plane. As at the Mauna Kea Beach Hotel, and before that the Kona Inn, the lack of fresh water required the drilling of a well, situated 2.5 miles inland.

While sharing many similar challenges, this new hotel differed radically from the AIA-award-winning design up the coast. Jackson left much of the terrain untouched by thinning out the dense *kiawe* stands by hand. The only major bulldozing done on the property involved the carving out of a 2,636-foot landing strip from the enveloping lava field. The lava did not yield without a battle, and Carl Vesy, the head of construction, went through two bulldozers completing the airstrip, now part of the entry drive.

Dismissed as "impractical and impossible"[20] by many in Honolulu's architectural community, the first phase of the resort, designed by John Russell Rummell of Honolulu, included thirteen Tahitian, seventeen Samoan, six Hawaiian, and seven Fijian *hale*, or houses, as well as a Tongan quadruplex, all spread over twenty-five acres. A large thirty-six-foot-long, twenty-eight-foot-wide, sixty-foot-tall Samoan longhouse served as the dining room and bar. Mere steps from the airstrip, it also functioned as a reception area for the then lobbyless hotel. This dramatic longhouse burned to the ground in 1972.

Opening in 1966, after four years of clearing and construction, the luxury property was the antithesis of a Waikīkī hotel and most hotels around the world. There was no lobby, no front desk, no bellboys, no elevators, no cement sidewalks, and no keys to the *hale*, although the units' sliding doors could be bolted from the inside for those desiring a secure repose. The local press repeatedly emphasized Kona Village Resort's unique quality and its embodiment of

top right *Kona Village Resort, Ka'ūpūlehu, island of Hawai'i , 1966, a sylvan setting of coconuts, lagoon, and thatched roofed houses*

bottom right *Kona Village Resort.* Ohia *beams and* lauhala *ceilings contribute to the tropic interior decor of the* hales.

opposite *Beach at Kona Village Resort*

the visitors' "little grass shack" image of Hawai'i. Kay Lund claimed, "Kona Village at Kaupulehu is the kind of Polynesian hideaway that people travel thousands of miles to find in Hawaii—and don't."[21] *Hawaii Building and Industry* declared the resort to be, "the most unusual hotel in Hawaii today."[22] The *Los Angeles Times* agreed, declaring Kona Village Resort to be, "strange and marvelous...remote and peaceful, one of the truly unusual resorts anywhere in the world."[23] Although now readily found throughout the Caribbean, Southeast Asia, Central and South America, thatch roofed visitor accommodations with modern conveniences were nearly nonexistent in an era that not only demanded but celebrated the comfort and pleasure of modern living. In Hawai'i, thatched roofs briefly graced Waikīkī's late-fifties landscape at Kaiser's Hawaiian Village, but had disappeared before the construction of Kona Village Resort. The Coco Palms on Kaua'i also offered a few thatch-roofed bungalows, but a modern wood-frame building provided most of the visitor accommodations. One would have had to travel to Tahiti, where Wimberly & Cook's recently completed Hotel Bora Bora stood,[24] if they wished to experience a thatch-roofed-hotel experience similar to Kona Village.

Harkening back to the nineteenth century's romantic infatuation with the "primitive," the Kona Village Resort brought select images of an earlier Hawai'i back to life, allowing dreams of a bygone era to stand still long enough for twentieth-century men and women to walk through them. Seemingly stepping back in time, the resort placed its guests in the midst of a South Seas idyll, to partake in the imagined unrestrained, carefree lifestyle of "natives." It was a casual place of shorts and sandals, at a time when sports coats were still de rigueur at the Mauna Kea Beach Hotel.

Although modeled after "primitive culture patterns," the resort's cottages contained almost all the modern conveniences, except the telephone. Constructed of redwood, the cottages had fireproof metal roofing under their thatch. The interiors originally featured Italian marble bathrooms and Italian slate floors. As the hotel's manager, Henry Rittmeister, informed the *Fargo Forum* in 1971, "we want to give people the chance to unwind, to hide away without giving up the modern conveniences of good food, a good bed and bathroom."[25]

Picturesquely built on the edges of the lava flow, overlooking the ocean and coastal, brackish-water-filled anchialine ponds, the hotel's peaceful atmosphere of isolation, oceanside beauty, and outgoing hospitality remain genuine to this day. In this magical environment, the visitor's own time and place seem to disappear, and the evocative architecture allows guests to move one step further away from the outside world. A self-defined domain, it remains an ultimate hideaway from the contemporary world, a tangible manifestation of a romantic notion, where guests meander from their accommodations through a sylvan neighborhood to indulge in tranquil delight. Unlike the nineteenth-century traveler intent on experiencing the different, guests at the Kona Village Resort are offered the opportunity to escape the daily expectations of the twentieth century through immersion in a panacean South Seas reverie, complete with a ship wreck bar made from the salvaged hulk of Johnno Jackson's forty-two-foot sailboat, the *Half Moon*, which had actually sunk in the bay when its bilge hole was left open in November 1966. In 1968, the shipwreck was cut in half and dragged along the shore until waning enthusiasm and energy dictated the bar's ultimate location.

Initially, short-wave radio was the only communication between the village and the outside world, as the isolated hotel could not obtain telephone service until 1968. With no easy overland access, guests reached the hotel by air from either Kona or Kamuela. The ten-minute flight in the Royal Hawaiian Air Service's five-passenger Piper Cherokee cost $3.50, roughly the same as taxi fare from Honolulu airport to Waikīkī. Upon arrival, electric carts transported guests and their baggage to their cottages, and then, armed with knowledge of the mealtimes, they were on their own, a routine that remains in place to this day.

Taking the reclusive character of Hotel Hana Maui one step further, this hideaway met with great acclaim. Reporter Bob Krauss well summed up the allure of the new hotel: "Picture a cluster of thatched cottages in an oasis of green beside a magnificently lonely beach. This is the perfect place for shattered nerves, for a nagging ulcer. Here there are no telephones, no crises, only endless hours of lazy, luxurious solitude."[26]

Indeed, travel writer Jonathan Rinehart found that "the specialty of the house, at least on the surface, is doing nothing," and *Honolulu Advertiser* columnist and author Cobey Black labeled the village a "retreat for romantic escapists."[27]

The resort met with immediate success with many of its initial guests extending their stays beyond their original reservations. Work immediately started on an additional twenty-five *hale* in 1967, as well as the dining room, named the Hale Moana, designed in a modern New Hebridean form by Maui architect Patrick Fitzpatrick of Dynamics Ltd. The splendid isolation of the village was somewhat compromised the following year, when a seven-mile-long access road up to the Māmalahoa Highway was paved, making Kailua-Kona only a little over a one-hour drive away. The Kona Village Resort's geographical solitude came to an end on March 25, 1975, when the Queen Kaʻahumanu Highway opened. The thirty-four-mile-long two-lane road had taken twelve years to build at a cost of sixteen million dollars; it opened the Kona-Kohala coastline for development and placed this thatched hideaway a mere ten minutes away from the Keāhole airport by car. Despite the

top *Hawaiian Village brochure cover, late 1950s. A thatched-roof cottage amidst lush tropical foliage forms a backdrop for images of model tourists capturing the Kodak moment, offering by proxy a firsthand experience well before the viewers' actual arrival to the islands.*
bottom *Stan Steubenberg, graphic embellishment rendered for Hawaiian Village brochure, late 1950s*

above *Kona Village Resort, cottage*
opposite *Kona Village Resort. The end of another day in paradise.*

ease of automobile access, some guests continued to fly into the resort until 1981, when the airstrip was finally closed. Additional *hale* were constructed in 1977 to raise the room count to 81; more appeared in the late 1980s, the work of Bob Marvich and Associates of Los Angeles. The complex now holds 125 units.

Kona Village Resort remains a one-of-a-kind place in Hawai'i. Tucked into the shoreline, visually removed from the passing highway by a rugged lava field, it retains a sense of separation from the remainder of the world. It rightfully continues to celebrate itself as a special and magic place, "Hawaii . . . As It Was Meant To Be."[28]

BY 1964, WITH the Mauna Kea Beach and Kona Village Resort Hotel on the verge of opening, and Kā'anapali and other more modest neighbor-island hotels already underway, the shape of tourism on the islands was quickly changing. As the *Star Bulletin* reported,

A momentous change has come over the Hawaii travel industry. For the first time, the hotel growth rate is faster outside Waikiki than in it. Waikiki still has five times as many hotel rooms as the rest of the State combined and is increasing more rapidly in absolute numbers. But outlying areas are beginning to close the gap, and Maui, Kauai and Hawaii all have more hotel rooms than Waikiki had just 18 years ago.[29]

Indeed, the years between 1960 and 1970 saw Hawai'i's visitor count increase sixfold and its hotel rooms increase from 9,522 to 30,323. Those who stayed at the Mauna Kea Beach Hotel, Kona Village Resort, or Hotel Hana Maui were the exception, not the norm. The majority of the new multitude who came to frolic on Hawai'i's shores was not of the leisure class, and over the decade, the average length of stay for an island visit declined statewide from seventeen days to eleven days. By 1970, Waikiki, which had geared itself more to the economy-minded masses, conventions, and group tours, was being referred to, in certain circles, as, "the highrise iron curtain."[30]

The neighbor islands were emerging as destinations in their own right with a prevailing air of quietude, exclusivity, and quality. By 1965, 30 percent of Hawai'i's visitors were repeat visitors, some of whom found the new Waikīkī too crowded for their tastes. These and others in search of paradise turned, with greater frequency, to the neighbor islands for extended vacations, rather than an overnight jaunt and in turn, the neighbor islands began to develop more visitor attractions to rivet guests to their domain. As a result, between 1955 and 1965 visitor length of stay increased for the main neighbor islands. The island of Hawai'i's numbers modestly climbed from 2.4 to 3 days; Kaua'i from 1.7 to 2.4 days; and thanks to Kā'anapali, Maui rose from 1 to 2.7 days.[31]

chapter 6

Grace and Style
THE REFINED MAGIC OF EDWARD KILLINGSWORTH

THE ANNOUNCED PLANS for the Mauna Kea Beach Hotel and Kona Village Resort had moved forward amidst wide acclaim, as the media portrayed them as tangible milestones in the advancement of Hawai'i's tourist industry and the state's economic progress. In contrast, when Conrad Hilton, the grand "innkeeper" of America, deigned to consider building a luxury hotel outside Waikīkī, the proposal for such an O'ahu hotel initially elicited a storm of controversy. Working in partnership with Honolulu developer Charles J. Pietsch, Hilton envisioned a hotel placed on a 12.5-acre parcel in Kāhala adjoining the Wai'alae Country Club.

Situated a scant ten minutes from the bustle of Waikīkī, in the midst of the posh Wai'alae-Kāhala neighborhood, the proposed beachfront Hilton hotel incensed the area homeowners, who foresaw it disrupting the serenity of their lives and their relationship to the Pacific. Despite Hilton's announced intention to construct one, low-density, seven-to-nine-story building, cries of doom resounded at public meetings, predicting, "another Waikiki at Waialae ... the beginning of a cancerous growth that could

opposite *Mauna Lani Bay Hotel, Kohala coast, island of Hawai'i , 1983, Canoe House Restaurant*

spread from Diamond Head to Koko Head"[1] and a shoreline of hideous high-rises.

As the site was residential, the lands needed to be rezoned for the project to move forward; prior to the rezoning, the city's master plan would have to be amended. The City and County's Planning Department, headed by Leighton S. C. Louis, declared complete opposition to zoning the area for hotel-apartment use and testified as such when the Master Plan Amendment came before the planning commission. By a vote of 5-1, with Commission Chair Cy Lemmon, a resident of Wai'alae-Kāhala, abstaining, the City and County of Honolulu Planning Commission agreed with the planning director and the over twelve hundred written protests submitted in opposition to the project. The commissioners expressed concern that any approval would open the way for further disregard of the city's master plan and would set a precedent to allow the entire coastline between Diamond Head and Koko Head to become a second Waikīkī, decimating residential use along O'ahu's southeastern shore. In addition, "the hotel would make inroads into the city's need for a higher class residential area" by opening an "exclusive residential area for commercial activities."[2]

The planning commission's recommendation was forwarded to the Honolulu City Council, where it was unanimously disregarded. The council members at their July 5, 1960, meeting voted 7-0 in favor of the plan amendment. Council member Herman Lemke noted that the overwhelming majority of testimony from people outside the Wai'alae-Kāhala district favored the hotel project and that "the hotel is important for the State's economic growth." Preliminary estimates indicated the construction of the project would add ten to fifteen million dollars to the state's economy, and once completed, the hotel would employ 550 to 600 full-time persons. In addition, Hilton offered to build a sand beach in front of the hotel, improve the stream channel that ran through nearby Wai'alae Public Park, and also upgrade the adjoining Wai'alae Country Club to championship caliber to attract "tournaments and players of world renown."[3] Wai'alae-Kāhala resident Jo L. Fuller saw a larger political agenda to the council vote, declaring that the council, composed exclusively of Democrats, was "not interested in the votes from the Republican 17th District" of Wai'alae-Kāhala.[4]

On August 18, 1960, Mayor Neal S. Blaisdell vetoed the Honolulu City Council's bill to rezone the Bishop Estate parcel. In a letter to the council, the Republican mayor declared that the measure "in effect is junking the general plan proposed by our professional planners" and that it was wrong to rezone the parcel merely to lure Hilton to Hawai'i.

> We shouldn't be panicked into ill-advised action based on unfounded fears that if Hilton is denied access to Waialae-Kahala, Hilton will not come to Hawaii. Hilton will come... because [he] can't afford to stay out.
>
> A general plan should be changed only if the change is compatible with existing surroundings or is necessary to serve and benefit the neighborhood. The operation of a commercial hotel at Waialae-Kahala isn't compatible with the single family residential uses in adjacent neighborhoods and the golf course facility.

He felt the promise of a new sandy beach was insufficient justification, and if the area needed a beach, the government should provide

opposite *Kahala Hilton Hotel, Honolulu, O'ahu, 1964. In 1993, the Hong Kong based Mandarin Hotel Company purchased the hotel and undertook an $80 million renovation, overseen by Ron Lindgren of Killingsworth, Stricker, Lindgren, Wilson & Associates, retaining much of the original character and ambiance.*

it. The mayor further countered the opinion that the Kāhala site was the only one on Oʻahu that offered what Hilton wanted and suggested both Punaluʻu and Mākaha as better locations, as "a tourist who is willing to pay a high price for hotel facilities would prefer a quiet Hawaiian atmosphere in which to spend his vacation rather than be quartered in a hotel in a residential area near the heart of the city."[5] While the mayor may have been theoretically correct concerning the council's apparent spot zoning, later developments proved Punaluʻu and Mākaha to be less than ideal resort locations, as subsequent hotels, Pat's at Punaluu and the Makaha Inn, have had fitful existences in their efforts to fend off failure.

On August 30, 1960, the county council overrode the mayor's veto by a vote of 7-0, giving the Kahala Hilton the green light to proceed. At a time when Waikīkī hotels increasingly focused on the economy-minded, middle-income traveler, and the length of stay in the islands was plummeting, Hilton announced his new hotel was to be a prestigious development catering to the international carriage trade. Turning its back on group packages, the hotel offered no convention facilities or banquet rooms. It was "designed purely for people who want to spend time in Honolulu in seclusion and in luxury," and for "people who want to visit Hawaii, get away from town, yet still be close to a city."[6] As local writer and founding editor of *Honolulu Magazine*, David Eyre, noted on the hotel's opening, "the Kahala Hilton has all the isolation of the outer Islands, but the bright lights [of Waikiki] are there when you want them."[7]

In December 1960, the hotel-chain owner made a weekend trip to Hawaiʻi to confer with Pietsch. He indicated that he planned

opposite *Kahala Hilton Hotel postcard, 1965, aerial view prior to construction of the cottages*

to construct a "very fine" hotel on the same level of quality as the Beverly Hilton (Beverly Hills, California). He anticipated spending $26,000 per room, and by the time construction was completed, he actually had expended $33,000 per room, at a time when the cost to construct a hundred-room hotel in the islands ran between $12,000 to $15,000 per room. This outlay of money momentarily made the Kahala Hilton not only the most expensive hotel in Hawaiʻi, but in the world, although soon surpassed by Rockefeller's Mauna Kea Beach Hotel.

The ten-story, eleven-million-dollar Kahala Hilton was called, "swanky," during its planning stages and upon its completion was considered of "palatial elegance ... one of the most plush establishments to appear in Hawaii."[8] According to a 1965 brochure, it was "a blend of architectural and tropical beauty," where guests would find, "classical elegance and relaxing comfort." The local magazine *Beacon* announced: "The Royal Hawaiian, supreme in its field since 1928, now has a challenger ... [The Kahala Hilton has been built in] the grand manner. It is going to knock this town on its ear."[9] A Hilton advertisement in the magazine advised readers to remember such words as "casually elegant, luxurious, gracious, stunning ... dedicated to superb service and sheer enjoyment"[10] when thinking of the hotel.

Hilton chose Killingsworth, Brady & Smith of Long Beach, California, to design the new hotel. Edward Killingsworth (1917–2004) had won four AIA National Honor Awards by 1960, with his buildings firmly grounded in a modern vocabulary with walls of glass and flowing, open plans, which emphasized environmentally harmonious, indoor-outdoor living. His work initially came to Hilton's attention when working in the office of Long Beach architect Kenneth Wing, where he designed the rooftop Sky Room for the Breakers Hotel, a Hilton property in Long Beach. Killingsworth

Kahala Hilton Hotel, lobby. The three chandeliers each weigh over 2,500 pounds, sparkling with 28,500 pieces of blue, emerald, topaz, amber, amethyst, turquoise, and moonstone white colored glass. The colors derive from the varying shades of glass found on the beach.

subsequently met Hilton in New York, and upon opening his own firm, he received commissions to design Hilton motor inns, including the Lafayette in Long Beach and one in El Paso, Texas, which became a prototype for the chain. Over the course of these projects, Killingsworth and Hilton established a solid client/architect relationship, and this, coupled with the firm's glowing reputation, made Killingsworth, Brady & Smith an ideal choice for Hilton's new Hawai'i project.

The Kahala Hilton was unabashedly modern in its design, yet also touched on a sense of Hawai'i and the late-nineteenth and early-twentieth-century ranchland heritage of Wai'alae-Kāhala. Project architect Waugh Smith explained that, "while using modern concrete, the planners sought a building that wouldn't look like a box and wouldn't seem to be going 60 miles an hour either. The goal they sought was a concrete building that, when finished, will look much like a wooden one and look as though it has been there for 50 years."[11]

Standing aloof, towering above the beach and ocean, the simple and direct building sends forth a poised sixties modern statement to the world. A distinctive concrete trellis, a motif earlier employed by Killingsworth in various residential projects, breaks up and softens the modern facade and makes the hotel immediately recognizable. Superimposing a near gossamer grid of prestressed-concrete beams over the primary elevations, the trellis ascends above the flat roofline to present an airy pergola profile against the clear blue sky. To further negate a boxy look, the building has outset lānai and follows an aberrant T-shape plan, with the ten-story head containing 288 guestrooms. The two guestroom wings jog in plan by half the depth of the building, resulting in five corner units per floor, rather than the rectangle's standard four. The jog allows modern floor to ceiling corner windows to illuminate each floor's elevator lobby while offering dramatic mountain and golf-course vistas. The guestrooms are enormous, offering a minimum of 550 square feet of space. A pair of bifold doors open on the bathroom with its separate his-and-hers bath facilities, a brand new concept in hotel design for Hawai'i. Such a luxurious amenity required space and had previously only graced top-of-the line suites in the mainland.

The more human-scale, pavilion-like lobby extends perpendicularly from the guest wings toward the ocean. Large, fixed wooden louver panels, reminiscent of Hawai'i's nineteenth-century residential doorways, add definition to the modern composition and soften the aluminum-framed entryways. The long, narrow lobby, with its thirty-foot high ceiling, exudes an air of formality. The *Honolulu Advertiser* declared it to be "one of the most outstanding [lobbies] of any Hilton hotel—or any other hotel built in modern times."[12] Although not as open as many of the more recent resort hotels, windows and sliding doors, draped in swagged curtains, line the length of the teak floored lobby on one side, not only providing views of the gardens and lagoons, but also a lambent atmosphere. Its lofty ceiling and "old Hawaiian monarchy decor"[13] presented a refined majesty, overseen by three large chandeliers. A curving stair with a hand-carved mahogany railing and an orchid-bedecked lava-rock wall lead down to the below-grade, beach-level dining facilities. Here, food and beverages are offered in a distinct indoor-outdoor Hawaiian atmosphere.

Slender, prestressed concrete support columns gracefully raise the lobby pavilion and guest wing thirty-eight feet above the sea-level grounds, allowing the gardens, water features, and building

top *Kahala Hilton Hotel, outdoor dining at Plumeria Restaurant*
bottom *Kahala Hilton Hotel, hotel and lagoon*

above left *Kahala Hilton Hotel, view from the Presidential suite*
above right *Kahala Hilton Hotel, stairway with lava rock and orchids*
right *Kahala Hilton Hotel, floor plan of typical guestroom with a distinctive*
bathroom layout

to literally flow into each other. The use of prestressed concrete was in its infancy at this time; the hotel's structural engineer, Alfred Yee of Honolulu, was one of the pioneers of its use.[14] The new material was capable of withstanding the pressure necessary to drive the columns as piles through the island's coral substrate, offering substantial time and money savings.

Wilbur Choi, who also handled the landscape installations at the Mauna Kea Beach Hotel and Kona Village Resort, oversaw the planting of the 6.5-acre property. The terrain was significantly altered to comport with visitor expectations: 150,000 cubic yards of sand were brought in to make an 1,800-foot beach in front of the property, and peninsulas and an island were built to protect the new beach and frame the oceanic horizon. A filtered 26,000-square-foot salt-water lagoon serves as a focal point for the lush gardens. Fed by a waterfall, the man-made lagoon, now populated by dolphins, flows under and intermingles with the building, while the garden's pathways afford immediate pedestrian-water interactions by bridging the waterways hither and yon. Garden cottages lining the lagoon were built in 1969 and added fifty units to the hotel; they provide a harmonious background as well as serve as a windbreak for the pool area.

With a high-priced daily room rate of $24 or more a night, the hotel was not an immediate success, with occupancy rates hovering in the 20 to 60 percent range for most of the first year. Under duress and to remain solvent, the hotel had to accept a few conventions and tour groups. Although attracting such renowned people as Barbara Hutton, Kirk Douglas, David Rockefeller, Henry Fonda, James Garner, and Lowell Thomas, during its opening year, the turning point for this posh retreat came after the National Broadcasting

right *Kahala Hilton Hotel, dolphins in the lagoon*

Corporation (NBC) chose the hotel for its annual meeting. The network booked the entire hotel and filled it with television stars, headed by Andy Williams. The NBC word of mouth, coupled with a heavy advertising campaign aimed at Hollywood's entertainment elite, brought the hotel to the fore in the minds of the famous and affluent. It became known as a hideaway for motion picture and television celebrities, and *Honolulu Advertiser* columnist Eddie Sherman renamed it the "KaHollywood Hilton." Standing on its reputation of isolated, end-of-road exclusivity, the hotel, by 1967, enjoyed a 90 percent occupancy rate. Every President of the United States since Richard Nixon has stayed in the 2,000-square-foot Presidential Suite, as has Queen Elizabeth, Emperor Hirohito, Prince Rainier and Princess Grace, Prince Charles and Princess Diana, the Dalai Lama, Indira Gandhi, and numerous other world leaders and celebrities. The architect hoped all of them took away impressions of "gracious rooms, lush gardens and elegant informality . . . an unobtrusive but lovely environment."[15]

The Kahala Hilton, one of his more restrained island projects, solidified Killingsworth's reputation as a hotel designer. Over the course of his career, his firm designed over two-dozen resort hotels internationally, including Hilton hotels in Bali, Jakarta, Malaysia, Saudi Arabia, Borneo, and Korea. Between 1975 and 1983, Killingsworth worked on three major resort-hotel commissions in Hawai'i: the Kapalua Bay Hotel, the Halekulani, and the Mauna Lani Bay Hotel and Bungalows. Of exceptionally high quality, all three probed and advanced the concepts laid out a decade before at Mauna Kea Beach Hotel, and exemplified the best in resort hotel design for the period. These Hawai'i works, supporting Killingsworth's contention that

opposite *Kapalua Bay Hotel, Kapalua, Maui, 1978, Gardenia Court Restaurant overlooking the lawn and Pacific Ocean*

Kahala Hilton Hotel, Presidential Suite bedroom

architecture is "delicacy and space,"[16] reflect the refinement of his distinctive design approach and his responses to on-going developments in the field of tropical resort architecture.

KAPALUA: A SOPHISTICATED INFORMALITY

The Kapalua Bay Hotel, the flagship hotel at Kapalua Resort on Maui, opened in 1978, fourteen years after the Kahala Hilton. However, the initial conceptualization of a hotel at Kapalua commenced less than nine months after the opening of Hilton's gem. In September 1964, Alexander & Baldwin (A & B), a sugar company and the largest landowner on Maui, who had been adverse to developing tourism on Maui throughout the 1950s,[17] announced plans to develop a resort area on its Honolua pineapple lands, six

Kapalua Bay Hotel, view toward Fleming Beach

miles north of Kāʻanapali. Company president C. C. Cadagan told reporters the anticipated $25 million project would be "a 'proud State landmark' rather than a quick return, minimum standard commercial development."[18] The new master-planned destination resort was to be exclusive, and "while not for the 'super carriage' trade would be a cut above anything to be found in the Kaanapali area."[19] Almost two years elapsed before Maui Pineapple, a subsidiary of A & B, hired Western Management Consultants to undertake an economic feasibility study for resort conversion of the area. Almost simultaneously Belt, Collins & Associates developed a preliminary engineering study and, subsequently, a master plan. The final master plan called for a second

inland relocation of the Honoapiʻilani Highway, as had previously occurred at Kāʻanapali. Work started on the new highway in 1977 and was completed to Office Drive by 1986.

Internal turmoil within A & B slowed the resort project, and in 1969, Maui Land & Pineapple formally separated from A & B, with all pineapple operations, including Honolua, coming under its control. Maui Land & Pineapple's president, Colin Cameron (1927–1992), the former general manager of Maui Pineapple and grandson of Harry A. Baldwin, cautiously moved forward with the resort plans; some observers doubted that the project would be implemented.[20] A major snag appeared when Ogden Development Company withdrew their financial support in June 1973. This was a difficult blow to absorb, as one of the chief constraints in resort development worldwide is the ability to raise the necessary up-front capital. Lending institutions have traditionally rated resort hotel enterprises as "speculative," and cash for pioneering efforts where no destination currently existed has usually proven difficult to procure. In an effort to attract moneys for resort projects, a number of governments around the globe have stepped forward to subsidize such development or guarantee loans, although the state of Hawaiʻi has found it unnecessary to provide such support and has steadfastly rebuked proposals to do so.

Undaunted, Maui Land & Pineapple decided to move ahead using their own financial resources. Relying on the profits from their pineapple operations, the company edged forward in a prudent manner. Cameron insisted on a company commitment to excellence, and the newspapers reported that the 579-acre Kapalua Resort "will be developed and operated for an affluent market."[21] An eight-year, 8.2 million dollar development loan from Bank of Hawaii and Bank of America secured in November 1974 provided the impetus to commence construction. First, a seven million dollar championship golf course, designed by Arnold Palmer, emerged upon the landscape in late 1975. The Bay Villa's 141 condominium units followed, injecting the first revenues into the resort project. They all sold before the end of 1976, with the announcement that Rockefeller's Rockresorts would manage Kapalua's proposed hotel providing a final sales impetus.

The company next decided to place the Golf Villas project on the market. With a list of 1,300 potential buyers, Kapalua Land Company, the subsidiary of Maui Land & Pineapple handling the resort development, decided to hold a lottery to determine who might be given the opportunity to purchase one of the 186 soon-to-be-built leasehold condominiums. Almost five hundred hopeful buyers showed up for the drawing on February 28, 1977, and in the matter of four hours, the Golf Villas, in a flurry of condomania, was sold out, based solely on architect drawings and Kapalua's aura of exclusivity. The units went for an average price of $134,000, plunking $23 million into the company's coffers and leading Cameron to half jokingly declare: "Kapalua is really just a money factory based on the tourist industry."[22] Condominium sales over the subsequent year and a half made this statement ring all too true, and resort developers at Kāʻanapali, Wailea, and elsewhere in the state took notice. Indeed, with the sharply rising appreciation of resort-condominium properties, the developers were confronted with a new problem, determining what the market demand would bear. As one executive noted, "the problem is no longer figuring a way to get a good return on our investment. Now, it's figuring how we can avoid leaving too much on the table."[23]

The incredible response to the initial residential offerings at Kapalua, and the equally unbelievable escalation in resale values of these units,[24] led Kapalua Land Company to upwardly revise its approach toward developing, marketing, and pricing their property.

Kapalua Bay Hotel, Gardenia Terrace embellished by a modest Japanese garden, with a shallow pool, stream, and a bridge that traverses the stream

The destination resort was trumpeted as a place of "quiet elegance for people who can afford it."[25] For Kapalua's next condominium development, Ironwoods, where Carol Burnett purchased a hideaway, rather than construct two hundred mid-rise units on an eight-acre site, the company opted to build ten high-end, two-story quadruplexes. Two hundred and fifty jet setters came by invitation from around the world to bid on the forty ocean-view units that sold for an average price of $442,000 each, making it Maui's highest-priced residential development up to that time. Another lottery was held in July 1978 for the 134 Ridge condominiums. This attracted some 1,500 potential owners, with some traveling from as far away as London, Hong Kong, Brussels, and Australia. The Ridge immediately sold out with units ranging in price between $165,000 and $270,000, providing Maui Land & Pineapple with end of day receipts of $28 million. The Cottages followed in 1980, twenty-one detached three-bedroom, three-bath luxury houses on ten acres of oceanfront property, each with a price tag of over one million dollars.

The then astronomical and meteoric residential sales at Kapalua Resort clearly overshadowed the development of its first hotel, the Kapalua Bay Hotel. Master planned from the beginning by Belt, Collins & Associates for a ten-acre parcel overlooking Kapalua Bay and Fleming Beach, the hotel's construction did not commence until 1977. Like other aspects of the project, it too was re-envisioned as the project's quality level evolved. Initially, the Kapalua Land Company turned to SOM, the architects of the Mauna Kea Beach Hotel, to design the hotel. However, in 1975, the company decided the plans for a six-hundred-room hotel, with three six-story towers, a ballroom, dining room, and specialty

top *Kapalua Bay Hotel, Gardenia Terrace*
opposite *Kapalua Bay Hotel,* makai *elevation*

restaurant, were inappropriate for the type of destination resort they envisioned. Desiring a more intimate, less ostentatious, lower profiled, and elegant hotel, they cancelled SOM's contract, and Killingsworth, Brady & Associates, based on their achievement at the Kahala Hilton, were hired to design the work.

Killingsworth's firm lived up to its reputation. Melding elements of his previous design penchants with the more open-air programs and ocean vistas introduced at the Mauna Kea Beach Hotel, design architect Ron Lindgren further refined the vocabulary of tropical resort design in Hawai'i with consummate taste. The hotel, with its modified pavilion plan, was sited above the three-hundred-foot-long Fleming Beach and Kapalua Bay, but sufficiently back from the cliff face to form a large, gently sloping, manicured landscape from which to view the vast Pacific. Following the lay of the land, two of the three low-rise guest wings framed the lush lawn and gracefully stepped down the eighteen-acre property.

The prestressed-concrete trellis work of the Kahala Hilton reappears to frame the Kapalua Bay Hotel's entry court. To better integrate interior and exterior, this motif is carried over into the lobby's columns and coffered ceiling. A porte-cochere defines the entry, marking a return of this architectural feature that had been all but absent from hotel use in Hawai'i for over fifty years. As in both the Kahala Hilton and Mauna Kea Beach Resort, the lobby is elevated a full floor above the resort's grounds, allowing for a dining terrace below.

Large, louvered awning shutters allow the lobby to be virtually open air on three sides. Glass, a strong element in the Kahala Hilton lobby, does not mitigate the interaction of inside and out,

top *Kapalua Bay Hotel. Reporter Thomas Rohr immediately recognized the entry court's white beams of prestressed concrete as evoking "visions of the spiffy Kahala Hilton."*
bottom *Kapalua Bay Hotel, lobby*

except as a later addition on the *mauka* side.[26] As opposed to the Kahala Hilton lobby's perpendicular orientation to the shore, the lobby of the Kapalua Bay Hotel runs parallel to the ocean, with a *mauka-makai* axis affording unobstructed views of the Pacific from the entry through the lobby. The lobby's lounge areas progressively step down toward the ocean, echoing the building's site and enhancing the views from all parts of the lobby. The stepped floors afford areas of discrete, residential-like intimacy within the greater volume of the public space. The lobby also reflects the building's pavilion floor plan as a centered opening in the stepped floors allows visitors to glimpse down to the terrace dining area below. At the lower level, the centered opening is embellished by a modest Japanese garden, with a shallow koi-filled pool and stream as a focal point. A bridge traverses the stream as it meanders outward to link the grounds with the building. Incredibly dynamic, yet serene, the impressive lobby offers a gentle, varied spatial experience, which has yet to be equaled in tropical resort design in Hawai'i. Gracious rather than majestic, the lobby's emphasis is on the vista, as the fifty-five-foot-tall openings between the lobby's column clusters frame the vast Pacific and the glorious year-round, daily drama of the sun setting between the islands of Lāna'i and Moloka'i.

At the hotel's opening ceremony Cameron expressed the vision behind the hotel and the resort:

> Our intentions at Kapalua . . . was and is to respect the land, its beauty, climate and history; to design buildings and facilities which are pleasing, yet not dominant, and are of the highest quality, structures which are different and distinctive, yet not monotonous in design, which are sophisticated in some respects, yet informal in others, and are welcoming and friendly.[27]

Halekulani Hotel, Waikīkī, O'ahu, 1983

As with the Kahala Hilton and Mauna Kea Beach hotels, the thirty million dollar Kapalua Bay Hotel, the "Rolls Royce of Maui,"[28] with its 196 units, set its sights on the independent traveler, the most-affluent 10 to 15 percent of the visitor market and avoided "the name tag crowd" of tours and conventions. With daily rates only 5 percent below that of the Mauna Kea Beach Hotel, Kapalua Bay Hotel opened with one hundred percent occupancy and an enviable twelve month reservation backlog.

THE HALEKULANI: THE HOUSE BEFITTING HEAVEN

Killingsworth, Stricker, Lindgren, Wilson & Associates had the redevelopment of the Halekulani Hotel on the drawing board as the Kapalua Bay Hotel was opening. When the Norman Clapp family of Seattle, the co-owners of Weyerhauser Lumber, and the owners of

the Halekulani Hotel since 1962, informed the press of their intention to expand the hotel's size from 189 to 480 rooms, many *kama'āina* in Honolulu were uneasy. They did not relish thoughts of the last garden cottage hotel on Waikīkī beach disappearing. Set slightly apart from the main bustle of the world famous beach resort on a "5.5 acre oasis in highrise Waikiki,"[29] this vintage, low-rise hotel was a romantic favorite of Hawai'i residents and visitors alike. Known for its casual, comfortable hospitality, and quiet atmosphere—a combination of qualities many enjoyed despite the snide mutterers who claimed the hotel was only fit for "the newly wed and nearly dead."[30]

The original building and its cottages epitomized the Hawaiian style of architecture, which its architect, C. W. Dickey, had popularized in the 1920s and 1930s. Their double-pitched hipped roofs, frequently referred to in island architectural circles as the "Hawaiian" or "Dickey" roof, coupled with extensive windows, wide doorways, lava-rock accents, and applied ornament utilizing island motifs, led Dickey to modestly note in 1927, "I believe I have achieved a distinctive Hawaiian type of architecture. The cottages seem to fit the landscape. They are simply designed, gathering character from the roof."[31] The challenge set forth to design architect Ron Lindgren was to integrate the old with the new on an extremely small lot.

The original hotel was set to close on November 1, 1979; however, problems in obtaining the funds necessary to build the new hotel delayed the closing. The high cost of financing pushed even the affluent Clapp family to search for a partner. Their unsuccessful quest led to the sale of the oceanfront property in November

top left *Halekulani Hotel, view of one of the property's two courtyards*
bottom left *Halekulani Hotel, Royal Suite living room. The coffee table, accented by a green granite slab, was fabricated from a Chinese opium bed.*
opposite *Halekulani Hotel, view of Diamond Head from Orchids Restaurant*

GRACE AND STYLE : 141

1980, for an undisclosed price, to Mitsui Fudosan, a subsidiary of Mitsui Real Estate Development Company, Japan's largest real estate group.[32] The new owners announced they would retain the Clapps' redevelopment team, which included the civil engineering firm of Belt, Collins & Associates and architecture firm of Killingsworth, Stricker, Lindgren, Wilson & Associates. Like the Clapps, the company intended to operate the Halekulani Hotel as a mid-range hotel; however, Shuhei Okuda (b. 1937), a senior executive of Halekulani Corp, a subsidiary of Mitsui Fudosan, prevailed upon the parent company to shift direction and pursue the upscale market, resulting in an expenditure of $125 million dollars on the new hotel, a staggering $275,000 per room.

Okuda envisioned a hotel grounded on "simplicity, serenity and elegance," the embodiment of his childhood memories of the Yamato Hotel, in Darien City, Manchuria, with its crisp, white decor.[33] Such an approach fit perfectly with Killingsworth's design proclivities, and the only significant changes made to the already completed contract drawings commissioned by the Clapps were the encasing and air conditioning of the single-loaded guestroom corridors and an increase of the typical guestroom width by four inches. Okuda revised the landscape concept from one of an informal "jungle" of tropical exotics to the more refined formality of lawns and palms accented with flowers, as designed by Dave Woolsey of the

opposite *Halekulani Hotel, courtyard. The historic hotel closed its doors on May 1, 1981, with a number of loyal patrons flying in from the mainland to have one final night of salubrious slumber. Demolition of the historic cottages began on June 4, 1981; however, the Dickey designed main building remained standing, incorporated into Killingsworth's plans.*

top right *Halekulani Hotel, Royal Suite, living room*

bottom right *Halekulani Hotel, Royal Suite, entry from private elevator lobby*

Halekulani Hotel, renovated lounge in 1931 building featuring Eucalyptus wood flooring and teak columns

Honolulu landscape architectural firm of Woolsey, Miyabara & Associates. The selection of Regent International Hotels to manage the property also boded well for the realization of Okuda's goals. Founded in 1970, by Robert H. Burns, the former general manager of the Kahala Hilton, the chain had attained a reputation for understated luxury and attention to detail. In addition to managing a number of hotels in Asia, they had previously operated the Hawaiian Regent Hotel in Waikīkī and had run the Kapalua Bay Hotel on Maui since 1980.[34] Under Burns' guiding hand, the Halekulani Hotel achieved the quality of Okuda's vision.

As an urban resort hotel, set on a very small lot, the new 456-room Halekulani Hotel presented design challenges that differed from the Kahala Hilton and Kapalua Bay hotels. The main problem was accommodating all of the necessary elements while maintaining ocean views and a sense of intimacy. Confined by the narrow distance between Kunia Road and the ocean, there could be no grand entry statement. Killingsworth's concrete trellis work disappeared; however, in its stead, unadorned concrete members appeared, ethereally defining the open-air foyer, gatehouse, a lounge area, and walkways. A porte-cochere serves as a simple transition from the street, smoothly flowing into a chic, low-ceilinged, octagonal-shaped reception area, with a ceiling finished in reeded maple with stained teak borders. White Bottorino marble agglomerate floors from Italy, trimmed with travertine, further accentuate the spare elegance of the space.

Openings from the enclosed lobby lead to a pair of grassed courtyards—physically separated from the bustle of the streets of Waikīkī by less than fifty yards, yet experientially a magical eternity away. At the *makai* end of one sits the Dickey-designed, two-story main building of 1931, its calm countenance grounding an air of tranquility. Three wings of guestrooms, all with Dickey roofs, step down to the ocean. Going from sixteen to two stories, the guestrooms frame the courtyards, which, in turn, soften the scale of the wings. The building resonates an exclusivity; subtly sedate, its crisp, clean lines impeccably set forth a tone of sophisticated refinement at its best. The orchid pool, in the second courtyard, composed of custom-made glass tiles from South Africa, is the only potentially ostentatious moment.

"Informal but stylish,"[35] the hotel catered to the carriage trade, yet retained the aura of gracious hospitality and simplicity traditionally associated with the earlier *kama'āina* hotel. The new building's use of the double-pitched hipped roof reintroduced the form to the architectural consciousness of Hawai'i. Its laudatory oceanfront scale and the accentuation of open green space within the confines of the hotel further enamored urban planners. Indeed, over a decade later, when the City and County of Honolulu set forth design guidelines to instill Waikīkī with a sense of Hawaiian place, the new Halekulani Hotel figured prominently as an example of appropriate regional design at its best.[36]

Although placed in an urban setting, the hotel embraced the finest features of a resort hotel within a friendly, accommodating atmosphere. Many doubted such a high-end operation could survive in Waikīkī, but after a slow start the Halekulani Hotel has not only survived, but has excelled. Only months after the hotel's opening, Michael Carlton, a travel writer for the *Denver Post*, declared,

> This is without question the best hotel in Waikiki and it has the potential of being one of the finest resort properties in the world, even though it has only a sliver of a beach, no golf course or tennis courts and no nightclub. You can find all of them elsewhere in Waikiki.
>
> What you can't find elsewhere is the caring, personal service, the wonderfully tasteful rooms and the magic of sitting beneath the old kiawa [sic] tree, sipping a mai tai, listening to the soft music of an Hawaiian quartet and watching a sunset that is as beautiful today as it was a century ago.[37]

Carlton's prediction concerning the hotel's potential has proven accurate as it has consistently appeared in *Zagat*'s top ten hotels in the U.S.; *Travel & Leisure* magazine's readers' poll ranked it the fourth best hotel on the planet in 2003, and *Gourmet* magazine's poll declared it the world's best hotel in 1999. A sanctuary unto itself, it emits a tenor of superb service and casual intimacy. It has reaffirmed the Killingsworth firm's exalted position in the pantheon of elegant resort architecture.

MAUNA LANI BAY HOTEL & BUNGALOWS: SUPPORTING A SPIRIT OF PLACE

Months before the opening of the Halekulani Hotel, the immaculate Mauna Lani Bay Hotel opened its doors in February 1983. The fifth of six hotel projects undertaken in Hawai'i by Killingsworth,[38] it displayed more dramatic flair than his earlier projects, but retained his high level of refined detail. Situated on the island of Hawai'i, around five miles south of the Mauna Kea Beach Hotel, the 345-room hotel was built as the flagship for the Mauna Lani Resort. This master-planned resort had been in the planning stage since 1972 when the Japan-based railroad, real estate, and development company Tokyu Corporation, headed by Noboru Gotoh, acquired the Hawaiian Regent Hotel in Waikīkī and 3,200 acres in South Kohala on the island of Hawai'i with three miles of ocean frontage. The Japanese company formed a subsidiary, Mauna Lani Development, headed by Kenny Brown, to handle the development of their Big Island resort. Brown is not only a former architect and state senator, but also a great-grandson of John Papa I'i, a member of Kamehameha I's court. He has an abiding interest in quality development in Hawai'i and, as early as 1973, advised a seminar on quality growth:

> Multiply, if you will, within the limits of productivity, but have infinite care where you put your houses, harbors and hotels, because you must protect your land's natural beauty and spirit of place if you are to retain and sustain your own spirit.[39]

It was within this spirit of enlightened stewardship strongly supported by Gotoh that the development of Mauna Lani Bay Hotel was undertaken. Aspiring to build a resort community of "world renown,"[40] Belt, Collins was hired to work on the master plan. Killingsworth, Stricker, Lindgren, Wilson & Associates were retained

for architectural design based on the high quality of their previous work in the islands.

Rising out of the black, rugged sixteenth-century Kanikū lava flow, the $72 million hotel sits in an oasis of palms and lush greenery. A blue tile-paved walkway, a variation on the Mauna Kea Beach Hotel's entry, delivers guests from the porte-cochere to the lobby. The entry walk passes over a shallow tropical pool, an appropriate forecast of the property's anchialine-pond-strewn grounds and reminiscent of some of Killingsworth's earlier residential work. The strong axis of the entry walk delivers guests to the brink of a lush and spectacular six-story, one-hundred-yard-long garden atrium that explodes from the floor below. Open to the sky, this area, with its palm-enshrouded lagoon, maximizes the potential that initially emerged with the Kapalua Bay Hotel lobby's central opening. A series of five sleek plexiglass waterfalls flank a central stairway to accentuate the journey down to the lagoon level. With an entry experience of this caliber-drawing upon the emanations of the Mauna Kea Beach Hotel, the Hyatt's atriums, and Killingsworth's own oeuvre—the deprivation of an ocean vista goes sublimely unnoticed.

The hotel itself strikingly discloses Killingsworth's love of "balance, a clear and compelling axis, careful proportion, [and] respect for tradition."[41] The building's Y-shaped plan allows 327 of its 350 rooms to have ocean views. Expansive ninety-square-foot lānai run the length of its facades, giving the structure a strong horizontality, despite its six-story height. As at the Mauna Kea Beach

left and opposite *Mauna Lani Bay Hotel, Kohala coast, island of Hawai'i, 1983. The stately atrium with its forty-foot palms and tranquil waterways never fails to make guests pause in awe. Los Angeles Times travel editor, Jerry Hulse found the atrium to be, "without exaggeration, unlike any other I've encountered in the world. It is simply breathtaking."*

Hotel, the oceanfront stories are stepped back, further tempering any vertical thrust and adding a sense of visual drama.

As with Killingsworth's other Hawai'i hotel projects, the impeccably detailed building made a profound impression, as expressed by *Los Angeles Times* writer Jerry Hulse: "The Big Island's stunning new Mauna Lani Bay Hotel is a welcome surprise: The moment one arrives beneath the impressive porte cochere it is evident this is no ordinary hotel. Seldom in this day of concrete extravaganzas does a new resort reflect this grace and style."[42]

The work of design architect Larry Stricker, this supremely confident building blends a bright white architectural formality with a lush, informal tropical landscape. The atrium's rampant flora—a veritable jungle at its nether regions—contrasts with the rigidity of its enframing structure. In turn, the atrium's waters flow outward beyond the building, offering a myriad of waterfalls, ponds, and streams teaming with tropical reef fish. Meandering out onto the twenty-nine-acre grounds, these water features commingle with much of the property's preserved natural landscape, including fifteen acres of natural anchialine ponds, which imbue the resort with an atmosphere of casual relaxation and a sense of unity with the place.

As at Mauna Kea and Kapalua, the hotel's main dining facility, the haut-cuisine Canoe House Restaurant, is detached from the central building. The restaurant manifests Japanese undertones in its rafter tails and latticed gablet and continues, in wood, the high level of finish found in the central building. Its double-pitched, hipped-gablet roof adds a tropical charm, and the wood-framed, folding-glass doors, which serve as three of the four walls, maximize the opportunities for indoor-outdoor dining and ocean vistas.

Beyond the restaurant, five "bungalows" stand on five acres of land. Built five years after the opening of the hotel, they also were

designed by Stricker. Representing the ultimate in luxury, these four-thousand-square-foot domiciles redefined the concept of a hotel bungalow, building on the Kahala Hilton's defunct Japanese-style Hideaway Cottage's concept of isolated exclusivity. Gracious worlds unto themselves and separate from the typical guest experience, each of the bungalows has two master bedrooms and a central living area. The expansive sliding doorways of all three rooms open onto a private swimming pool, whirlpool spa, and ocean view. The four-hundred-square-foot master bathrooms each include his-and-her grooming areas and a glass wall that looks onto a meditation garden. Of course, twenty-four-hour butler service is included in the price of the suite, as is limousine transportation to and from the airport.[43] With such amenities, *Lifestyles of the Rich and Famous* in 1990 named the Mauna Lani Bay the best resort hotel in America.

At the time of its opening, Laurance Rockefeller found the new hotel to be "a truly remarkable complex . . . a triumph of thoughtful, considerate planning."[44] The *Honolulu Advertiser*, looking at a broader picture, noted,

> Hawaii's future in tourism probably depends on a mixture of hotels in various price ranges. The Mauna Lani is in a top price class almost by itself.
>
> But quality has to be a hallmark of whatever we do. And in that sense the time and effort put into the Mauna Lani has produced a standard of excellence for other hotel developments to follow.[45]

left *Mauna Lani Bay Hotel, view of Waipuhi Pond. Mauna Lani Development preserved the ancient Waipuhi Pond, which the resort continues to use to harvest fish for its restaurants.*
opposite *Mauna Lani Bay Hotel. Water is a dominant element inside and outside the hotel.*

Recognized by the *Honolulu Advertiser* as a "special hotel" of high quality, it was a fitting summation of Edward Killingsworth's first two decades of work in the islands.

Rather than pursue the modest simplicity of the Hotel Hana Maui or the thatched romanticism of the Kona Village Resort, Killingsworth's hotels invigorated Hawai'i's resort architecture with the sophisticated simplicity of modern design at its best. Absorbing the aura of the Mauna Kea Beach Hotel, the understated, yet refined, elegance of his four hotels took tropical resort hotel design out of the realm of the ordinary. Linked by their high attention to detail, they present an amazing diversity of memorable spatial experiences, each hotel addressing the needs of its individual situation in its own distinctive way. Their open, flowing designs excel in their response to, and celebration of, the semitropical environment of Hawai'i. Amazingly, in November 1990 *Condé Nast Traveller* ranked the Halekulani, Mauna Lani Bay, Kahala Hilton, and Kapalua Bay hotels as the top four tropical resort hotels in the world,[46] an incredibly impressive testament to the wondrous magic of Edward Killingsworth's architectural savoir-faire.

top right *Mauna Lani Bay Hotel, entryway. The blue tiled entry walk traverses a shallow tropical pool—a forecast of the property's anchialine pond-strewn grounds and reminiscent of Killingsworth's earlier residential work.*
bottom right *Mauna Lani Bay Hotel, view from the lānai of a bungalow*
opposite *Mauna Lani Bay Hotel. The desire to maximize ocean views led to the development of the Y-shaped plan. By siting the base of the Y perpendicular to the ocean, the architects provided splendid ocean views up and down the Kohala coastline.*

chapter 7

Fantasy Becomes Reality, and Beyond

AT THE HAWAI'I International Longshore and Warehouse Union's (ILWU) 1969 statewide convention, San Francisco's architectural critic Allan Temko, the 1990 Pulitzer Prize recipient for his architectural writings, praised the quality of the Mauna Kea Beach Hotel, and warned the union members that Hawai'i needed to maintain a high level of resort hotel design. He informed them that many of the hotels at Kā'anapali were the "wrong hotels—Waikiki hotels . . . monuments to corporate stupidity."[1] He had a point; a large majority of the hotels, not only at Kā'anapali but throughout the islands, were uninspired stacked boxes, rectilinear in form and devoid of enduring character.

Temko's advice went unheeded throughout the 1970s as Hawai'i's travel industry continued to prosper, with visitor numbers more than doubling, from 1,745,904 in 1970 to 3,966,192 ten years later. This period saw the introduction of the Boeing 747 Jumbo Jet to Hawai'i in 1970. Capable of carrying over four hundred passengers, this four engine, wide body jet more than doubled the capacity of the popular Boeing 707 and made possible large-scale, affordable long-distance travel. In addition, the rise of group

opposite *Hyatt Regency Maui, Kā'anapali, Maui, 1980, Grotto Bar. Behind the waterfalls, Glenn presides over the bar, with a fish tank ironically in the seawall.*

left *Members of the Hawaii Visitor Bureau, in hopes of expanding Hawai'i's visitor market, undertook a promotional tour of Japan from May 4–20, 1962. Posing on the gangway prior to departure are, from left to right, top row: musician Nelson Waikiki, Richard MacMillan, the HVB's director of advertising and publicity, musician Joe Kahaulelio; center row: Rose Marie Alvaro, Marilyn Honan; bottom row: Arville Reed, a cast member of the Honolulu television show* Lucky Luck, *Mae Beimes. Hawai'i would have to wait until the end of the decade, after Japan relaxed its currency exchange restrictions, before it could reap the reward of its early cultivations.*

right *Paradise Aloha Tours brochure featuring Rose Marie Alvaro, 1977*

TV Guide, *September 4–10, 1971.* Hawaii 5-0, *starring Jack Lord, premiered in September 1968, and for the next twelve years brought the presence of Hawai'i into American living rooms on a weekly basis at the time the Boeing 747 made it possible to efficiently transport more and more people to the islands.*

and agriculture, a position it has maintained until the present. In the midst of such robust activity, the Kapalua Bay Hotel was a design exception in an era characterized by the burgeoning town of Kīhei on Maui,[3] and the appearance of a multitude of utilitarian hotels across the state.

The opening of the Hyatt Regency Maui in April 1980, however, made some tourism industry leaders take pause and reevaluate their approach, momentarily returning Kā'anapali to the forefront of resort design and operation in Hawai'i. Popular opinion held that there were two types of island visitors: the mass market tourists who made Waikīkī their base of operations and the carriage trade that stayed at the Kahala Hilton, Mauna Kea Beach, Kapalua Bay, and other smaller, high-end neighbor-island venues, such as the Kona Village, Waiohai, and Hotel Hana Maui. The $80 million Hyatt Regency Maui tapped into a new market sector, the successful thirty-something baby boomers, whom *Time* magazine referred to as "The Over-the-Thrill Crowd": "Children of inflation, born with credit cards in their mouths, and oriented to spending rather than saving. They are part of the instant gratification, self-indulgent, 'me' generation which has a taste for high-priced gadgets and little interest in self-denial." This new clientele, according to marketing professor Louis W. Stern of Northwestern University, "wants the outward visible things that say, 'I have made it and I want to live comfortably.'"[4] With this population segment coming of age in the early 1980s, the number of Free and Independent Travelers (FITs), individuals traveling without the service of guided tours, rose.[5]

The triple-towered mid-rise Hyatt Regency Maui promised its upwardly mobile guests a "world class hotel . . . a Garden of Eden with hot running water."[6] The largest resort hotel on a neighbor island, the 815-room marvel was designed by Wimberly, Whisenand, Allison & Tong, with Chris Hemmeter (1939–2003), founder

inclusive tours (including airfare, accommodations, set itineraries, ground transportation, and tour guides) catering to groups organized by travel agents emerged in 1971 and handled almost 70 percent of Hawai'i's tourist business by the end of the decade. Also during the period, eastbound travelers, primarily from Japan, became a more pronounced part of the visitor population, rising from 17 percent of the tourist mix in 1965 to a readily noticeable 22 percent in 1975.[2] In 1976, visitor expenditures became the prime source of revenues for Hawai'i, surpassing defense spending (revenue from military bases) and agriculture. Two years later, tourism grew sufficiently to exceed the combined total of defense spending

Hyatt Regency Maui, atrium

and head of Hemmeter Corporation, as the developer. This team had previously undertaken the Hyatt Regency Waikiki project in 1975, which featured a distinctive arcade first floor and an open atrium with a dramatic three-story waterfall. The atrium, a hallmark of Hyatt hotels since John Portman's resurrection of the form in the late 1960s, played a prominent role in the Hyatt Regency Maui but in a decidedly tropical, nature-oriented manner. Its focal point, a seventy-foot-high banyan tree, was transplanted on the site, with the hotel constructed around it.[7]

Visitors, upon entering the building, are greeted by a giant garden/atrium rather than a hotel lobby. Reception and concierge desks are discretely tucked into corners near the entry, allowing the eye to be overwhelmed by verdant foliage embellished by exotic statuary from Asia, set amidst meandering pathways. Framed by the eleven-story Atrium Tower, the atrium's off-axis *makai* side completely opens on the grounds and glorious ocean views, further dissolving the boundaries between building and the great outdoors. The graciousness of Hawai'i's delightful climate receives further reinforcement at the periphery of the atrium. Here, the diminutive Weeping Banyan Bar, with its rounded seating peninsulas intimately extending into a placid pond complete with South American Black-Necked swans, transitions the hotel to the grounds. This theme is expanded in the hotel's serene lower-level indoor-outdoor Swan Court Restaurant, a terrace with an intimate Pacific vista serving as a backdrop to the immediacy of a waterfall-fed, swan-filled lagoon. A splendid prospect and refuge setting, the Swan Court has been selected by "Lifestyles of the Rich and Famous" as one of the ten most romantic restaurants in the world.

The hotel innovatively and tastefully extended many of the concepts initially set forth by the Mauna Kea Beach Hotel and subtly paid homage to the SOM masterpiece through the use of similar cruciform-shaped columns in its lobby. Hemmeter further followed the lead of Rockefeller and installed, with the aid of Los Angeles interior designer Howard Hirsch, two million dollars worth of art in the Hyatt, thereby enshrining under one roof the two primary deities of the late twentieth century's tourism pantheon: art and nature. However, where Rockefeller perceived the works he displayed in terms of a statement on humanity's universal aesthetic sensibility and refined appreciation, the pieces at the Hyatt served more to astound and impress, if not overwhelm.

In addition to ingeniously expanding upon the legacies of SOM and Portman, the Hyatt took resort design in Hawai'i to a new level through its treatment of the surrounding grounds. The eighteen acres of lushly planted gardens were filled with streams, waterfalls, lagoons, and Japanese landscaping. Although many of these elements had previously been incorporated at the Kahala Hilton, it had never been handled on such a grand scale in Hawai'i. Furthermore, the grounds were populated by macaws, cockatoos, flamingos, African crowned cranes, swans, and penguins. Hemmeter, inspired by his stay at Mexico's Acapulco Princess Hotel (designed in 1971), felt the introduction of exotic birdlife and myriad water features engendered the resort with "a magical atmosphere."[8] The developer also brought from the Acapulco Princess another new element, a large splash of water, for Hawai'i's resort equation: a one-acre swimming pool, the largest in the state at the time. To exhilarate the spirit of playful adventure, the sprawling pool included rope bridges, waterfalls, a 150-foot waterslide that twisted

top *Hyatt Regency Maui, Kā'anapali, Maui, 1980, Swan Court Restaurant*
bottom *Hyatt Regency Maui, Swan Court Restaurant. The indoor-outdoor restaurant looks out on a waterfall-fed, swan-filled lagoon that flows out toward the Pacific Ocean.*

through lava-rock archways, and the Grotto Bar that offered cocktails behind the waterfalls.

Following the spirit of Bachman Turner Overdrive's 1974 hit, "You Ain't Seen Nothing Yet," the Hyatt seemingly challenged the guest at every turn with another "here's something you're never gonna forget" experience within an immaculate, clean-line context. Discussing the success of the Hyatt Regency Maui, its general manager, Gordon Hentschel, in 1983, observed, "people were ready for this kind of resort. You can't lose sight of the fact that the deluxe traveler is looking for a fantasy, and the ultimate is a hotel with international flavor and maximum pampering."[9] Phantasia, the site where imagination dwells in the soul,[10] sprang to life at the Hyatt. As a series of memorable moments, the hotel brought an entirely new aura to resort design in Hawai'i by augmenting the natural beauty of the islands and its East-meets-West culture with equally elaborate human constructs to astound the imagination. While Hotel Hana Maui, Kona Village Resort, and Kahala Hilton promoted themselves as tropical hideaways, Hyatt Regency Maui proclaimed, "You don't just come here to get away from it all; you come to be a part of it all." Rather than subjugate itself to Hawai'i's superb setting, the Hyatt demanded equal time. It remains a commanding presence, offering a plethora of delightful spaces and high-toned energies that inspired the emergence of entirely new resort idioms for the islands.

With construction costs hovering near $100,000 per room, some economists predicted the Hyatt Regency Maui would flop.

top right *Hyatt Regency Maui, newlywed reception at Weeping Banyan Bar*
bottom right *Hyatt Regency Maui, grounds designed by landscape architect Richard Tongg*
opposite *Hyatt Regency Maui. The swimming pool was the largest in the state when the hotel opened and made all previous pools in Hawai'i appear staid. It blended a "natural" setting into the traditional tiled pool deck, blurring the distinctions between hotel and nature.*

However, the hotel enjoyed occupancy rates in the 90 percent range during the first three years of its existence, during a period of national economic recession. Such success is even more astounding since during 1979 and 1982, Maui's visitor volume slipped 5 percent while its hotel/condominium inventory increased 30 percent.[11] The incredibly high occupancy rates of the Hyatt Regency Maui and the Hyatt Regency Waikiki, the highest-priced hotels in their respective resort areas between 1980 and 1982, led others to venture into the expanding stratosphere of luxury resort hotels.

The success of the two Hyatts certainly encouraged Hemmeter, referred to by *Lodging Hospitality* in 1989 as "Mr. Fantasy Resort,"[12] to further explore the wonderland he had conceived. Since the 1960s, with the Disneyfication of the world, media-induced credibility gaps, and the popularizing of psychedelic drugs, the definition of reality had become increasingly blurry within American culture. In his ensuing projects, the transformation of the Maui and Kauai Surf hotels into the "Disneyesque"[13] Westin Maui and Westin Kauai in 1987 and 1988, respectively, and the development of the even more extravagant 1,240-room Hyatt Regency Waikoloa on the island of Hawai'i, the self-made developer further celebrated and elaborated upon the fantastic, pushing it to new levels. The latter, a $360 million extravaganza sited on sixty-two oceanfront acres in North Kona, opened in September 1988 as the largest development project ever undertaken in Hawai'i up to that time. Draped in Palladian elements, the Hyatt Regency Waikoloa featured towering atriums, a choice of boat or monorail transport to guest rooms, a seven-million-dollar art collection, three action

left *Hyatt Regency Maui, Kā'anapali, Maui, 1980*
opposite *Hyatt Regency Waikoloa, Waikoloa, island of Hawai'i, 1988*

pools with slides, waterfalls, grottos, and hot tubs, an opportunity to swim with dolphins, as well as the first hotel spa facility in Hawai'i. As British novelist David Lodge noted in *Paradise News*, the Hyatt Regency Waikoloa "looked like the set for a Hollywood epic that hadn't quite decided whether it was to be a sequel to *Ben Hur*, *Tarzan of the Apes*, or *The Shape of Things to Come*."[14] It was, indeed, adventure land, fantasyland, and tomorrow land all rolled into one. Its operators declared, "We want to offer so many things to do that it would be unthinkable to go anywhere else."[15] A world unto itself, the Hyatt Regency Waikoloa took the resort hotel as resort destination to a new level, or in the words of Lodge, it was "not so much a hotel as a whole resort. Not so much a resort as a way of life."[16] Unlike Rockefeller's Mauna Kea Beach Hotel, it was not designed for people that relied upon their "inner resources" but for those wanting to be bedazzled. Pursuing a more recreational or entertainment tourism, the hotel property became the main attraction, moving the concept of a resort hotel well beyond simple lodging or a getaway retreat or hideaway, to a spectacle in and of itself.

From Waikōloa, Hemmeter Corporation took wing to other parts of the globe. Claiming to be the only developer in the world specializing in fantasy mega-resorts, the corporation, at its zenith between 1989 and 1990, claimed to have seventeen resorts under development in California, Arizona, Florida, the Caribbean, Canary Islands, and Australia.[17] All were based on the newly emerging resort realm of entertainment tourism, a la Disney and Las Vegas, and its accompanying "architainment": "I tell my architects, 'Don't draw anything until you can write the script. Build a marvelous experience; don't just provide good sleeping facilities. Fulfill the guests' fantasies, consider the psychic value of the trip.'"[18]

In his exuberance, Hemmeter overextended himself and with the Westin Kauai and Hyatt Regency Waikoloa pushed the edges of credibility, transparently offering an overwhelming, ersatz opulence skirting the fringes of plausibility. The hotels did not dissolve the boundary between the real and artificial, but rather made that thin line a bit too apparent. Great fun, but definitely unreal, this larger-than-life tendency transcended the islands' more traditional resort emphasis on luxury and refined recreation. Glitzy, teetering on the gauche and garish, Hemmeter's later hotels' emphasis on all-encompassing amazement overshadowed the essence of Hawai'i.

OTHER DEVELOPERS TOOK the vitality and lessons of the Hyatt Regency Maui and moved in a slightly different direction than the one pursued by Hemmeter. They re-embraced the atmosphere of the palatial country homes of the rich that Rockefeller had strove to embody in the Mauna Kea Beach Hotel so many years before and tangibly presented Hawai'i as the "Paradise of the Pacific." These new developments were largely financed by a burgeoning Japanese economy eager to invest in Hawai'i and the promising future projected by the Hawai'i State Tourism Functional Plan.

The State Tourism Functional Plan, adopted by the 1982 Hawai'i State Legislature, predicted a continued, albeit slower, growth of tourism in the islands. It pointed to studies that foresaw tourism as Hawai'i's most important growth industry for at least the next decade and projected that visitation would reach 6.43 million by 1990 and 7.83 million by the end of the century. The planners felt such increases would enable Hawai'i to maintain an unemployment rate under 6 percent. To accommodate this moderate expansion, when compared to previous decades, the plan anticipated a need for an additional 26,100 hotel rooms to be constructed between 1980 and 1990. Over two-thirds of these rooms were proposed for the neighbor islands, to be constructed in existing designated resort areas.

The plan's visitor projections for 1990 were fairly accurate, as in the decade following the opening of the Hyatt Regency Maui, Hawai'i's visitor count jumped from 3,928,906 to 6,723,530. This increase did, indeed, lead to further expansion of the neighbor islands' room count, including a large number of high-end, high-priced resort hotels.[19] As the 1980s turned into the 1990s, *grande luxe* resort hotels appeared on Lāna'i as well as at Po'ipū on Kaua'i and Wailea on Maui, each of these new hotels seemingly more splendid, more lavish, and more distinctive than the last. They celebrated Hawai'i's incredible climate and lush vegetation, establishing a sense of place through their open, flowing spaces, and coupled the casual, informal tropics with a less-than-sedate sense of opulence. Rather than try to one-up Hemmeter's over-the-top projects that had dominated the mid-1980s, a number of these decade-ending projects sought to recapture the gentle luxury and consummate taste established by Killingsworth's Mauna Lani Bay and Halekulani hotels of the early 1980s. Most retained, in one guise or another, the precepts set down by the Mauna Kea Beach Hotel twenty years earlier as refracted by and commingled with the Hyatt Regency Maui. They all resonated with luxury and a strong sense of place that correlated with romantic notions of an exotic, slow-paced South Seas paradise. The developers of these new resort hotels seemed to be in total agreement with the observations Hank Koppelman made at the Governor's Tourism Congress in December 1984.

> Dream fulfillment and image fulfillment are the prime motivators behind the need for quality investments such as those we have mentioned [the Halekulani and the Hyatt Regency Maui]. Dream fulfillment and image fulfillment are also the motivators behind the successful marketing and promotion of these quality type investments and Hawaii itself.[20]

LĀNA'I: HAWAI'I'S MOST EXCLUSIVE ISLAND

David Murdock (b. 1924), who took over as chairman of Castle & Cooke in 1985, led the new, super-charged explosion in luxury resort development by announcing his intention to open the island of Lāna'i to tourism. The sixth largest island in Hawai'i's chain, with a 1990 population of approximately 2,300, Lāna'i's primary industry since 1922 had been pineapple cultivation. With Castle & Cooke owning 98 percent of the island, Hawai'i's tourism boom had seemingly passed by the "Pineapple Isle," and up until 1990, the ten-room Hotel Lanai satisfactorily handled the island's modest visitor accommodation needs.

Under Murdock, Castle & Cooke shifted direction, building two high-end hotels, the Lodge at Koele and Manele Bay Hotel, and an eighteen-hole Greg Norman golf course on the island during 1989 and 1991. The Jack Nicklaus Challenge course followed in late 1993, and less than a year later, all pineapple operations terminated. The near overnight shift to tourism as the island's sole industry was as traumatic as it was dramatic for the residents of the island.[21] Although the change was a major upheaval from the residents' perspective, Lāna'i, with its sparse thirty miles of paved roadways and no traffic lights, remained bucolic. Pineapple fields were displaced by equally green pasturelands used to produce hay and for small-scale grazing by horses and cattle. As George Lidicker, general manager and vice president of Rockresorts, the initial operators of the two hotels, noted, "These are non-tour-group hotels, that cater to high-end independent travelers. They employ the most amount of people with the least impact on infrastructure. I know it's hard for the community because they can't compare, but imagine what a Holiday Inn or a Hemmeter property would do to this island. It would be a sin."[22] Even before the hotels opened, Honolulu newspapers warned potential visitors that Lāna'i would not be "for the

faint of wallet";[23] the exclusivity of the new resort was firmly established in the public mind in 1994 when Bill Gates booked the entire island for his New Year's Day wedding, excluding all paparazzi and reporters. To further assure the privacy of the marriage ceremony, the thirty-eight-year-old billionaire rented every helicopter on the island of Maui to prevent any spying from the sky.

Castle & Cooke dedicated almost the entire 140.6 square mile island of Lānaʻi to resort purposes. A near mind-boggling concept, Castle & Cooke Resorts, the company formed to develop the hotels, and the island of Lānaʻi brought the idea of a destination resort into the realm of wide screen and high definition. The company sank $360 million into upgrading the island's facilities and building the two new hotels, transforming a land formerly dominated by a pineapple plantation into "Hawaii's Most Exclusive Island." Upon deplaning, guests registered for their stay at the newly constructed airport terminal, emphasizing the image that they had checked into the island, rather than one of its two luxury resort hotels. Eight miles apart, the two hotels offer the best of two worlds, the mountains, and the sea. Regardless of which hotel guests call their home-away-from-home, they have open access to the varied atmospheres, amenities, and hospitality extended by both establishments. Minibuses shuttle guests between the two hotels with stops in Lānaʻi City, the sole town on the island, as well as the airport.

Lānaʻi offers a truly unequaled approach to an island getaway, made incomparable by the high degree of excellence maintained by both hotels. Each is annually ranked among the best resort hotels in the world, each for its own individual merits. *Zagat*

---

opposite *Lodge at Koele, Lānaʻi, 1990. The large pineapple, painted by Calley and Adan O'Neill, adorning the entry gable serves not only as a reminder of the island's economic past but also revitalizes the nineteenth-century symbol for hospitality.*

declared the Lodge at Koele to be the finest resort hotel in the United States in 2002, while *Condé Nast Traveller* placed it number one in its 2002 list of the "World's Best Places to Stay" and also selected it as the best resort hotel in the U.S. in both 2001 and 2002. The larger Manele Bay Hotel has usually always ranked close behind the Lodge at Koele, with the 2003 *Condé Nast Traveller*'s readers poll including it at number six among Pacific Rim resorts. The two hotels clearly live up to their advertised "timeless luxury for the new millennium."

The hotels, both designed by the Honolulu firm Group 70 International, set forth new resort design paradigms for Hawaiʻi. Group 70 was formed by Gus Ishihara in 1971; two years later, Francis Oda, a graduate of Cornell University, joined the company as its president. Under Oda, it steadily grew to become one of Hawaiʻi's preeminent architecture, planning, and interior design firms of the late twentieth, and early twenty-first centuries. In addition to numerous Hawaiʻi projects, the visionary architects of Group 70 have undertaken hotel and resort projects in Australia, Indonesia, Tahiti, and the Philippines, as well as a housing project in China. They received the Lānaʻi hotel commissions as the winner of an invited competition. The two hotels each address their distinctive environments in a compelling manner, maintaining a strong commitment to developing architectural forms appropriate for the islands and recognizing Hawaiʻi's little-known, but broad, range of microclimates that adds considerable depth to the Lānaʻi resort experience.

The Lodge at Koele, sited at a 1,760-foot elevation, was the first to open, and the two-story, 102-room "mountain retreat" remains the largest wood-frame building in the state. To set the tone for the lodge prior to its opening, management likened it to the Hotel Hana Maui, which they imagined to be their closest competition.[24] Like the remote Maui resort hotel, the Lodge at Koele, at its

clockwise from top left *Lodge at Koele, Great Hall; dining room; Fireplace Garden Suite; octagonal shaped library with its parquet floors and coffered ceiling*

opening, had no in-room televisions or radios, and marketed itself as an opportunity "to find peace, solitude, and a taste of real paradise. Life as it used to be. Life as it should be. Life as it is on the island of Lāna'i."[25] Standing alone amidst former pasturelands, the lodge emphasizes a rural tranquility and solitude, softly embellished by a pair of genteel croquet courts and an eighteen-hole putting course.

Unlike the less-pretentious Hotel Hana Maui, with its understated refinement, the $46 million hotel dripped "subdued elegance" and offered a late 1980s and early 1990s sense of grandeur and majesty. Conceived as a Victorian country estate, the Lodge at Koele emits a neo-Queen Anne revival aura with its octagonal corner turrets, large lānai, gabled dormers, and widow's walk. The rambling composition's broad, gracious lānai serve as outdoor covered passageways connecting the main body to the guest wings, their cushioned wicker furniture inviting tranquil moments of repose.

A baronial hall, replete with two large stone fireplaces and a thirty-five-foot-high ceiling, resonates with a dense sumptuousness. The tenor of the Great Hall is intimately sustained by four rooms symmetrically situated off each corner of the entry hall. The octagonal-shaped library, game room, and music room each sport a fireplace, and each features a distinctive decor embodying its proclaimed function. Embellished by such distinctive accoutrements as elephant-hide-covered chairs, with floors, ceilings, and doors hand painted with island floral motifs, a pervasive posh elegance permeates the atmosphere. Lavishly adorned, costing over $430,000 a room to construct, the lodge includes a pair of 2,200-square-foot one-bedroom suites, each with their own fireplace and balconies. Removed from the ocean, the Lodge at Koele's high-end rustic

Lodge at Koele, Great Hall. The eclectic decor brings together Asia and the American Southwest.

design fits its setting, serving as an alternate environment to its island partner, the Manele Bay Hotel.

Located eight miles away from Lāna'i City, down a twisty mountain road, the 250-room oceanfront Manele Bay Hotel opened in April 1991, its three stories making it the tallest building on Lāna'i. It gracefully embodies a sense of Hawai'i by reviving an earlier local style of architecture, inspired by the 1931 Kamehameha School for Girls in Honolulu designed by C. W. Dickey and Bertram Goodhue & Associates. Costing approximately $112 million, $450,000 a room, to build, the hotel is a series of pavilions connected to the main lobby by covered breezeways enframing sumptuous gardens that amble down its twenty-eight-acre site and turn the trudge to one's hotel room into a special joy unto itself. The masonry structure features the green tiled, double-pitched hipped roofs and detailing, such as the masonry grillwork, of the Kamehameha School. Like many other major seaside resorts, openness prevails, with grand terraces, a loggialike lounge, and spacious public spaces, including the larger-than-life, commodious, Chinese-themed Kailani Terrace. A restrained, but obvious, use of marble and the lobby's expansive volume instill a soothing sense of grandeur. Carved out of the hillside, the hotel follows in the seaside tradition of the Mauna Kea Beach and Kapalua Bay hotels by overlooking the white sands of Hulopo'e Beach, the finest swimming beach on Lāna'i. Most guestrooms enjoy magnificent ocean views, animated by the near-shore frolicking of spinner dolphins and whales.

top right *Manele Bay Hotel, Lāna'i City, Lāna'i, 1991. Fu Dogs frame the entry court fountain.*
bottom right *Manele Bay Hotel, pool*
opposite *Lodge at Koele. A reservoir that served the ranch lands where the Lodge now stands was refurbished as a water feature.*

top left *Manele Bay Hotel, Haleaheahe Lounge*
bottom left *Manele Bay Hotel, lobby*
right *Manele Bay Hotel, Hawaiian garden*
opposite *Manele Bay Hotel, Chinese garden*

top, left and right *Manele Bay Hotel, Chinese garden*

bottom left *Manele Bay Hotel, Bromeliad garden. Designed by Walters, Kimura Motada, Inc., each of the five courtyard gardens has a distinct theme: the Japanese garden, Chinese garden, Hawaiian garden, Bromeliad garden, and Cosmopolitan garden.*

bottom right *Manele Bay Hotel, view of Hulapoʻe Beach from the lānai of an oceanfront room*

Addressing the emerging globalized sensibility of localism, the hotel strove to crystallize an image of appropriate regional architecture in Hawai'i and admirably succeeded. A number of Hawai'i's other resort hotels, as well as corporate and commercial structures, have since embodied the form. The design guidelines developed by Group 70 for the new city of Kapolei on the island of O'ahu also endorsed this style by requiring its incorporation in all public and commercial buildings. Thus, a form from an earlier time was reinvigorated to provide a resort hotel with a strong Hawai'i connection and has come to architecturally define a sense of place for the entire state.

HYATT REGENCY KAUAI: A HAWAIIAN CLASSIC

The Hyatt Regency Kauai in Po'ipū closely followed the design precedents of the Manele Bay Hotel but opened five months before it, in November 1990. It is "a Hawaii hotel that feels like a Hawaii hotel."[26] The developers, Kaua'i businessman Mel Ventura and two Japanese partners, Hawaii Takenaka Development and Toko Development Hawaii, wanted to avoid "probably at some perceived risk, the trend toward fantasy resorts."[27] Instead they imagined an architecture recalling an earlier Hawai'i and commissioned WATG to conceive such a hotel. Design architect Kevin Chun delivered a gem of the first order, "built in the style of Hawaii of the 1920s and 1930s."[28]

Stucco walls with masonry grilles, and green tiled, double-pitched hipped roofs dominate the four-story hotel, while an invitingly open floor plan incorporates an atrium and a myriad of arcades that open on spacious lawned gardens, the work of Honolulu

top right *Hyatt Regency Kauai, Po'ipū Kaua'i, 1990, Seaview Terrace surrounded by a water feature that cascades down to the lagoons below*
bottom right *Hyatt Regency Kauai, Ilima Terrace restaurant*

landscape architects Tongg Clarke & Mechler. The building, with its 602 guestrooms and suites, sprawls along the length of its fifty-acre oceanfront site with wings zig-zagging off either side of the central lobby. The plan maximizes ocean vistas, while meandering pathways, lānai, and open passageways emphasize a strong interaction with the climate. Although built in a windy area, the hotel's indoor-outdoor spaces remain unruffled, as they are all sited in wind saddles, frequently sheltered by other parts of the structure.

The wonder of Hawai'i's tropical environment is immediately impressed upon guests the moment they exit their vehicles at the porte-cochere, as a compelling view of the ocean greets them through the openness of the lobby and a lushly planted atrium. By a structured sequence of events, the guest moves from the initial glimpse of sky and sea, through the lobby and gently sloping, verdant atrium, down a stairway to the Seaview Terrace. From here, the space flows out to the terrace's edge where a stunning view of the entire shoreline and property presents itself.

The Ilima and Seaview terraces both offer opportunities for outdoor dining and imbibing, graced by the trill of waterfalls, a pool with swans—a la the Hyatt Regency Maui—and vistas of the vast Pacific across the landscaped gardens and five acres of artificial lagoons; the latter defines a transition space between the higher level hotel and the ocean. The Tidepools Restaurant, sited in the lower coastal plain area, adds a different dimension of tropical ambiance. Its thatched-roofed pavilions sit in and above koi ponds,

top right *Hyatt Regency Kauai, swimming pool. Although more restrained than a number of 1980s extravaganzas, the pool still reflected the new spirit with its meandering waterways and a giant slide.*
bottom right *Hyatt Regency Kauai, Tidepools Restaurant.*
opposite *Hyatt Regency Kauai, the man-made, salt-water lagoon with a mini-version of an isolated tropical isle, accessible only to swimmers*

top *Hyatt Regency Kauai, a garden guest wing*
bottom *Hyatt Regency Kauai, garden room*

beside a waterfall, whose waters originate at the lobby level. The dining area is broken into small intimate pods, each seemingly its own private structure, while the interior decor continues the romantic mood of the idyllic tropics with lauhala- and bamboo-clad walls and tapa-patterned ceilings.

The hotel's atmosphere differed remarkably from the fantasy-based resorts; as reporter Jan Ten Bruggencate observed, "Visitors will not exclaim loudly their surprise, but they'll nod, pleased, at numerous fine touches."[29] The building's foyer, with its two large calabashes and deco mirrors, elicits a subtle allusion to a manor house; the lobby sparks all the signals of opulent 1990s luxury with its travertine and marble floors, thirty-foot-high, open-beam ceiling, koa-paneled walls, massive, deco-inspired chandeliers, and refined level of ornament. Sugar cane, a reference to the former use of the area's lands, serves as a recurring motif in a variety of materials, appearing in the entry's bronze gateways, doorframes and transoms, in the koa reception desks, and in torchieres and other light fixtures. Other images of the islands pervade the hotel's decorative program and include shell-shaped wall sconces, pineapple-and-maile-motif light fixtures, and kapa patterns in the masonry grilles. The paintings behind the concierge and bell desks continue the hotel's evocation of 1920 and 30s architecture by depicting an ocean liner and airplane.

What's refreshing about the Kauai Hyatt is that it has a strong sense of place. Even though it is a big resort hotel, it feels Hawaiian. This hotel is proof that large resorts can be designed with a real awareness of what Hawaii hospitality is all about. It is one of the most successful designs of any large resort in the Islands.[30]

WAILEA COMES OF AGE

Similar to Lāna'i and Po'ipū, Kaua'i, Wailea on Maui also underwent a late-1980s surge of up-scale hotel development. The 1,400-acre area with its 1.4 miles of ocean frontage and 4,400 feet of sand beach had been proposed for resort development since the time of the state's 1960 Visitor Destination Areas Report. Matson Navigation, prior to the sale of its Waikīkī hotels to Sheraton in 1959,[31] had acquired these lands from 'Ulupalakua Ranch in 1957 with visions of converting it into a master-planned resort along the lines of Kā'anapali. In 1960, Wolbrink prepared "A Plan for Wailea Resort Development, Island of Maui" for Matson. As at Kā'anapali, the landowner did not intend to develop the property, but rather lease or sell parcels to others who would undertake the improvements. The plan envisioned two hotels, a golf course, two hundred deluxe apartment suites, and 750 residences on 530 acres, and an undersea bar and restaurant off the coral reef. Despite this early planning, steps to develop the area did not commence until after Matson's parent company, Alexander & Baldwin, acquired the property in 1969 and entered into partnership with Northwestern Mutual Life Insurance Company to form Wailea Development Company. Grovsener & Company was hired to execute a new master plan; they produced an innovative new town concept, a "City of Flowers," which excluded cars from the resort. A total "escape from the noise and bustle of city traffic,"[32] the resort was to include a small boat harbor, childcare facilities, and extensive open space. Like its predecessor, this plan, too, was shelved, and Belt, Collins and Associates was hired to develop yet another master plan.

As at Kā'anapali, and later at Kapalua, the first tangible indication of change was the construction of a golf course. Wailea's Blue Course opened in 1972, and in 1974, the resort's first condominium cluster, appropriately named Ekahi, the Hawaiian word for "one,"

Four Seasons Maui at Wailea, Wailea, Maui, 1990

was placed on the market. It was followed a year later by Elua (two), and then Ekolu (three) in 1978. As at Kapalua, condomania set in, and drawings were held to determine the buyers for Ekolu and the additional units constructed during the second phase of building at Elua. The latter project consisted of sixty-six units, mostly three-bedroom units selling for approximately $350,000 each. This represented a jump of $185,000 over the Ekolu sales prices of the previous year. The escalating returns on Wailea's residential sales led to a scaling back on the number of units built, as higher quality was favored over density.[33]

The first hotel, Pan American's 558-room Intercontinental, did not open until 1976, followed by United Airlines' Wailea Beach in 1978. With the momentary tourism recession of 1980, Alexander & Baldwin realized "that Wailea had simply been catching Kaanapali's overflow, so we had to establish an identity."[34] The Wailea Destination Association was formed in 1981, and the slogan, "A Place Apart," was selected to market the resort.[35] Contrasting itself with Kāʻanapali, which had gained a reputation as "an action-oriented hotspot of activity,"[36] Wailea moved to position itself as a peaceful getaway, addressing itself to the "50/50 crowd," those over fifty years old and earning over $50,000.

However, Wailea continued to be overshadowed by Kāʻanapali and Kapalua, and it was not until the construction of the Four Seasons Maui at Wailea and the Grand Hyatt Wailea, both owned and developed by Japan-based TSA International, that this resort destination

opposite *Four Seasons Maui at Wailea, pool fountain at night*
top right *Four Seasons Maui at Wailea, Spago restaurant with views overlooking the pool and Wailea Beach*
bottom right *Four Seasons Maui at Wailea, elevator lobby. The tropical flora in the hand-painted ceilings injects a sense of the tropics into a baroque sky.*

garnered critical acclaim.[37] The former was the Four Seasons' first project in Hawai'i and also their first "from the ground up" resort hotel.[38] The Toronto-based hotel company primarily operated luxury business hotels; however, like the Hyatt and Embassy Suites chains, it decided to venture into the realm of resort hotels. Having already established an extensive business traveler base with a very high rate of repeat customers, the company felt it could build on its reputation and offer its clients high-end vacation venues as well.

Rather than try to play the fantasy extravaganza game, the Four Seasons came up with what it thought to be "a better formula for success [in Hawai'i]: good old-fashioned luxury."[39] The company consciously declared its intention of becoming the best hotel in the islands and expended $140 million on its 374-room facility. WATG, who had previously worked with the Four Seasons on their Newport Beach, California, hotel, was commissioned to design the new hotel, with instructions to build a palace. Officially opening in May 1990, before the Manele Bay Hotel and Kauai Hyatt Regency, the resort addressed the client's desires, but also expressed a strong connection to Hawai'i through its openness and landscaping. It sedately effused a gentle air of affluence, presenting a formal classical dignity within a concinnity of casual, flowing open-air spaces.

A substantial building with massive postmodern columns and shouldered archways, its solid masonry walls are gently subverted by courtyards, lānai, and open-air lounge areas. The primary public spaces focus on the lower-level, palm-enshrouded courtyard, with its pools, urn fountains, and formal parterre-forms desired by the owner. The courtyard expands and complements the classical atmosphere of the building while injecting a palatial sense

top *Four Seasons Maui at Wailea, Maile Suite living room*
bottom *Four Seasons Maui at Wailea, Maile Suite master bedroom*

of opulence. Refined use of materials, including white Simena limestone floors, brown Clooney Ribbon Flame limestone accents, and cast-stone framed openings, coupled with coffered ceilings, elaborate fountains, and a grand staircase to gracefully infuse a sense of nonchalant luxury. Art is found here and there, as focal points in appropriate places, handled in a much quieter manner than in a number of 1980s hotels. As Harry Eager noted in the *Maui News*, "Four Seasons' style is somewhat understated elegance. Not too understated—the bathrooms are full of real marble—but something less than a Chris Hemmeter fantasy resort. There will be fountains, but they won't have live dolphins in them."[40]

Sited above the beautiful Wailea Beach, named America's best beach in 1999, the eight-story building sits on a long, narrow, very tight 14.48-acre parcel. The hotel gently negotiates this hillside property through a series of terraces, which beguilingly conceal the building's actual height. Through such an approach, the Four Seasons Maui at Wailea, like the Halekulani, maintains a small-scale oceanfront presence. Design architect Chun further used the sloping terrain to great advantage by siting the parking lot on the uphill side, connecting it directly to the upper-level guestrooms and thereby facilitating convenient room-to-automobile access. Placement of the hotel's entry on the downhill portion of the resort afforded guests an immediate ocean greeting as they approach the porte-cochere.

Another successful adaptation to the narrow lot's constraints resulted in the daring placement of the 6,930-square-foot ballroom in the core of the hotel's public area, at lobby level, overlooking the pools and the Pacific. Rather than being shunted to the side, meetings and events remain in the heart of activity, an integrated part of

top *Four Seasons Maui at Wailea, lobby*
bottom *Four Seasons Maui at Wailea, open-air lobby*

Grand Wailea, Wailea, Maui, 1991. Jan Fisher's sculptural group of hula dancers extend a welcome to guests along their walk to the reception desk.

the hotel's ebb and flow. Framed open-air courtyards soften the interstice between hotel and meeting functions, creating a balmy and successful transition between business and pleasure. On the ballroom's roof, the architect placed a large, lawned courtyard accented by a linear water feature and a sculpture garden, appending additional open space to the grounds.

Maximizing the use of every square foot of its parcel, the hotel has a strong ocean orientation, offering horizon-encompassing panoramas from almost all of its public spaces. In addition, most of the guestrooms enjoy an ocean view from spacious lānai, thanks to a herringbone-pattern plan laid out at a forty-five-degree angle from the hallway. The finely appointed 550-square-foot rooms include 100-square-foot marble bathrooms with double vanities and lānai furnished in teak.

Costing just under $400,000 a room to build, the Four Seasons Maui at Wailea offered the highest-priced rooms in Hawai'i at the time of its opening, with units ranging from $325 to $5,000 a night. The Maile Suite, sitting atop the hotel's north tower, commanded the latter price and acquired the reputation of the most expensive room in the islands. Offering such luxuriousness, the well-proportioned hotel lived up to initial aspirations and consistently appears on *Zagat*'s highly touted list of the world's foremost resorts. In 2002, *Travel & Leisure* named it the best hotel in Hawai'i and the fifth best resort in the world; while *Condé Nast Traveller's* 2003 reader's poll listed it as the second best Pacific Rim resort.[41]

The Four Seasons Maui's neighbor on Wailea Beach, the $600-million, 787-room Grand Hyatt Wailea was touted by the *Honolulu Advertiser* to be "easily Maui's, if not Hawaii's grandest hotel"[42] at the time of its 1991 opening—a reputation it arguably maintains to this day. A tour de force designed by Previn Desai, of

CDS International, who studied architecture under Killingsworth at USC, it coalesced the past three decades' development of resort hotels in an extraordinary way. It heartily embraced the 1980s sense of a fantastic larger-than-life opulence as a major resort element, refining the directions set forth by Hemmeter's previous projects and bringing an ever-evolving sense of paradise to the fore with great finesse. Recognizing that the fantasy concept had been extended too far, it tempered the cartoonlike moments of fantasy and established a more credible architectural context.

An invigorating Caribbean red-orange facade, accented with bulbous cream colored lānaʻi, establishes an immediate energy for the nine-story building, whose height is mitigated through a careful utilization of the sloping terrain. The open central core of the sprawling hotel presents a strong *mauka-makai* axis and offers a series of pedestrian constrictions and releases, accented by water features and changes in elevation. Architectural elements dissolve into the astounding space they define, while plantings, sculptures, murals, and mosaics establish a sense of an exotic land bathed in opulence. The highly structured space reveals elements a little at a time, resulting in a spectacular processional of the highest order.

A sense of wonder commences at the circular entry drive, certainly the most dramatic in Hawaii. Herb Kane's statue of Kamehameha the Great reigns over the landscaped center and a sumptuous waterfall seemingly cascades down from the mountains, accentuating the roadway's sense of arrival. Amazement builds along an elongated variation on Mauna Kea Beach Hotel's and Mauna Lani Bay Hotel's entry walks, and explodes at an open-air atrium replete with a reflecting pool circumscribing a classical, copper-roofed pavilion and culminates a floor below with a view through the dining room to the Pacific laid out beyond a Mughal-inspired series of formal pools and fountains. This staggering introductory state-

Grand Wailea, view from the Grand Dining Room. Inspired by the Shalamar Gardens at Lahore, royal palms line an allée with its multiple fountains, lending an air of formal Mughal majesty to Hawaiʻi's paradise.

ment, carried off with supreme architectural aplomb, sets the tone for the remainder of the astounding Grand Wailea experience.

Sitting on forty fully developed acres, with over a million square feet under roof, the resort offers a variety of different, yet complementary, settings and includes five restaurants, twelve bars, and a 28,000-square-foot ballroom. The 4,850-square-foot, adults-only Hibiscus pool, inlaid with Mexican glass mosaic tiles, recalls the Halekulani Hotel's orchid pool; a 2,000-foot-long, 25,700-square-foot "action pool" features "whitewater" rapids, waterfalls, a water elevator, rope swing, and thirty-foot-high slides. The latter, the work of Howard Fields of Los Angeles, takes aquatic delight and exhilaration beyond Hemmeter's wildest dreams at the Hyatt Regency Maui and Waikoloa, two earlier Fields projects.

The Grand Hyatt Wailea also includes a thirty-million-dollar art collection. Previn Desai, who formerly sat on the board of Hawai'i's State Foundation on Culture and the Arts, commissioned contemporary Hawai'i art, placing island-themed sculptures, murals, mosaics, and stained glass throughout the hotel and its grounds as a major design component. Unlike some of its predecessors' use of art, most all of the Grand Wailea's works were produced by artists with a link to Hawai'i or its culture. They accentuate the hotel's celebration of the islands, with many of the pieces tangibly expressing a native-Hawaiian cultural dimension, a too frequently

top right *Grand Wailea, Humuhumunukunukuapuaa Restaurant. Water abounds on the Grand Wailea's grounds. The resort has 2.2. million gallons of water circulating in pools, ponds, lagoons, and streams.*

bottom right *Grand Wailea, Kincha, a Japanese restaurant. The structure housing the restaurant was built in Japan and disassembled and reassembled on site without the use of nails. It overlooks a landscape replete with eight hundred tons of rock imported from the base of Mount Fuji.*

opposite *Grand Wailea, Humuhumunukunukuapuaa restaurant*

neglected resort element amidst the clamorous images of exotic nature and climate. To augment this distinguished collection of contemporary Hawai'i art, the owner brought in works by Fernando Botero, Pablo Picasso, Andy Warhol, and Ferdinand Leger.

In addition to the numerous sculptures and water features, several ancillary buildings dot the expansive grounds. A New England-style wedding chapel used primarily for Japanese weddings sits on a small island of its own and features stained-glass windows executed by Yvonne Chang. Kincha, a Japanese restaurant, which overlooks a landscape replete with eight hundred tons of rock imported from the base of Mount Fuji, was built in Japan, disassembled, and reassembled on site without the use of nails. In a far corner of the property, the thatched roof Humuhumunukunukuapuaa Restaurant stands near a waterfall, surrounded by a salt-water lagoon and recalls the Kauai Hyatt Regency's Tidepools Restaurant.

Masterfully combining the spirit of Hemmeter's fantasy resorts with the refinement of the other early 1990s luxury resort hotels, the Grand Hyatt Wailea is a superb scripted space.[43] It tweaks all the right sensations in an impeccable manner to bedazzle and elicit paroxysms of amazement as well as evoke a sense of paradise and well being. In 1966, *Architectural Forum* asked the question, "Should resort hotels be judged by normal architectural standards?" and then went on to note that one "specialist in the design of such pleasure palaces" defended his work by claiming it to be "stage sets, fantasies, man-made mirages—not buildings." The

article dismissed this designer's hotels as "simply bad stage sets," but went on to applaud the Mauna Kea Beach Hotel for showing "that a stage set can be splendid architecture, and vice versa."[44] The Grand Hyatt Wailea accomplished the same sensitive balance, utilizing a dramatic vocabulary that embraces a baroque ebullience in a modern manner.

In contrast to the two oceanfront luxury hotels, the less ostentatious, less exuberant, but equally immaculate Diamond Resort of Hawaii was constructed at Wailea on the hillside, three hundred feet above the coastline. Diamond Resort Corporation, which operates twenty resorts in Japan, originally built this complex as a private hotel for its Japanese membership, but has since extended its hospitality to everyone. Opening in February 1990, the work of architect Takashi Okamoto of the Tokyo-based architectural firm, Nikken Sekkei Ltd., the resort offers a relaxed, self-assured alternative to its more elaborate neighbors.

Removed from Wailea's main roadway and hub of activity, the 72-unit cottage hotel is scattered on fifteen acres of grounds, making it one of the least dense resorts in Hawai'i. Its main building, a modern, yet rustic, craftsman design, further sets this small hotel apart. Recalling a medieval castle for inspiration, broad, squat turrets ground the corners of the main stone building. The lobby rotunda's thirty-six-foot-high, Japanese parasol-inspired ceiling is balanced by a capacious, lateral running lānai and a slightly smaller corner turret. The low-pitched, overhanging Chinese-slate rooflines combine with Kaua'i coral pillars and India sandstone floors and walls to impart an earthiness to the main building. A long, dual-story waterfall forms an incredible facade-length tropical moat. It cascades down to a below-grade koi pool, dramatically flows under the building, and emerges on the *makai* side as a stream that meanders brooklike through Japanese gardens

opposite, left *Grand Wailea, Napua Tower courtyard*
opposite, top right *Grand Wailea, Spa Grande*
opposite, bottom right *Grand Wailea. A roofed pavilion housing the Botero Bar stands on its own island in the middle of the Napua Tower's courtyard, with Jan Fisher's mermaid in the reflecting pool.*

and the remainder of the property. Dotting the landscape, eighteen quadruplexes house guests in nine-hundred-square-foot, one-bedroom suites, each with an ocean-facing lānai offering panoramic sunset views.

The decor jarringly contrasts with the muted natural forms of the main building in a manner often associated with modern Japanese architecture. Dramatic, ultramodern light fixtures in bold primary colors attract the eye, and large tapestries emulating the works of the Spanish artists João Miró and Pablo Picasso hang from the walls. The hotel, although outside the flow of Hawai'i's mainstream of resort design, nevertheless addresses the islands' compelling climate with its casual, flowing openness and gentle landscape harmony. It stands as a late-twentieth-century reminder of Hawai'i's on-going role as a place where East truly does meet West.

The new resort hotels at Wailea, coupled with those on Lāna'i, were the culmination of a shift in thinking for Maui County's visitor industry, as it moved from an emphasis on quantity to one of quality. The need for such a shift had been steadfastly advocated by Maui County Mayor Elmer Cravalho throughout the 1970s. It took root on Maui with the Kapalua Bay Hotel and was then accentuated by the success of the Hyatt Regency Maui. The latter tangibly heralded, in dollars and cents, the expanded luxury resort market, to which an increasing number of late 1980s resort hotels appealed. As a result, in 2004, Maui County accounted for 45 percent of Hawai'i's luxury class visitor accommodations.[45] In large measure, their successful provision of a paradise environment has led to Maui being annually selected as the "Best Island in the World" by *Condé Nast Traveller*, since 1994. If only Allan Temko could see them now.

top *Diamond Resort, Wailea, Maui, 1990, lobby. The mobilelike "surfboards in the moonlight" atop the rotunda's fluted columns add an eclectic contemporary craftsman flair with a touch of Hawaii.*
bottom *Diamond Resort, Taiko Restaurant*
opposite *Diamond Resort. A long, dual-story waterfall cascades down to a below grade koi pool and forms an incredible, facade length tropical moat for this hospitable castle.*

above *Diamond Resort. Falling Water Maui style: the facade's waterfall flows dramatically under the building and emerges on the* makai *side as a stream that meanders through Japanese gardens and the remainder of the property.*
opposite *Diamond Resort, grounds and cottages. A county-required run-off basin for storm water was made into an attractive water feature on the property.*

chapter 8

The Close of an Era

THE INTEGRATED MASTER-PLANNED destination-resort idea pioneered at Kāʻanapali in 1960 had come a long way. Hawaiʻi had, by 1991, eighteen such resorts, and others could be found wherever warm climates caressed the body, soothed the mind, and brightened the soul. Along with Mexico and the Caribbean, integrated destination resorts had, by this time, appeared in places such as Australia, Malaysia, and Thailand.[1] The United Arab Emirates, South Africa, Indonesia, Brazil, and India soon followed. These large-scale, self-contained developments, usually encompassing anywhere from 400 to 4,000 acres, followed the success of Hawaiian resort ventures and combined tourist accommodations with a broad range of support activities within a single location. Controlled by a master developer, each destination usually emerged slowly through a succession of phases, with construction following market demand and development needs. Without a doubt, the ideas of Donald Wolbrink, Walter Collins, and others have profoundly determined the environments in which many travelers worldwide now choose to relax. Resort hotels, sumptuous islands

opposite *Four Seasons Hualālai at Historic Kaʻupulehu, island of Hawaiʻi, 1996, King's Pool.*

unto themselves, have sparkled, all the while drawing inspiration from the sophistication of hotels such as the Mauna Kea Beach and the energy of the Hyatt Regency Maui. The experiences of SOM, Edward Killingsworth, and WATG have shaped a generation of resort hotel design.

In 1991, Hawai'i's visitor count topped 6.5 million, and a state-sponsored conference on resort development in Hawai'i and Japan optimistically projected that "much of future tourism development will be in the form of vacation resorts."[2] It certainly appeared that the islands were on track to hit their projected 7.83 million visitors by the end of the century. However, all was not as carefree as it appeared. Following the successes of those that came before, numerous new high-end hotels opened in the early 1990s and resulted in a glut of rooms for this market. In 1990 alone, 1,790 new luxury rooms appeared via new hotels and additions to existing operations, an 18.6 percent increase over 1989's count. With the onset of a worldwide economic recession, the Japanese investment bubble in Hawai'i popped in 1992. As early as May 1992, some people were predicting the end of megaresort development in Hawai'i. At a Pacific Rim resorts-and-golf conference, Malcolm Tom of Peat Marwick Management Consultants noted some disturbing signs: the occupancy levels at some Hawai'i resort hotels had dropped down to forty percent, and in some cases below twenty percent. The Grand Hyatt Wailea, which was expected to generate room rates of $500 a day, could only charge $200 to $250.[3] Soon a number of resort hotel owners found themselves in untenable financial situations, unable to repay the loans borrowed to develop their properties, resulting in liquidations at fire-sale prices. Hemmeter's Hyatt Regency Waikoloa, a $360 million project in 1987, sold for $55 million in 1993 and emerged as the Hilton Waikoloa. Similarly, the Ritz Carlton Mauna Lani, designed by WATG and completed in 1990 at a cost of $175 million, was acquired by Colony Capital in 1996 for $75 million and reopened as the Orchid at Mauna Lani.[4]

In the midst of these difficult times, Kajima Corporation decided to move forward with the construction of a Four Seasons Hotel on forty acres at Ka'ūpūlehu, the centerpiece of the first phase of a proposed 11,000-acre resort development on the island of Hawai'i. The previous owners and developers, IDG Development Corporation of Irvine, California, and Cosmo World Corporation of Japan, had obtained their zoning approvals in October 1988 and had announced a resort project for this property the following year. Cosmo World, which had developed golf course resorts in Japan, Europe, and the United States, envisioned an eighteen-hole, Jack Nicklaus-designed golf course and a five-star, six-hundred-room "grand hotel." Construction started on the golf course, roads, infrastructure, and the hotel's initial 350 rooms; however, Cosmo World soon found itself over extended, and in 1991, all work on the project halted. In order for Cosmo World to avoid possible bankruptcy, Kajima Corporation, a Japan-based construction company, who was Cosmo World's prime contractor at Ka'ūpūlehu and, in turn, their prime creditor, acquired the property.

The new owners, one of the largest construction companies in the world, completing projects in over twenty nations in Asia, Africa, Europe, and the U.S., quickly realized that their expertise lay in construction, not the development of a major resort project. Kajima Corporation undertook a search for someone to handle the development aspects of the project. Dr. Shoichi Kajima, a director and senior advisor to the Board of Kajima Corporation, hired Kim Richards, the president of the Athens Group, who had recently completed the environmentally sensitive Loews Ventana Canyon Resort outside Tucson, Arizona. Richards, Jeff Mongan, and Sam Ainslie arrived in August 1992 to operate the Kajima subsidiary in charge of the development that would eventually be known as Hualālai Development Corporation. They felt a new direction was necessary if the project was to differentiate itself from other resorts in Hawai'i. Richards looked around, listened, and quickly realized,

> The most successful luxury resorts on the Big Island—the Mauna Kea Beach and Kona Village among them—have succeeded over the years despite recession and increased competition. The secret? They are understated. They have preserved a pristine ocean environment, provided a Hawaiian sense of place and fostered interaction between staff and guests.[5]

Rejecting the trends of the past fifteen years, the new developers went back to the 1960s sources of resort development. Ed Kennedy, the *Honolulu Advertiser*'s travel editor, came to a realization similar to Richards and found,

> Tourists who come to Hawaii, especially those who come for the first time, are not looking for gimmicks. They are looking for Hawaii itself. And architecture—how the tourists' physical surroundings blend with the natural environment of the Islands—is playing an increasingly important role in the Islands' tourist dollar. Tourists are getting picky about where they stay and why.[6]

Interpreting a sense of Hawai'i through the lenses of the 1960s, simplicity re-emerged as part of the paradise paradigm. As a result, Richards urged the scrapping of the plans for a megaresort

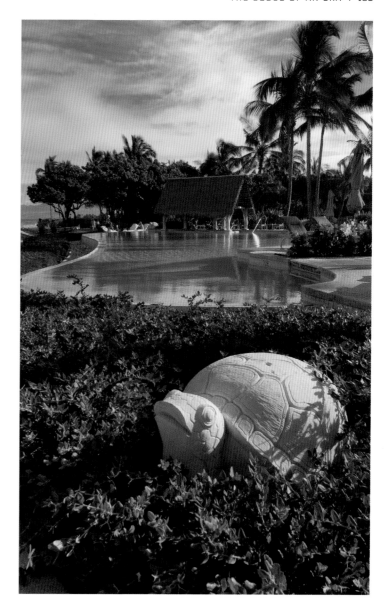

Four Seasons Hualālai, Sea Shell Pool.

above *Four Seasons Hualālai, Sea Shell Pool. The structure shading the hot tub was inspired by native Hawaiian canoe houses. Its roof is made from fountain grass woven into small tufts and applied to the frame.*
opposite *Four Seasons Hualālai, ocean view from the entry court over Beach Tree Pool*

hotel and the demolition of the partly built concrete highrise hotel, which Cosmo World had started to build and which already loomed three stories in the air. Belt Collins & Associates was retained to produce a new master plan, and in early 1993, Kajima Corporation gave its nod to the new direction.

The new plan of the Four Seasons Hotel drew upon the Mauna Kea Beach Hotel and Kona Village Resort for inspiration, combining the latter's low density and clusters of cottages with the former's immaculate landscaping, warm hospitality, and sophistication. Richards favored simplicity, going back to the basics, "the ocean, the earth and the people. . . . Our philosophy is, don't build anything that interferes with any of that."[7] With this in mind, Hill Glazier Architects from Palo Alto, California, were awarded the architectural commission, having previously worked with the Athens Group on the Loews Ventana Canyon Resort. John Hill and Robert Glazier founded their firm in 1983 and had established a reputation of successfully designing buildings that respected regional architectural traditions and natural site features, thereby reflecting the essence of a project's location and reinforcing a sense of place. The Four Seasons Resort Hualālai at historic Ka'ūpūlehu was their first project for Four Seasons and led to subsequent work for the hotel chain in Egypt, Dubai, Marrakech, Jerusalem, Tobago, Scottsdale, Baltimore, and Jackson Hole.[8]

The positive interaction between Richards' ideas, community leader Hannah Springer's insights, Belt Collins' site planning, and John Hill's designs resulted in a quiet, intimate hotel with an overwhelming residential neighborhood quality. A refined cottage hotel, in some ways reminiscent of the original Waiohai, the Four Seasons Resort Hualālai offers 243 rooms in thirty-six two-story cottages nestled along the shoreline, every room with an ocean view from its inset lānai. The Dickey-roofed abodes are grouped in four

crescents, each clustering around either a natural anchialine pond or a swimming pool. Each pool offers a different bathing experience, including a man-made, brackish-water King's Pond filled with tropical fish and stingrays—a snorkeler's delight. Each crescent seems to be a resort within the resort, giving the guests the impression of staying in a fifty-unit, rather than two-hundred-fifty-unit, hotel.

Although seemingly modest in character, a refined atmosphere makes it clear that this is a luxury retreat in Hawai'i. The guestrooms are commodious, almost suitelike, each over six hundred square feet in size. An entry foyer separates the living space from the bathroom, which in the ground-floor units includes an outdoor shower in an orchid-bedecked garden. High lava-rock walls allow the shower/garden to be open air yet private, and a glass wall allows bathers to view the shower/garden from the tub. The living area's decor is in a tasteful Hawaiian style.

The hotel's entry court is designed with a turning radius insufficient to accommodate buses, making it clear that this is not a package-tour-oriented establishment. From the entry court, guests are immediately presented with a view of the ocean and sky, across a gently sloping lawn and an infinity pool. Unobtrusively tucked in a corner of the drive, the lobby pavilion offers an unimposing, single-story facade that blends with the landscape. Built of mahogany, the lobby has wide openings and is capped with a Dickey roof; its interior is "grander in space than it was in attitude."[9] Wrap-around lānai overlook the landscaped grounds with glimpses of the cottages and ocean beyond. Paintings of old Hawai'i, by D. Howard Hitchcock and Lionel Walden, adorn the lobby, a rare glimpse of art in its public spaces. Most of the hotel's extensive collection is primarily found in the guestrooms, drawing heavily on John Kelley's Hawaiian prints of the mid-twentieth century. The hotel, with a

sensitivity rarely found in a resort setting, highlights the host culture: a Hawaiian cultural center sits at the heart of the property in the lobby pavilion's lava-rock-walled first floor and a canoe house, used by local paddlers, stands at one end of the property. In addition, a variety of cultural programs, including night presentations on Polynesian star navigation, are offered.

Like the art and architecture, the landscape design of the grounds is also subdued. The work of the Thailand-based Bill Bensley Design Group, it avoids colorful tropical exotics, working softly with a simple palette on a theme of greens and whites. The landscape seemingly appeared overnight, as Hualālai Development Company was able to reasonably purchase Mauna Lani Resort's entire nursery of mature plants during the travel-industry recession. Linking hardscape and terrain, the winding walkways are paved with concrete colored to match the lava flows surrounding the resort, and steps and pathways leading to the cottages feature lava-rock pavers specially sawn for the project. The free-standing oceanfront restaurant, Pahu i'a, continues the design tradition of Kapalua's Bay Club and Mauna Lani's Canoe House Restaurant, with its warm-wood construction and all-encompassing openness.

The resort's soothing, casual ambiance lends itself to the spirit of Hawai'i. Intentionally built "small to cater to an easily defined market segment—the top,"[10] the Four Seasons Resort Hualālai has positioned itself at the very highest tier of the luxury class. Its splendid service, excellent execution, and sedate sensibility have allowed the hotel to repeatedly appear at or near the top of numerous travel magazine polls. *Zagat*, in 2003 and 2005, named it the best resort in the United States, while *Condé Nast Traveller* has consistently named it the best resort spa on the planet, and, in 2002, the top Pacific Rim Hotel; the Travel Channel selected it as the World's Best Honeymoon site in 2005. As Ed Kennedy of the

Honolulu Advertiser observed, "It is designed to enhance the island's charms rather than shut them out. I got the feeling that someone had put intelligent thought into what Hawaii—and the Hawaiian tourist experience—is really about."[11]

In addition to housing its guests and providing a serene, relaxed version of paradise, the Four Seasons Resort Hualālai serves another well-recognized hotel function, which extends back at least to Kā'anapali:

> The little hotel is meant, not only as a place to stay and luxuriate, but also as the centerpiece of the much larger, exclusive residential development known as Hualalai that is growing up around it. In fact, one of its developers expressed the idea that it eventually would be viewed as a kind of "clubhouse" for the well-heeled owners of the more than 800 homes and condos planned for the development.[12]

As in other destination resorts, the Four Seasons Resort Hualālai serves as a major amenity to attract buyers for the surrounding condominium and single-family residential projects. The latter lots were initially priced between $600,000 and $5 million— from the start, the developers envisioned "an exclusive 'country club' type of community aimed at the top of the market."[13] Setting the tone for the surrounding community, the Four Seasons Resort Hualālai, like Honolulu's nineteenth-century Canton Hotel, offers room service to those dwellings situated in close proximity; resort residents have all the privileges of hotel guests.

top *Four Seasons Hualālai, lobby*
bottom *Four Seasons Hualālai, Pahu i'a restaurant*

When the Four Seasons Resort Hualālai opened in September 1996, it was touted to be "the end of an era in Hawaii hotel development…the last resort in Hawaii."[14] Although the latter statement was optimistically doubted by many, all seemed to agree that it would be the last built for some time. Investment money had completely evaporated, and as a result of spiraling costs to construct a megaextravaganza resort, hotel properties of the caliber developed over the preceding ten years were now fiscal impossibilities. Even more importantly, the prime, beautiful beachfront locations zoned for tourism development have all but disappeared in Hawai'i. To date, the "last resort" claim still holds true, and with Hawai'i's visitor count plateauing between 6.9 and 7.1 million a year during the opening five years of the twenty-first century, there appears to be little incentive to build more hotels. Indeed, several oceanfront destinations originally reserved for hotel development are now occupied by multimillion-dollar beach houses. The days of developing a luxurious hotel overlooking an incredible beach in Hawai'i seem to truly have come and gone.

Equally lost are the days of astronomical increases in visitor numbers to Hawai'i. The advent of aggressive global-tourism competition, coupled with Hawai'i's limited and fragile natural resource base, has led to a shift in thinking about tourism in Hawai'i. *Ke Kumu, Strategic Directions for Hawai'i's Visitor Industry*, a tourism plan that was adopted by the visitor industry statewide in 2002, formally announced a new priority for the state's number-one industry. Rather than measure success in terms of how many visitors came to the islands, industry success, henceforth, would be gauged in terms of revenues generated: Hawai'i has chosen to attract those people who will spend *more*. Obviously, such thinking had been around since at least the 1970s, as evidenced by the development of high-end resort hotels. However, absent a compelling

fiscal need, Hawai'i's travel leaders let the idea shift for itself. The assertion as an official industry goal will hopefully translate into an improved physical environment.

On October 14, 2004, the Hawai'i Tourism Authority adopted the *Hawai'i Tourism Strategic Plan, 2005–2015*, which set forth actions to implement the new strategic direction. It, as well as the 2002 plan, differs from almost all of Hawai'i's previous long-term tourism plans, as neither calls for an expansion in the number of hotel rooms.

> With Hawaii's focus on those segments which have higher per day and per trip spending, the destination must offer the type of accommodation necessary to attract higher-spending visitors across budget categories.…With visitors becoming more sophisticated and competing destinations developing exciting new hotels and attractions, keeping the major physical elements of Hawaii's tourism product up-to-date, competitive and in line with visitor expectations is critical.[15]

The strategic plan recommends a number of measures to encourage property owners to improve and renovate their holdings, including state tax incentives and expedited permitting. The plan also noncommittally marked a growing trend to convert hotels into time-shares. Travel experts noted that the time-share market was the quickest segment to recover after 9/11; it is viewed as a more stable clientele source, for the rooms have already been purchased. In 2004, time-shares comprised 8.3 percent of Hawai'i's visitor accommodations, and this number is anticipated to rise as time-shares present an opportunity for higher immediate returns on an

opposite *Four Seasons Hualālai, anchialine pond and guest cottages*

investment. The proposed 2006 demolition of the Kapalua Bay Hotel stands as a dramatic indicator of this new direction. David Cole, the chairman of Maui Land & Pineapple, says Kapalua's proposed "members only" resort center will be aimed at "'super premium' tourists."[16] Encouragingly, the design of the proposed 150-room, 300-million-dollar replacement for the Kapalua Bay Hotel has been awarded to Kevin Chun of Watanabe, Chun, Iopa & Takaki, who earlier designed both the Four Seasons Maui at Wailea and the Kauai Hyatt Regency while at WATG. The potential for something of architectural worthiness is present, but only time will tell what perceived market forces and owners may dictate.

The proposed demolition and redevelopment of the twenty-eight-year-old Kapalua Bay Hotel is not without precedent. The Waikiki Biltmore Hotel, the tallest building in the Territory of Hawai'i and a proud symbol of the advancement of Hawai'i's travel industry in 1955, was a pile of rubble a mere nineteen years later. Its successor, the Hyatt Regency Waikiki, heralded the coming of the Hyatt Regency Maui and the Halekulani hotels, with their distinctive approaches for presenting paradise to Hawai'i's visitors. Hopefully, whatever new tourism directions emerge with the rising of tomorrow's sun, the lessons learned and the beauty produced over the past four decades at Hawai'i's premier resorts will not be forgotten.

Built in an era of optimistic energy, which witnessed Hawai'i's visitor count leap from 686,928 in 1965 to over seven million in 2005, the distinguished environments of the premier resort hotels are an enduring legacy. Their elegant embodiment and relaxed perpetuation of a buoyant vision of enchanted isles, the Paradise of the Pacific, continue to cast a spell. May their gracious sway continue to influence not only the future design of tropical destination-resort accommodations, but also the human spirit.

above *Aloha!*
opposite *Four Seasons Hualālai, Palm Grove cottages bordering a natural anchialine pond*

NOTES

CHAPTER ONE: NINETEENTH-CENTURY VISITORS

1. Most historians point to the opening of Tremont House in Boston in 1829 as the first hotel in the United States. Designed by Isaiah Rogers, it differed from the tavern tradition by having distinctly defined public spaces for dining, lounging, and reception, with a clerk assigned exclusively to its front desk. In addition, it had private single and double bedrooms, with keys and interior water closets. This hotel also introduced to the world "rotunda men," who were later referred to as bellboys. "With the opening of the Tremont House in October 1829, the concept of hotel building and hotel keeping changed once and for all. Now it was the guest who mattered." Leslie Dorsey and Janice Devine, *Fare Thee Well: A Backward Look at Two Centuries of Historic American Hostelries, Fashionable Spas, and Seaside Resorts* (New York: Crown Publishers, 1964), 186. The book *A Description of Tremont House with Architectural Illustrations* (Boston: Gray & Bowen, 1830) became the standard reference for hotel building in the U.S. for over a half century.

2. For mention of Manini's Hotel or Oahu Hotel, see Ross H. Gast, *Don Francisco de Paula Marin* (Honolulu: Hawaiian Historical Society, 1973), 30, 296, 302; "Honolulu in Primitive Days," *Thrum's Hawaiian Annual for 1901* (Honolulu: Honolulu Star-Bulletin, 1901), 81, 83, 86; Adelbert von Chamisso, *A Voyage around the World with the Romanzov Exploring Expedition in the Years 1815–1818* (Honolulu: University of Hawaii Press, 1986), 185. Manini was Marin's Hawaiian name.

3. On occasion the terms "*mauka,*" "*makai,*" "Ewa," and "Diamond Head" are used to provide geographical orientation. *Mauka* denotes a direction toward the mountains, *makai* toward the ocean, Ewa toward the district beyond Pearl Harbor, and Diamond Head toward the famous crater.

4. Kamehameha I, or Kamehameha the Great, united the Hawaiian islands under his rule in 1810. The islands remained an independent kingdom until 1893 when Queen Lili'uokalani was overthrown. A Provisional government ruled Hawai'i from 1893 to 1894, at which time a republic was established. In 1898, the United States annexed the islands as a territory, a status it retained until 1959 when it became the fiftieth state.

5. Hiram Bingham, *A Residence of Twenty One Years in the Sandwich Islands* (Rutland, VT: Charles E. Tuttle Company, 1981), 95. Navarro's marital difficulties and banishment were recorded by Marin in his journal. See Gast, *Don Francisco de Paula Marin*, 296, 298. Reference to Novara's Inn may also be found in James Macrae, *With Lord Byron at the Sandwich Islands in 1825* (Honolulu: William F. Wilson, 1922), 43, 69.

6. Chester Lyman, *Around the Horn to the Sandwich Islands and California, 1845–1850* (Freeport, NY: Books for Libraries Press, 1971), 64.

7. Anthony Allen was born in 1774 and raised in New York, where slavery was legal until 1799. His mother was likely a slave and his father a freeman and mariner. Allen was freed at age twenty-four and fled to Boston. Like his father before him, he took to the sea and shipped out to China, the West Indies, the northwest coast of the U.S., and Hawai'i, where he settled in 1810 or 1811. Called Alani by the Hawaiians, he served as steward to Kamehameha the Great and acquired a six-acre parcel of land from the High Priest Hewa Hewa. Allen suffered a fatal stroke in December of 1835 and was buried near his dwelling. For more information on Allen, see Marc Scruggs, "Anthony D. Allen: A Prosperous American of African Descent in Early Nineteenth Century Hawaii," *Hawaiian Journal of History*, 1992, 55–94. For a mention of Allen's tavern activities, see Samuel Kamakau, *Ruling Chiefs of Hawaii* (Honolulu: The Kamehameha Schools Press, 1992), 304.

8. Charles Samuel Stewart, *Journal of a Residence in the Sandwich Islands, during the Years 1823, 1824, and 1825* (Honolulu: University of Hawaii Press, 1970), 157.

9. For information pertaining to the history of the building constructed by Major Warren, see "Business Building Changes," *Thrum's Hawaiian Annual for 1910*, 40–47; Thomas Thrum, "Honolulu in 1853," *Thrum's Hawaiian Annual for 1914*, 91; Mark Twain, *Letters from the Sandwich Islands* (New York: Haskell House Publishers, 1972), 26. References to Warren's hospitality may be found in James Hunnewell, "Honolulu in 1817 and 1818," *Papers of the Hawaiian Historical Society, Number 8* (Honolulu: Hawaiian Gazette Company, 1909), 16; Gast, *Don Francisco de Paula Marin*, 302; *Sandwich Island Gazette*, February 4, 1837, December 22, 1838, January 2, 1839. Reference to the Canton Hotel can be found in *Polynesian*, August 24, 1844.

10. Brief descriptions of Ka'ahumanu's residence, which was relocated and converted to the Blonde, may be found in Andrew Bloxam, *Diary of Andrew Bloxam* (Honolulu: Bernice P. Bishop Museum, 1925), 34; Charles Samuel Stewart, *A Visit to the South Seas in the U.S. Ship Vincennes, During the Years 1829–1830* (New York: Praeger Publishers, 1970), 2:115; and Gorham D. Gilman, "Early Streets of Honolulu," *Thrum's Hawaiian Annual for 1904*, 76–77.

11. Kamakau, *Ruling Chiefs of Hawaii*, 276. Kamakau further noted that Boki's saloon was called Polelewa, which referred to those people who lived off the monarch through their associations with the royal court. It was most likely a Hawaiian slang name for the Blonde.

12. Gilman, "Early Streets of Honolulu," 76–77. For Booth's advertisement for the Blonde, see *Polynesian*, July 10, 1847, 1 .

13. *Friend*, August 1, 1844, 72.

14. Gilman, "Early Streets of Honolulu," 98. For other references to activities at the Mansion House, see James Gleason, *Beloved Sister, Letters of James Henry Gleason, 1841–1859*, (Glendale, CA: A. H. Clark Co., 1978), 55, 62, 64, 68, 69.

15. *Friend*, January 15, 1847, 12.

16. Carl Skogman, *His Swedish Majesty's Frigate Eugenie at Honolulu, 22 June 1852 2 July* (Honolulu: Loomis House Press, 1954), 4.

17. For information on the French Hotel, see "Another Vanishing Landmark," *Thrum's Annual for 1915*, 153–54; "Last of Adobes is being Razed, Honolulu Landmark Soon to Disappear," *Pacific Commercial Advertiser*, October 13, 1914, 7; advertisements in *Polynesian*, September 9, 1848, January 13, 1855. For information on the Commercial Hotel, see Gilman, "Early Streets of Honolulu," 92; *The Polynesian*, January 3, 1846, January 13, 1855, June 27, 1857, contain typical advertisements. For information on the Globe Hotel, see Gilman, "Early Streets of Honolulu," 91; *Polynesian*, January 13, 1855, contains an advertisement providing further description of the premises. For information on the National Hotel, see *Hawaiian Star*, June 10, 1893, 5; *Polynesian*, October 13, 1855, announces Booth's intention to open the National Hotel Billiard Saloon on October 17th; The *Polynesian's* advertisement, June 27, 1857, is typical for the hotel; the advertisement, November 23, 1861, announced that the hotel was for sale and included a good description of the property; various September 1867 issues of the *Pacific Commercial Advertiser* again describe the hotel in an advertisement for its sale.

18. Thrum, "Honolulu in 1853," 91.

19. "Commercial Hotel No More," *Pacific Commercial Advertiser*, March 1, 1903, 1.

20. Mention of the two billiard tables in 1825 may be found in Bloxam, *Diary of Andrew Bloxam*, 30; the quotation derives from an advertisement for Merchant Exchange Billiard Saloon, W. E. Cuttrell, proprietor, *Polynesian*, June 27, 1857, 58. Billiard tables were a common inn feature since the 1700s. The 1807 innovation of the leather-tipped cue stick revolutionized the game. A score of years later, the introduction of chalk made "controlled spin" a consistent possibility. Wooden balls were soon supplanted by ivory ones, and the table also improved dramatically when slate tops started to replace wood in 1826 and when vulcanized rubber cushions were introduced in 1845. The British game usually utilized three balls and six pockets, while a popular American version involved four balls and four pockets. The now familiar American fifteen-ball pool game did not appear until the 1870s and did not gain great popularity until the twentieth century.

21. "Hulahula," letter to editor, *Pacific Commercial Advertiser*, November 13, 1856, 2.

22. Editorial, *Pacific Commercial Advertiser*, January 15, 1857, 2.

23. For the *Polynesian*'s perspective on the dance houses, see the issues January 17, 1857, January 22, 1857. This trial was yet another indication of the on-going social dynamic between Hawaiian, American, and European cultures during this still highly charged transitional period.

24. For information on the hula and its shifting relationship with the law, see Dorothy B. Barrere, Mary Kawena Pukui, and Marion Kelly, *Hula: Historical Perspectives* (Honolulu: Bernice Pauahi Bishop Museum, 1980). Following the 1857 acquittal of the National Hotel owner, the government again attempted to regulate the public performance of the hula by amending the 1851 law to explicitly state, "Any person who shall set up or promote any such theatre, circus, Hawaiian hula, show or exhibition" must obtain a license and eliminated the earlier loophole by making no reference to admission fees.

Feminine allure, especially in the form of the hula dancer, has played a role in the marketing of the islands to tourists since at least the late nineteenth century. See Jane C. Desmond, "Picturing Hawai'i: The 'Ideal' Native and the Origins of Tourism, 1880–1915," *Positions: East Asian Cultures Critique*, 1999, 459–501.

25. George Washington Bates, *Sandwich Island Notes* (New York: Harper & Row, 1854), 294–95. To better regulate hotels, sections 72–82 of the civil law of 1859 authorized the Minister of the Interior to grant a license "to any person applying therefore, in writing, to keep a hotel or victualing house for the term of one year, upon receiving the sum of $50." The applicant also had to post a $500 bond and pay a fee of $25 for each billiard table and bowling alley. The hotel could not be "a noisy or disorderly house," nor could it harbor deserting sailors, sell or furnish "any spirituous liquor" without a license, house prostitutes, or allow gambling. In addition, it had to close by ten o'clock at night. Unlike the U.S., the Kingdom of Hawai'i did not confine the selling of alcohol to taverns or hotels. Rather, the kingdom issued a liquor license, which by 1853, cost $1,000 annually. For information on the sale and regulation of alcohol in Hawai'i prior to 1850, see Richard Greer, "Grog Shops and Hotels: Bending the Elbow in Old Honolulu," *Hawaiian Journal of History*, 1994, 35–67.

26. Phebe Finnigan, "Our Lady Correspondence," *Pacific Commercial Advertiser*, December 29, 1866, 1.

27. Charles Nordhoff, *Northern California, Oregon, and the Sandwich Islands* (Berkeley, CA: Ten Speed Press, 1974), 66.

28. Katharine Fullerton Gerould, *Hawaii: Scenes and Impressions* (New York: Scribners, 1916), 87–88.

29. Bates, *Sandwich Island Notes*, 189. For a description of a stay at Deborah's Inn, see Lyman, *Around the Horn*, 171, 180.

30. Lyman, *Around the Horn*, 181.

31. Advertisement in *Polynesian*, July 9, 1853, 35.

32. Advertisement in *Polynesian*, October 13, 1855, 87. For a history of the Mansion House, see Ethel Damon, *Koamalu* (Honolulu: Star Bulletin Press, 1931), 365–75.

33. William Ellis, *Journal of William Ellis* (Rutland, VT: Charles E. Tuttle Company, 1979), 164–66.

34. S. S. Hill, *Travels in the Sandwich and Society Islands* (London: Chapman & Hall, 1856), 257–61. Also see H. M. Whitney, "Volcano House: Of the Old and the New," *Pacific Commercial Advertiser*, December 29, 1891.

35. "Notes of the Week: Ahead of Honolulu," *Pacific Commercial Advertiser*, January 13, 1866.

36. This advertisement ran in both *Pacific Commercial Advertiser* and *Hawaiian Gazette* starting April 14, 1866.

37. "Trip to the Volcano," *Hawaiian Gazette*, March 13, 1867, 2.

38. Twain, *Letters from the Sandwich Islands*, 212–13.

39. Dr. Samuel Kneeland, *Volcanos and Earthquakes* (Boston: D. Lothrop, 1888), 20–22.

40. Isabella Bird, *Six Months in the Sandwich Islands, Among Hawai'i's Palm Groves, Coral Reefs, and Volcanoes* (Honolulu: Mutual Publishing, 1998), 57–58.

41. See A. B. Hulbert, *Pioneer Roads and Experiences of Travelers* (Cleveland: A. H. Clark Company, 1904).

42. Information on the 1877 Volcano House derives from a Wilder Steamship brochure and is quoted in Gunder E. Olson, *The Story of the Volcano House* (Hilo: Petroglyph Press, 1974), 73. This book also contains information on the succeeding buildings. For additional information on the 1891 building, see Whitney, "Volcano House: Of the Old and the New."

43. "Notes of the Week: Hotel Meeting," *Pacific Commercial Advertiser*, April 8, 1865.

44. *Friend*, March 1, 1866, 17.

45. "American House," *Hawaiian Gazette*, March 3, 1866, 3.

46. Twain, *Letters from the Sandwich Islands*, 25.

47. Minister of Finance's Report to the Legislature of 1872, quoted in Ralph S. Kuykendall, *1854–1874: Twenty Critical Years*, vol. 2, *The Hawaiian Kingdom* (Honolulu: University of Hawaii Press, 1966), 173.

48. For information on the planning and later construction of the Hawaiian Hotel, see "The Hotel Project," *Pacific Commercial Advertiser*, January 28, 1871; "The New Hotel," *Pacific Commercial Advertiser*, May 13, 1871, 2; "The Hotel," *Hawaiian Gazette*, May 17, 1871, 2; "A Landlord," *Hawaiian Gazette*, August 23, 1871, 2.

49. Henry M. Whitney, *The Hawaiian Guidebook of 1875* (Rutland, VT: Charles E. Tuttle & Company, 1970), 13.

50. Information on the original character of the Hawaiian Hotel derives from Whitney, *The Hawaiian Guidebook of 1875*, 7–11; "The Hawaiian Hotel," *Hawaiian Gazette*, April 30, 1873, 2.

51. Advertisement in *Hawaiian Gazette*, March 20, 1872, 3.

52. Whitney, *The Hawaiian Guidebook of 1875*, 7–11.

53. Ibid., 13.

54. Nordhoff, *Northern California, Oregon, and the Sandwich Islands*, 19–20.

55. Bird, *Six Months in the Sandwich Islands*, 23–24.

56. For a brief history of the Hawaiian Hotel, see William E. Fisher, Jr., "Old Royal Hawaiian Hotel," *Paradise of the Pacific*, April 1935, 30.

CHAPTER TWO: HAWAI'I AS A TOURIST DESTINATION

1. All visitor industry statistics derive from numbers in the *State of Hawaii Data Book* (Honolulu: Office of Information, Department of Planning & Economic Development, State of Hawaii) and Robert C. Schmitt, *Historical Statistics of Hawaii* (Honolulu: University Press of Hawaii, 1977), unless otherwise noted.

2. Philibert Commerson, letter to a friend, quoted in Gavan Daws, *A Dream of Islands* (Honolulu: Mutual Publishing, 1980), 4. Commerson was a scientific member of Captain Louis Antoine de Bougainville's expedition that landed in Tahiti in 1768.

3. A. Grenfell Price, ed., *The Explorations of Captain James Cook in the Pacific as Told by Selections of His Own Journals, 1768–1779* (New York: Dover Publications, 1971), 252; Mark Twain, *Roughing It* (New York: New American Library, 1962), 341; Una Hunt Drage, *Hawaii Deluxe: Compiled from Her Own Diaries and Letters in 1901* (Honolulu: Star-Bulletin, 1952), 70; Isabella Bird, *Six Months in the Sandwich Islands, Among Hawai'i's Palm Groves, Coral Reefs, and Volcanoes* (Honolulu: Mutual Publishing, 1998), 23.

4. According to the first issue of the *Paradise of the Pacific*, January 1888, the appellation "Paradise of the Pacific" was apparently bestowed upon Honolulu by a New York journalist in the 1870s. Advertisements for the Hawaiian Hotel in the *Hawaiian Gazette*, as early as April 1873, referred to Honolulu as "The Famed Paradise of the Pacific." Hawai'i was frequently alluded to as a "fairyland" and "paradise." For example, see James Gleason, *Beloved Sister: Letters of James Henry Gleason, 1841–1859* (Glendale, CA: A. H. Clark Co., 1978), 26, 31.

5. Reprinted in *Paradise of the Pacific*, September 1895, 133.

6. See "Prospectus," *Paradise of the Pacific*, January 1888, 1.

7. Quoted in Ralph S. Kuykendall, *1874–1893: The Kalakaua Dynasty*, vol. 3, *The Hawaiian Kingdom* (Honolulu: University of Hawaii Press, 1966), 115.

8. For information on the increased steamship service to Hawai'i, see *Thrum's Hawaiian Annual for 1931*, 32, 53; "The Oceanic Company's New Steamships," *Thrum's Hawaiian Annual for 1902*, 176; William L. Worden, *Cargoes: Matson's First Century in the Pacific* (Honolulu: University Press of Hawaii, 1981).

9. "Alexander Young Hotel Opened with Ceremony and Merry Making," *Pacific Commercial Advertiser*, August 1, 1903. In referring to only one hotel of equal size and general attractiveness, the editor of the newspaper was thinking most likely of San Francisco's seven-story Palace Hotel, which opened in 1875 with 755 rooms. The editor was apparently oblivious to the ten-story Brown Palace built in Denver in 1892, the 339-room Hotel Del Coronado erected in 1888 in San Diego, and the block-long, five-story, four-hundred-room Plankinton House in Milwaukee, razed in 1915. For information on the Alexander Young Hotel, see Don Hibbard, "In Memorium: The Alexander Young Building," *Hawaii Architect*, November 1981, 6–9.

10. "The Moana Hotel: Waikiki's New Attraction," *Thrum's Hawaiian Annual for 1901*, 161–65. For the opening of the Moana Hotel, see "Moana Hotel Opened Last Evening with Glitter and Good Cheer," *Pacific Commercial Advertiser*, March 12, 1901, 2. For a history of the hotel, see Stan Cohen, *The First Lady of Waikiki: A Pictorial History of the Sheraton Moana Surfrider* (Missoula, MT: Pictorial Histories Publishing Company, 1995).

11. "Moana Hotel Opened Last Evening with Glitter and Good Cheer," *Pacific Commercial Advertiser*, March 12, 1901, 2.

12. Ibid.

13. Information on the Haleiwa Hotel may be found in "Hawaii's Finest Hotel," *Evening Bulletin*, August 5, 1899, 1; "Waialua's New Attraction," *Thrum's Hawaiian Annual for 1900*, 130–33; Leverett H. Mesick, "Discovery of Haleiwa Hotel," *Pacific Commercial Advertiser*, May 24, 1904, 5; "Waialua Revisited," *Thrum's Hawaiian Annual for 1904*, 101–2.

14. *Paradise of the Pacific*, August 1902, 16. This issue printed the entire three-page report.

15. In July 1919, the Hawaii Promotion Committee changed its name to the Hawaii Tourist Bureau (HTB). From 1903 until the advent of World War II, the territorial government consistently made annual appropriations in support of the committee and, subsequently, the bureau. The organization retained this name until 1945 when it became the Hawaii Visitor Bureau (HVB).

16. *Honolulu Advertiser*, February 1, 1927. This issue of the newspaper was a special Royal Hawaiian Hotel edition and covered the Royal Hawaiian Hotel in depth. For a history of the hotel, see Stan Cohen, *The Pink Palace: The Royal Hawaiian Hotel* (Missoula, MT: Pictorial Histories Publishing Company, 1986).

17. To help stay afloat during the economic depression of the 1930s, the hotel company encouraged the formation of the Waialae Country Club. This private club eventually acquired the golf course in 1942—after the golf clubhouse went up in flames and the military took control of the Royal Hawai'ian. For a history of the golf course, see Thomas Kemper Hitch and Mary Ishii Kuramoto, *Waialae Country Club: The First Half Century* (Honolulu: Waialae Country Club, 1981).

18. "Good for Hilo: Old Hilo Hotel Will Soon be Replaced," *Pacific Commercial Advertiser*, February 26, 1897, 1. For a history of the Hilo Hotel, see *Paradise of the Pacific*, April 1956, 20.

19. "Kona Hotel Will Benefit Tourist Trade," *Honolulu Advertiser*, October 28, 1928, 8.

20. "New Addition to be Built at Kona Inn," *Honolulu Advertiser*, August 4, 1929, 13.

CHAPTER THREE: THE INCIPIENT BOOM

1. Between 1950 and 1955, U.S. residents increased their expenditures on foreign travel by 53 percent.

2. In response to World War II, the Hawai'i Tourist Bureau suspended operations after June 30, 1942. The organization reopened as the Hawai'i Visitors Bureau in October 1945, with Mark Egan (1905–2001) at its head. Egan had come to Hawai'i during the war as an Army officer and had previously built up the convention and visitors bureaus in Pittsburgh, Cleveland, and Cincinnati. It was he who recommended the bureau be renamed the Visitors Bureau and worked hard to have the term "visitor," with its connotations of hospitality, supplant "tourist" throughout Hawaii's travel industry. In April 1959, the HVB separated from the Chamber of Commerce to become its own nonprofit organization.

3. In 1959, the HVB received $800,000 in government funds, while Bermuda obtained $1.5 million and the Bahamas spent close to $2 million. Florida boasted a tourist promotion budget of $6 million for the year 1960. Although the HVB was primarily supported by government funds, the private sector remained Hawai'i's primary source of promotional materials, with United, Pan American, and Northwest Orient airlines and Matson Navigation providing the lion's share. The airlines quickly discovered that their computerized reservation systems could facilitate the booking of other traveler needs, and their customers soon found they could not only purchase tickets from the airlines, but also hotel reservations and tours. Hawai'i also received prime time attention when *Hawaiian Eye* premiered October 7, 1959. The show ran until 1963, broadcasting the magnificence of Hawai'i weekly to a national audience.

4. "Plan for World Playground with Hawaiian Background," *Maui News*, August 8, 1945, 1.

5. "Fagan Hotel Project Underway," *Maui News*, March 6, 1946, 1.

6. James W. Carey, "Old Hawaii Blends with Modern Comfort at Hana Ranch Hotel," *Star Bulletin*, February 17, 1947, 4. Prior to coming to Hawai'i, Albert Ely Ives worked for Delano

& Aldrich and for Addison Mizner. He was asssociated with the alterations and additions to the Dupont Mansion to house Henry Francis Dupont's collections. In the 1950s, he designed Barbara Hutton's Japanese-style residence in Mexico.

7. For descriptions of the Hotel Hana Maui, see *Maui News*, August 24, 1946, 1; Ezra Crane, "Ranch Hotel Reopens June 15," *Maui News*, May 10, 1947, 1; James W. Carey, "Many Attractions at Hana Ranch Hotel are Old Hawaii," *Star Bulletin*, February 13, 1947, 4; Carey, "Old Hawaii Blends with Modern Comfort at Hana Ranch Hotel," 4; "Opening of Hotel Hana Ranch is Triumph Over Many Obstacles," *Star Bulletin*, June 20, 1947, 10; "Hana Attracts World's Wealthy, Noted Guests," *Star Bulletin*, January 27, 1961, Maui section, 6. For a more contemporary description, see Bruce Shwartz, "Splendid Isolation" *Distinction*, January 2004, 91.

8. Charles Nordhoff, *Northern California, Oregon, and the Sandwich Islands* (Berkeley, CA: Ten Speed Press, 1974), 35–36.

9. For further information on the history of Hawaiian Airlines, see Ray Thiele, *Kennedy's Hawaiian Air* (Kailua, HI: Olomana Press, 1994).

10. "Coco Palm Lodge at Wailua is Leased by Honolulu Hui," *Garden Island*, January 28, 1953, 1.

11. "Lihue Hotel is Purchased by Inter-Island," *Honolulu Advertiser*, January 8, 1946, 1.

12. "What is Kauai Going to Do About Tourists?" *Garden Island*, January 22, 1946, 8.

13. Jack Bryan, "Hotel Rooms Doubled on Garden Isle," *Star Bulletin*, February 25, 1964, 21.

14. "Coco Palm Lodge at Wailua is Leased by Honolulu Hui; Plans Being Considered for Expansion," *Garden Island*, January 28, 1953, 1.

15. "$125,000 Expansion Set for Kauai Coco Palms," *Honolulu Advertiser*, October 25, 1956, C4. For further information on Lyle Guslander and Island Holidays, see "Lyle Guslander of Island Holidays," *Hawai'i Business and Industry*, October 1966, 20–29; Robert Allen, *Creating Hawai'i Tourism* (Honolulu: Bess Press, 2004), 78–90.

16. Bryan, "Hotel Rooms Doubled on Garden Isle," 21.

17. See chapter four, page 93 for further information on George "Pete" Wimberly.

18. Charles A. Ware, "Architect of the Pacific Area—Tropic Air About His Planning," *Honolulu Advertiser*, October 10, 1965, A8.

19. "Why Waiohai?" *Beacon*, October 1963, 22.

20. Joe Arakaki, "New Resort is Striving for Old Hawaii Charm," *Star Bulletin*, April 15, 1962, magazine section, 21. Also see "Resort Hotel on Beach," *Architectural Record*, August 1966, 134.

21. "Hotel on Kauai Sold to Guslander," *Honolulu Advertiser*, July 24, 1964, 1.

22. "HVB Report Sees Waikiki as Tourist Bottleneck," *Star Bulletin*, March 27, 1948, 1.

23. "High Rise or Low Taste?" *Paradise of the Pacific*, July–August 1962, 42.

24. "The Million Dollar Image," *Paradise of the Pacific*, March 1962, 34.

25. For further information on the history and development of Waikīkī, see Don Hibbard and David Franzen, *The View from Diamond Head* (Honolulu: Editions Limited, 1986).

26. Act 150 of the 1957 Legislature formed the Territorial Planning Office, which, among other mandates, was charged with the responsibility to plan for the integrated and coordinated development of the tourist industry. The legislature indicated that the development of tourist facilities was an imperative need for which the planning office should provide direction.

27. John Child and Company, *Structure and Growth Potential of Tourism in Hawaii*, (Honolulu: Hawaii State Planning Office, 1960), 66.

28. Donald Wolbrink, "Planning, Designing New Resort Areas for Hawaii's Isles," *Landscape Architecture*, January 1963, 101. See chapter four, pages 88–89 for more information on Donald Wolbrink.

29. Ibid., 102. The projection of 20,000 rooms for Waikīkī proved conservative, as the district now houses over 37,000 rooms and still manages to maintain a green, tropical sensibility.

30. Hawaii State Planning Office, *Visitor Destination Areas in Hawaii: An Action Program for Development*, part 4, 9.

31. "Major New Visitor Destination Areas Will be Developed on Neighbor Islands," *Star Bulletin*, January 27, 1961, tourism section, 3.

32. Charles A. Ware, "Walter Collins: A Maui Boy Now Plans for Many Islands," *Honolulu Advertiser*, December 19, 1965, A10. See chapter five, pages 104–5 for more information on Walter Collins.

33. A memorandum, dated July 12, 1960, from Governor Quinn to the chair of the state's Department of Land and Natural Resources indicates, "I consider the spreading of Oahu's prosperity to the Neighbor Islands as one of Hawaii's most pressing needs, I wish also to assure you that I stand ready to put the entire support of the Administration behind the carrying out of this [destination resorts] program." See Economic Development, Material on Tourism file, Governor Quinn papers, Hawai'i State Archives, Honolulu.

The simultaneous mechanization and economic decline of the sugar and pineapple industries resulted in dramatic population drops on the neighbor islands. Between 1930 and 1965, the population of the island of Hawai'i went from 73,000 to 60,000; Maui from 49,000 to 39,000; and Kauai from 36,000 to 26,000. Hawai'i's leaders thus looked to tourism as a possible way to bolster the neighbor islands' economies. With both the governor and legislature in full support, government action had started by 1962 on 70 percent of the recommendations set forth in the 1960 tourism plans.

CHAPTER FOUR: HAWAI'I'S FIRST MASTER-PLANNED DESTINATION RESORT

1. For information on these 1950s planned communities, see "Diversity of Forms Marks New Italian Resort," *Progressive Architecture*, April 1959, 87, for coverage of Torre Del Mare, Italy; "Brazil: A New Oceanside Community," *Architectural Record*, June 1954, 188–91, for Pernambuco Beach. *Architectural Record*, July 1959, 205–7, also covers the reconstruction of Glyfada Lido, a beach resort property with a bath house, hotel, and twenty bungalows near Athens, by architects P. Sakellarios, P. Vassiliadis, and E. Vourekas.

2. Quoted in Walter A. Rutes and Richard Penner, *Hotel Planning and Design* (New York: Whitney Library of Design, 1985), 84.

3. "The Tourist Wave Lapping on Maui's Shores," *Star Bulletin*, July 7, 1960, 8.

4. "Resort Work Not Started," *Star Bulletin*, August 8, 1959, 2.

5. Charles Young, "Maui: Off and Running," *Paradise of the Pacific*, April 1962, 22.

6. Jack Bryan, "Neighbor Island Resort Industry Spurred by Maui Development," *Star Bulletin*, February 26, 1964, 6.

7. "Upside Down Hotel," *Maui News*, January 23, 1963, 16. For a discussion of the Sheraton Maui at Kaanapali, see "Hanging Garden on the Rocks in Hawaii," *Architectural Record*, March 1964, 149–54; "Biggest, Best Aloha, Tuesday," *Maui News*, January 19, 1963, 1; *Maui News*, January 23, 1963, 16–24.

8. "Hanging Garden on the Rocks in Hawaii," 149–54.

9. Ibid.

10. "Architect's Dream," *Maui News*, January 23, 1963, 24.

11. See the WATG website, www.watg.com. WATG's hotels can be found on all the populated continents. Over the course of fifty years the firm has received commissions for hospitality and leisure projects in California, Washington, Oregon, Florida, the Virgin Islands, the

Bahamas, Mexico, French Polynesia, Fiji, American Samoa, Guam, New Zealand, Australia, Korea, Japan, Thailand, Malaysia, Singapore, Indonesia, India, South Africa, Jordan, Egypt, the United Arab Emerites, Spain, England, and France.

12. Charles A. Ware, "Architect of the Pacific Area—Tropic Air About His Planning," *Honolulu Advertiser*, October 10, 1965, A8.

13. "A Resort Hotel on a Hawaiian Island," *Architectural Record*, July 1968, 148.

14. Peggy Dunsmoor, "Kona Hilton Set for Dedication," *Star Bulletin*, February 1, 1968, D1. For further information on the Kona Hilton, see Eugene Tao, "Kona Hilton Opening Set Friday Afternoon," *Hilo Tribune Herald*, February 1, 1968, 10; Dee Dickson, "The Kona Hilton Design: Blending with Hawaiiana," *Hilo Tribune Herald*, February 2, 1968, 4.

15. Eugene Tao, "Newest Hotel Opens," *Hilo Tribune Herald*, February 4, 1968, Orchid Isle section, 1.

16. The first regular direct air service between the mainland and a neighbor island started in 1967 when Hilo greeted sixteen such flights a week. By April 1968, the number of mainland arrivals into Hilo had increased to thirty-two. ". . . And Progress in the Air," *Hilo Tribune Herald*, February 4, 1968, 4.

17. "Kona Hilton Becomes Largest Hotel on Big Island," *Honolulu Advertiser*, February 5, 1969, C8.

18. Young, "Maui: Off and Running," 21.

19. "Kaanapali, the New Look in Master Planning," *Hawaii Business and Industry*, April 1966, 61.

20. Frederick Simpich, Jr., *Dynasty of the Pacific* (New York: McGraw-Hill, 1974), 196–97.

21. "Kaanapali, the New Look in Master Planning," *Hawaii Business and Industry*, April 1966, 61.

22. Glenn Kimura, "Resort Destinations in Hawaii and the Resort Master Planning Process" *Hawaii-Japan Resort Development Workshop* (Honolulu: Hawaii State Office of International Relations, 1991), 21.

23. Since 1988, this figure has remained fairly constant, with 32 percent of Hawai'i's visitors staying exclusively on only one neighbor island in 2003. Of the slightly over two million people who visited only one neighbor island, 57 percent chose Maui as their venue. As articulated in the tourism plans prepared in 1960, the diversion of a portion of Hawai'i's visitors to the neighbor islands was consciously intended for the establishment of destination resorts. This redirection of visitors did not profoundly impact the economic success of Waikīkī. Although an increasing percentage of tourists stayed exclusively on a neighbor island, the total number of visitors staying in Waikīkī continued to climb, as Hawai'i's visitor count continued to grow until the early 1990s.

CHAPTER FIVE: WHERE GOD LEFT OFF: THE DIAMOND TIARA OF LAURANCE ROCKEFELLER AND A POLYNESIAN VILLAGE

1. Marnie Bassett, *Realms and Islands* (London: Oxford University Press, 1962), 155.

2. Hawaii State Planning Office, *Visitor Destination Areas in Hawaii, An Action Program for Development*, Part 3 (Honolulu: Hawaii State Planning Office), 57.

3. Hawaii State Planning Office, *Visitor Destination Areas in Hawaii, An Action Program for Development*, Part 4 (Honolulu: Hawaii State Planning Office), 13.

4. Information on Laurance Rockefeller's first trip to Hawai'i was garnered through Robert Butterfield and George Mason, interviews with author, 2004 and 2005, respectively, and from the following sources: "Laurance Rockefeller on Recreation Survey," *Star Bulletin*, July 16,

1960; "Man in Know—Rockefeller—Lauds Isle Tourist Planning," *Honolulu Advertiser*, July 18, 1960, B1; George Eagle, "Rockefeller to Build Resort," *Honolulu Advertiser*, February 5, 1961, A1; "Rockefeller Selects Big Island Hotel Site," *Honolulu Advertiser*, May 26, 1961, A1; "Miscellaneous Letters, Laurance Rockefeller," Governor Quinn papers, Hawai'i State Archives, Honolulu.

5. Gwilym S. Brown, "Pioneers in Every Sense," *Sports Illustrated*, June 28, 1965, 75.

6. For information on Belt, Collins & Associates, see David Cheever, *Belt Collins* (Mulgrave, Australia: The Images Publishing Group, 2003). For further information on Robert Belt and Walter Collins, see Perry Edward Hilleary, *Men and Women of Hawaii* (Honolulu: Honolulu Business Consultant, 1954), 34, 109; Charles Ware, "Walter Collins a Maui Boy Now Plans for Many Islands," *Honolulu Advertiser*, December 19, 1965, A10; "Robert Belt Named Engineer of Year," *Honolulu Advertiser*, February 26, 1967, B5; "Planning Firm Sees Hope for Honolulu's Problems," *Hawaii Business and Industry*, February 1967, 21–24.

7. "Rockefeller 'Sleep Tests' Hotel Plan," *Honolulu Advertiser*, August 15, 1962, B1.

8. "A Shocking Approach to Tranquility," *Sports Illustrated*, June 28, 1965, 76–79.

9. In 1956, SOM's Istanbul Hilton received an AIA award of merit, as did John Carl Warnecke's Mark Thomas Inn in DelMonte, California (now the Hyatt Regency Monterey). Victor Lundy's Warm Mineral Springs Inn in Venice, Florida (now a motel), was also given an award of merit in 1957, and I. M. Pei's Denver Hilton received a similar award in 1961. In addition to the Mauna Kea Beach Hotel, SOM received four other Honor Awards in 1966—a hefty 25 percent of the awards presented—clearly placing them at the architectural apex of America.

10. AIA jury comment is quoted in the *AIA Journal*, June 1967, 60.

11. For information on the *Esquire* and *Fortune* articles, see Jim Becker, "Jim Becker's Hawaii," *Star Bulletin*, December 15, 1966, H20; "Two Island Hotels Win High Rating," *Honolulu Advertiser*, November 18, 1967, C12; Richard Joseph, "The Three Greatest Hotels in the World," *Esquire*, December 1967, 205ff.

12. "Hawaiian Hotel Opens to Landscape," *Architectural Review*, August 1966, 79. For other professional coverage, see "Hawaiian Hotel at Mauna Kea Beach," *Architectural Record*, October 1964, 174–75.

13. For an informative history of the hotel, see Adi Kohler and Catherine Tarleton, *Mr. Mauna Kea* (Indian Wells, CA: McKenna Publishing Group, 2003). Laurance Rockefeller integrated a sophisticated selection of primitive and folk art from various Asian and Pacific rim cultures at his Hawai'i Hotel. He apparently followed in his brother's footsteps—in 1957, Nelson A. Rockefeller established the Museum of Primitive Art in New York City. When the museum closed in 1976, its collection became the basis for the gallery of primitive art at the Metropolitan Museum of Art.

14. Joseph, "The Three Greatest Hotels in the World," 122.

15. Caskie Stinnett, "Mauna Kea—One on the Isle," *Holiday*, March 1966, 26.

16. Leavitt Morris, "New Hawaiian Hotel Assessed with a Critical Eye," *Christian Science Monitor*, December 14, 1965, 12.

17. Horace Sutton, "The Mauna Kea Caper," *Saturday Review*, August 21, 1965, 34.

18. Brown, "Pioneers in Every Sense," 79.

19. Cobey Black, "Rockefeller's Regal Roost," *Paradise of the Pacific*, July–August, 1965, 26.

20. Kay Lund, "Unique Kona Village 'Couldn't be Built,'" *Star Bulletin*, March 30, 1966, A14.

21. Ibid.

22. "Isolated Big Island Hotel to Open Soon," *Hawaii Building and Industry*, May 1965, 61.

23. *Los Angeles Times*, November 6, 1966, section l, 15.

24. The Hotel Bora Bora was completed in 1961.

25. *Fargo Forum*, January 23, 1971.

26. Bob Krauss, "Life is Happy-Go-Lucky at Remote Kona Village," *Star Bulletin*, October 11, 1966, B1.

27. Unidentified travel article in a scrapbook at Kona Village Resort; Cobey Black, "Who's News with Cobey Black," *Star Bulletin*, August 18, 1965, E14; Lund, "Unique Kona Village 'Couldn't be Built,'" A14.

28. Advertising campaign slogan used at various times by the Kona Village Resort.

29. Jack Bryan, "Neighbor Island Resort Industry Spurred by Maui Developments," *Star Bulletin*, February 26, 1964, 6.

30. *Denver Post*, March 22, 1970.

31. The length-of-stay statistics for the neighbor islands derive from Belt, Collins & Associates, *The Kohala Coast Resort Region/Island of Hawaii* (Honolulu: Belt Collins and Associates, 1967).

CHAPTER SIX: GRACE AND STYLE: THE REFINED MAGIC OF EDWARD KILLINGSWORTH

1. See "Another Waikiki at Waialae," *Star Bulletin* July 26, 1960, 8; *Star Bulletin*, November 2, 1961, 1.

2. "Planning Board Rejects Hilton Hotel," *Star Bulletin*, May 5, 1960, 1; "Letter Indicates Hilton Does Seek Zoning Shifts," *Star Bulletin*, July 26, 1960, 1.

3. "Letter Indicates Hilton Does Seek Zoning Shifts," 1. The construction of the Kahala Hilton and the neighboring Kahala Beach condominium led to the elimination of the Waialae golf course's oceanfront holes and a redesign of sections of the course. The championship tournament arrived in the form of the PGA's Hawaiian Open in 1965, which continues today as the Sony Open. See Thomas Kemper Hitch and Mary Ishii Kuramoto, *Waialae Country Club: The First Half Century* (Honolulu: Waialae Country Club, 1981), 57–58.

4. "Hilton's Isle Realtor Not Surprised by Vote," *Star Bulletin*, July 7, 1960, 1.

5. "Blaisdell Vetoes Hilton Rezoning," *Honolulu Advertiser*, August 19, 1960, A1. Time did prove the mayor correct in his assessment that Hilton could not ignore the lure of the islands, as the world's second largest hotel chain opened its first Hawai'i location in 1961, when it acquired Henry Kaiser's Hawaiian Village in Waikīkī, three years before the opening of the Kahala Hilton.

6. "Cost of Hilton Luxury Hotel Placed at $10–$15 Million," *Star Bulletin*, July 27, 1960, 1; "Plush Kahala Hilton Hotel to Open in December," *Honolulu Advertiser*, November 1, 1963, B1.

7. David Eyre, "Kahala Hilton, This Sumptuous Hostelry Has a Significance Not Fully Realized by Many Honolulu People," *Beacon*, November 1963, 31.

8. Shideler Harpe, "Council Seen Approving Waialae Rezoning Plan," *Star Bulletin*, July 26, 1960, 1; Kay Lund, " Kahala Hilton—Newest Jewel in Global Necklace," *Star Bulletin*, January 18, 1964, 13.

9. Eyre, "Kahala Hilton," 14, 30.

10. See *Beacon*, January 1964, 5.

11. "Structure Gains World Attention," *Star Bulletin*, February 3, 1964, 20.

12. "Luxury is Feature of New Hotel," *Honolulu Advertiser*, January 15, 1964, B1.

13. Ibid. For further coverage of the Kahala Hilton, see Ted Kurrus, "The Kahala Hilton," *Star Bulletin*, November 28, 1963, 15; Mary Cooke, "Art and Local Research Shaped Kahala-Hilton Hotel at Waialae," *Star Bulletin*, January 19, 1964, D1; Howard M. Y. Wong, "Kahala Hilton Has Elegance," *Star Bulletin*, March 13, 1966, A10; Charles Turner, "Expanding Waikiki Adds a New Hotel, " *New York Times*, January 19, 1964, xx22.

14. "Visiting Engineers Eye Hawaii's Prestressed Concrete Structures," *Engineering News-Record*, October 24, 1963, 22–23.

15. Quoted in Herbert Weisskamp, *Hotels: An International Study* (New York: Frederick A. Praeger, 1968), 196. For a history of the hotel, see Ed Sheehan, *The Kahala: The Hotel that Could Only Happen Once* (Honolulu: Kahala Hilton Hotel, 1990). For additional information on the initial year of operation and marketing strategies, see Tomi Knaefler, "Kahala Hilton Low in Occupancy, but High in Quality," *Star Bulletin*, October 10, 1964, 13. The article "Isle Beauty and Vitality Amaze Hotelman Hilton," *Star Bulletin*, November 2, 1961, A1, notes Hilton's vision of his hotels combating communism, which is further examined in Annabel Jane Wharton, *Building the Cold War* (Chicago: University of Chicago Press, 2001).

TWA purchased the Kahala Hilton in 1968. As the primary promoters of travel destinations airlines gradually expanded into the hotel business in order to get more bang for their buck. PanAm would build the InterContinental Hotel at Wailea, and Hawai'i's other major carrier, United Airlines, purchased the nationwide Western (now Westin) chain, which included the Ilikai Hotel and Makaha Inn in Hawai'i, and also purchased an interest in Amfac's Island Holidays holdings.

16. Esther McCoy, *Case Study Houses, 1945–1962* (Los Angeles: Hennessey & Ingalls, 1977), 164.

17. Charles Young, "Maui Off and Running," *Paradise of the Pacific*, April 1962, 21.

18. "$25 Million A&B Maui Resort," *Star Bulletin*, September 18, 1964, 1.

19. Emil A. Schneider, "A & B Plans 750 Rooms in Maui Resort Complex," *Honolulu Advertiser*, October 1, 1964, A1A.

20. Frederick Simpich, Jr., *Anatomy of Hawaii* (Toronto: Coward, McCann & Geoghegan, 1971), 110.

21. "Kapalua, Maui, Resort to Be for the Affluent," *Honolulu Advertiser*, May 22, 1975, C1.

22. "MLP's Money Machine," *Hawaii Business*, May 1977, 52.

23. "Putting a Price on Paradise," *Hawaii Business*, May 1979, 17.

24. Between 1975 and 1979, units that originally were purchased for $135,000 were being resold for at least $500,000.

25. Robert McCabe, "Luxury Development Approved on Maui," *Star Bulletin*, February 19, 1976, B5.

26. To protect against the wind, the original lobby design included enormous double-hung window elements whose sash weights planned to be hung within the concrete column clusters. Budget constraints eliminated this winter-storm protective amenity.

27. Roy Nickeson, "Luxury Resort Formally Dedicated, From Kiawe to Kapalua," *Maui News*, October 27, 1978, 1.

28. Don Debat, "Kapalua," *Star Bulletin*, December 14, 1978, F1. For additional information about the hotel, see Horace Sutton, "The Pineapple Paradise of Kapalua," *Star Bulletin*, September 17, 1978, E1; "Kapalua Bay Hotel Opens," *Star Bulletin*, October 30, 1978, D4

29. "Halekulani Hotel Gets a Reprieve," *Honolulu Advertiser*, August 22, 1979, A2.

30. Simpich, *Dynasty in the Pacific*, 104.

31. "Hawaii Needs Distinctive Building Type," *Honolulu Advertiser*, February 27, 1927, 12.

32. Japanese investment into Hawaii's hotels began in 1963, when Kenji Osano purchased the Princess Kaiulani hotel from Sheraton. By 1977, he owned 4,200 hotel rooms on Oahu, 20 percent of Waikīkī's total, including the Moana, Surfrider, Royal Hawaiian, and Sheraton Waikiki. During the early 1970s, Hawai'i Governor George Ariyoshi encouraged foreign investment in the islands, and the number of Japanese-owned hotels rose. During the late 1970s, the yen soared in value, resulting in another surge of Japanese investment in Hawai'i. The purchase and renovation of the Halekulani was but one of a number of major acquisitions. See Kit Smith, "Osano: Rags to Royal Hawaiian," *Honolulu Advertiser*, July 21, 1977, A1; "Japan's

Investment in Hawaii," *Star Bulletin*, April 19, 1979, A12; "Japanese Lead in Island Investments," *Star Bulletin*, July 27, 1979, B11.

33. Susan Hooper, "Halekulani's Visionary Retiring," *Honolulu Advertiser*, March 29, 2002, C1.

34. Anne Harpham, "Halekulani, New Hotel Clings to Its Heritage," *Honolulu Advertiser*, August 29, 1983, B1; Kit Smith, "Regent-Kid's Young, But Well-Muscled," *Honolulu Advertiser*, May 9, 1982, F5. Initially, Maui Land & Pineapple wanted Regent International Hotels to manage the Kapalua Bay Hotel when it opened in 1978. However, as the company had not yet established an international reputation, the resort developer acquiesced to the financiers' desire to have Rockresorts as the operators. For biographical information on Robert Burns, see Wallace Mitchell, "Man on the Move at Kahala Hilton," *Honolulu Advertiser*, December 15, 1965, A26.

35. Harpham, "Halekulani: New Hotel Clings to Its Heritage," B1. For further information, see Thelma Chang, *Memories of Our House Befitting Heaven: A Halekulani History* (Honolulu: Halekulani Corporation, 2002).

36. For detailed information, see *Waikiki Special District Design Guidelines* (Honolulu: City and County of Honolulu Department of Land Utilization, 1997).

37. Michael Carlton, "A Rebuilt Halekulani Returns to Waikiki Glory," *Honolulu Advertiser*, October 9, 1983, D6.

38. In addition to the hotels discussed in this chapter, Killingsworth's office also designed the Waikiki Parc Hotel in conjunction with the redevelopment of the Halekulani property and in 1992 designed the Ihilani Hotel (1993) as the signature hotel for the Ko Olina Resort on O'ahu's leeward coast.

39. Quoted in Glenn Mason, *Kenneth Francis Brown, FAIA* (Honolulu: American Institute of Architects/Hawaii State Council, 2004), 13.

40. Leigh Critchlow, "Mauna Lani Opens: 'Beauty and Bucks,'" *Hilo Tribune-Herald*, February 15, 1983, 1.

41. Peggy Cochrane, "Killingsworth, Edward A(bel)," in *Contemporary Architects*, ed. Emanuel Muriel, 427 (New York: St. Martin's Press, 1980).

42. Jerry Hulse, "Mauna Lani Bay Hotel Reflects Grace and Style," *Star Bulletin*, April 15, 1984, F11. For other reactions to the hotel, see Ronn Ronck, "Mauna Lani: Splendor Along the Coast," *Honolulu Advertiser*, February 13, 1983, E1; Michael Carlton, "Two Different Settings for Big Island Romance," *Star Bulletin*, March 18, 1984, D1.

43. To better comprehend the delectability of a stay at one of the Mauna Lani's bungalows, see Julia Reed, "Relax It's Yours," *Condé Nast Traveller*, September 1998, 110ff. For information on the bungalows' conceptual predecessor, the exclusive Hideaway Cottage at the Kahala Hilton, see Burt Anderson, "For $150 a Day: Cottage Plus Waterfall," *Honolulu Advertiser*, April 11, 1965, E1.

44. Critchlow, "Mauna Lani Opens," 1.

45. "A Special Hotel," *Honolulu Advertiser*, February 16, 1983, A8.

46. See *Condé Nast Traveller*, November 1990, 207. The top four were ranked in the order presented. Hawai'i garnered eight of the top ten spots in the poll. The Mauna Kea Beach Hotel was ranked fifth, the Hyatt Regency Maui eighth, Hotel Hana Maui ninth, and the Stouffer Waiohai tenth.

CHAPTER SEVEN: FANTASY BECOMES REALITY, AND BEYOND

1. Russ Lynch, "Push Drive for Beautification," *Star Bulletin*, September 10, 1969, A12.

2. In 1965, 36,400 Japanese visited Hawai'i. Five years later, after Japan eased its restrictions on tourist spending abroad, the number of visitors more than tripled to 131,500. By 1977, the total reached 440,000. These figures derive from Hank Sato, "Japanese Take over Isles as Tourists," *Star Bulletin*, February 20, 1979, progress section, 4. Throughout the 1970s, eastbound visitors, primarily from Japan, accounted for 22 to 24 percent of Hawai'i's tourist population. In 1984, eastbound visitation topped the one million-visitor mark and by 1990 had exceeded two million, 32 percent of Hawai'i's visitors.

3. The beachfront town of Kīhei on Maui exploded without the benefit of a master plan, from 305 units in 1970 to 3,109 units by 1979. Most were all housed in concrete boxes, transforming a quiet village into a strip of hotels, condominiums, and shopping centers.

4. "The Over the Thrill Crowd," *Time*, May 28, 1979, 39.

5. The advent of toll-free 1-800 numbers contributed to the growth of FITs, facilitating individuals who wished to make their own travel arrangements. Toll-free dialing, "interstate INWARD WATS," was introduced by AT&T in 1967; however, it was not until the early 1980s that it gained wide use, following the development of centralized databases allowing businesses to have a single, nationwide 1-800 number, rather than different numbers for each state. By 1991, 40 percent of AT&T's long-distance network would be toll-free calls.

6. Ruth Ann Becker, "Doing It Right!" *Hawaii Business*, May 1983, 70.

7. One morning in 1988 or 1989, guests descended the elevator to the lobby to be greeted by a tangle of banyan branches—the mighty tree had been toppled by high winds in the wee hours of the night. Even without the tree, the majestic space remains compelling. For media response to the hotel, see Lois Taylor, "An Unfinished Symphony," *Star Bulletin*, April 21, 1980, B1; Anne Ray, "The Guest is in a Fantasy World," *Maui News*, April 25, 1980, Light Life, 2. Ronn Ronck, "He Designs Homes Away from Home, " *Honolulu Advertiser*, September 4, 1989, B1, considers the interior design.

8. Linda Kephart, "All in Favor?" *Hawaii Business*, July 1985, 19–24.

9. Becker, "Doing It Right!" 70.

10. Norman M. Klein, *The Vatican to Las Vegas: A History of Special Effects* (New York: The New Press, 2004), 6.

11. Ruth Ann Becker, "Doing It Right?" *Hawaii Business*, May 1983, 63.

12. Megan Rowe, "Westin's Hawaiian Reality," *Lodging Hospitality*, October 1989, 112–15.

13. This term was applied to the two Westin hotel projects in Linda Kephart, "All in Favor?" *Hawaii Business*, July 1985, 19–24.

14. David Lodge, *Paradise News* (New York: Viking, 1992), 260–61.

15. Linda Kephart, "Hot Spot," *Hawaii Business*, November 1984, 64–65.

16. Lodge, *Paradise News*, 261.

17. Madelin Schneider, "Hemmeter Builds Multi-billion Dollar Fantasy Resort Empire," *Hotels & Restaurants International*, July 1989, 15. For information on Hemmeter's later activity, see Gina Mangieri, "The Incomparable Hemmeter Returns," *Pacific Business News*, October 10, 2003, 1. Hemmeter's obituary appeared in *Pacific Business News*, November 28, 2003, 1.

18. Schneider, "Hemmeter Builds Multi-billion Dollar Fantasy Resort Empire," 16.

19. Between 1980 and 1990, visitor accommodations in Hawai'i increased by 17,020 rooms, with the neighbor islands accounting for all but 2,500 of those units. According to the *Honolulu Advertiser*, August 13, 1989, B4, a 1990 Pannell Kerr Forster report found that the state added 1,790 rooms in the luxury category, an 18.6 percent increase over the 1989 luxury room inventory of 9,600.

20. Hank Koppelman, "Quality and Quantity of Tourism for the Future," *Proceedings of the Governor's Tourism Congress December 10 and 11, 1984* (Honolulu: Department of Business and Economic Development, 1985), 35.

21. In 1990, people anticipated that the new hotels would bring an additional 40,000 to 60,000 people to Lāna'i annually. In 2003, the number of persons visiting the island exceeded 91,000, which added 853 persons to the daily population of Lāna'i. In addition, the development of upscale housing increased the population from 2,300 in 1990 to approximately 3,193 in 2000, an almost 30 percent increase.

22. Susan Hooper, "One Man's Island," *Hawaii Business*, May 1991, 26–28.

23. Ken Miller, "Little Lanai Will Take Big Bucks," *Star Bulletin*, August 25, 1989, A8; "Murdock: Style Awakes Sleepy Lanai," *Star Bulletin*, March 24, 1989, A8.

24. Miller, "Little Lanai Will Take Big Bucks," A8.

25. Promotional brochure for Lāna'i, 2002.

26. Jan TenBruggencate, "New Hyatt Regency Kauai Has the Feel of Old Hawaii," *Honolulu Advertiser*, November 18, 1990, D1.

27. Ibid.

28. Russ Lynch, "Hyatt Regency Kauai to Open on Thursday," *Star Bulletin*, November 13, 1990, C1. Other luxury hotels to follow in this genre included the Ritz Carltons at Mauna Lani (1990) and Kapalua (1992), both also designed by WATG.

29. TenBruggencate, "New Hyatt Regency Kauai Has the Feel of Old Hawaii," D1.

30. "Kauai Bouncing Back," *Honolulu Advertiser*, February 5, 1995, D6.

31. Matson sold the Moana, Surfrider, Royal Hawaiian, and Princess Kaiulani for $18 million in 1956, as they were concerned that the lease on the Royal Hawaiian was due to expire in 1977.

32. Mansel Blackford, *Fragile Paradise: the Impact of Tourism on Maui, 1959–2000* (Lawrence, KS: University Press of Kansas, 2001), 195.

33. For a brief summary of the development of Wailea, see Liz Janes, "The Greening of Wailea," *Maui News*, February 2, 1999, C1. The Belt, Collins & Associates master plan anticipated Wailea having a population of 9,000. Thanks to the positive response to the more up-scale residential offerings and attendant scaling back of the resort, Wailea only had a population of a little over 5,000 in 2000.

34. Becker, "Doing It Right?" 67.

35. Promotional organizations for the various counties commenced in 1974, when the Maui County Visitor Association was formed as a means of augmenting the HVB's efforts. Individual resort associations followed, with the Kaanapali Beach Operators Association being among the first.

36. Becker, "Doing It Right?" 67.

37. TSA International's investments in Wailea were part of a major infusion of Japanese capital into Hawai'i in the late 1980s and early 1990s. As a result of the 1985 Plaza Accord, which significantly realigned international currency rates and sharply appreciated the Japanese Yen, Japanese investment in Hawai'i between 1985 and 1995 has been estimated to have been between $12 and $18 million. In comparison, Japanese investment from 1975 to 1985 totalled $850 million. See University of Hawaii Economic Research Organization, *Japanese Investment in Hawaii Past and Future* (Honolulu: University of Hawaii, 1998) and Rick Dayson, "Isle Real Estate is Bleeding Bargains," *Star Bulletin*, September 9, 1997, A1.

38. Earlier, the company had purchased existing resorts in Santa Barbara, Dallas, and Northern Ontario.

39. Greg Wiles, "Four Seasons Likes Climate in Hawaii," *Honolulu Advertiser*, August 13, 1989, B4.

40. Harry Eagar, "Service Seen as the Key as Four Seasons' Doors Open," *Maui News*, March 15, 1990, 1.

41. For a discussion of the Four Seasons Maui at Wailea, see Mary Scoviak-Lerner, "Aloha from Hawaii's 3 New Resorts," *Hotels*, March 1992, 40; Edwin Tanji, "Four Seasons Enters Isles' Resort Market," *Honolulu Advertiser*, March 5, 1990, D2; Harry Shattuck, "The Four Seasons Resort is Pure Luxury," *Star Bulletin*, December 21, 2003, F6. Other information was obtained through Kevin Chun, interview with author, March 2005.

42. Edwin Tanji, "A Truly Grand Hyatt," *Honolulu Advertiser*, September 1, 1991, E1.

43. Norman Klein grapples with a definition of the term "scripted space" in *The Vatican to Vegas: A History of Special Effects* (New York: The New Press, 2004), 2, 43. "These spaces were set up to provide only the fragrance of desire, for political or financial profit. But most of all, they were set up to release a 'marvel,' a briefly eloquent stupefaction. . . . It is an epic narrative, where the tangible is a membrane standing in for the powerful. It is a catholicity, a hint of the immutable—but also a warning that power is out of reach." Also see "Imaginary Space: Building the Impossible," *Nevada Historical Society Quarterly*, winter 1993, 274–82; "The Politics of Scripted Spaces: Las Vegas and Reno," *Nevada Historical Society Quarterly*, summer 1997, 151–59. In the latter, he defines the term as "a space to be walked through as a narrative, a story where the audience is the central character."

44. J. Bailey, "Sand, Sea, & SOM," *Architectural Forum*, May 1966, 80.

45. In 2004, Maui County had 2,658 luxury rooms that commanded prices over $500 per night. This represented 45 percent of the state's stock in that price range. Rooms in the deluxe and luxury range, commanding prices over $250 per night, accounted for 54.2 percent of Maui's units in 2004. Statewide in 2004, the 5,196 luxury rooms accounted for 10.8 percent of the total hotel units, while deluxe and luxury units constituted 52.9 percent of the total.

CHAPTER EIGHT: THE CLOSE OF AN ERA

1. Larry Helber, "Resort Planning, Design and Construction," in *Hawaii-Japan Resort Development Workshop* (Honolulu: Hawaii State Office of International Relations, 1991), 40–41.

2. Chuck Y. Gee, "Resort Industry Trends and Issues," in *Hawaii-Japan Resort Development Workshop* (Honolulu: Hawaii State Office of International Relations, 1991), 7.

3. Greg Wiles, "Mega-Resorts are Out, Conference Here Told," *Honolulu Advertiser*, May 29, 1992, B5.

4. "Hotels: Experts Say Fire Sales are Ending," *Honolulu Advertiser*, March 25, 1996, C1–C2.

5. Stu Glauberman, "New Resort Downsizes to Lure Upscale Guests," *Honolulu Advertiser*, July 23, 1996, A1.

6. Ed Kennedy, "A Hotel for All Seasons," *Honolulu Advertiser*, October 6, 1996, E2.

7. Stu Glauberman, "New Resort Downsizes to Lure Upscale Guests," *Honolulu Advertiser*, July 23, 1996, A1.

8. Since the Four Seasons Hualālai, Hill Glazier Architects has designed hotels for the Westin, Hyatt, and Ritz-Carlton chains. Its relationship with the Athens Group has continued with such projects as the Ritz-Carlton Bachelor Gulch in Vail, the Ritz-Carlton Half Moon Bay near San Francisco, and the Montage Resort and Spa at Laguna Beach, California.

9. Heather Smith Macisaac, "Four Seasons Hualalai," *Travel & Leisure*, February 1997.

10. Glauberman, "New Resort Downsizes to Lure Upscale Guests," A1.

11. Kennedy, "A Hotel for All Seasons," E2.

12. Ibid., E1.

13. Ed Kennedy, "Investment Era May Close at Hualalai," *Honolulu Advertiser*, September 27, 1996, A2.

14. Ibid., A1; Kennedy, "A Hotel for All Seasons," E1.

15. *Hawaii Tourism Strategic Plan, 2005–2015* (Honolulu: Hawaii Tourism Authority, 2004), 51.

16. Harry Eagar, "Kapalua Hotel is History," *Maui News*, January 13, 2005, A1.

BIBLIOGRAPHY

Aanavi, Don. *The Art of Mauna Kea: Asian and Oceanic Art at Mauna Kea Beach Hotel*. Honolulu: East-West Center, 1990.

Abraben, E. *Resort Hotels: Planning and Management*. New York: Reinhold Publishing, 1965.

Allen, Robert C. *Creating Hawai'i Tourism: A Memoir*. Honolulu: Bess Press, 2004.

Bangert, Albrecht and Otto Riewoldt. *Designer Hotels*. New York: Vendome Press, 1993.

Barrere, Dorothy B., Kawena Pukui, and Marion Kelly. *Hula: Historical Perspectives*. Honolulu: Bernice Pauahi Bishop Museum, 1980.

Bates, George Washington. *Sandwich Island Notes*. New York: Harper & Row, 1854.

Belknap, Jodi Parry. *Kaanapali*. Honolulu: Amfac Property Corporation, 1981.

Bell, Claudia and John Lyall. *The Accelerated Sublime: Landscape, Tourism and Identity*. Westport, CT: Praeger, 2002.

Belt Collins and Associates. *The Kohala Coast Resort Region/Island of Hawai'i*. Honolulu: Belt Collins and Associates, 1967.

Berger, Molly W. *Journal of Design and Propaganda Arts 25: The Americal Hotel*. Cambridge, MA: MIT Press, 2005.

Bingham, Hiram. *A Residence of Twenty One Years in the Sandwich Islands*. Rutland, VT: Charles E. Tuttle Company, 1981. First published 1847 by H. Huntington.

Bird, Isabella. *Six Months in the Sandwich Islands: Among Hawai'i's Palm Groves, Coral Reefs, and Volcanoes*. Honolulu: Mutual Publishing, 1998. First published 1875 by J. Murray.

Blackford, Mansel. *Fragile Paradise: The Impact of Tourism on Maui, 1959–2000*. Lawrence, KS: University Press of Kansas, 2001.

Bloxam, Andrew. *Diary of Andrew Bloxam*. Honolulu: Bernice Pauahi Bishop Museum, 1925.

Buck, Elizabeth. *Paradise Remade: The Politics of Culture and History in Hawai'i*. Philadelphia: Temple University Press, 1993.

Chamisso, Adelbert von. *A Voyage Around the World with the Romanzov Exploring Expedition in the Years 1815–1818*. Honolulu: University of Hawaii Press, 1986.

Chang, Thelma. *Memories of Our House Befitting Heaven: A Halekulani History*. Honolulu: Halekulani Corporation, 2002.

Cheever, David. *Belt Collins*. Mulgrave, Australia: The Images Publishing Group, 2003.

Cohen, Stan. *The First Lady of Waikiki: A Pictorial History of the Sheraton Moana Surfrider*. Missoula, MT: Pictorial Histories Publishing Company, 1995.

———. *The Pink Palace: The Royal Hawaiian Hotel*. Missoula, MT: Pictorial Histories Publishing Company, 1986.

Coleman, Simon and Mike Crang. *Tourism: Between Place and Performance*. New York: Berghahn Books, 2002.

Craft, Mabel Clare. *Hawaii Nei*. San Francisco: William Doxey, 1899.

Damon, Ethel. *Koamalu*. Honolulu: Star Bulletin Press, 1931.

Daws, Gavan. *A Dream of Islands*. Honolulu: Mutual Publishing, 1980.

———. *Shoal of Time*. Honolulu: University of Hawaii Press, 1968.

Dorsey, Leslie and Janice Devine. *Fare Thee Well: A Backward Look at Two Centuries of Historic American Hostelries, Fashionable Spas, and Seaside Resorts*. New York: Crown Publishers, 1964.

Drage, Una Hunt. *Hawaii Deluxe, Compiled from Her Own Diaries and Letters in 1901*. Honolulu: Star-Bulletin, 1952.

Ellis, William. *Journal of William Ellis*. Rutland, VT: Charles E. Tuttle Company, 1979. First published 1825 by Crocker.

Emanuel, Muriel. *Contemporary Architects*. New York: St. Martin's Press, 1980.

Farrell, Bryan H. *Hawaii: The Legend That Sells*. Honolulu: University Press of Hawaii, 1982.

———. *The Social and Economic Impact of Tourism on Pacific Communities*. Santa Cruz, CA: Center for South Pacific Studies, 1977.

———. *The Tourist Ghettos of Hawaii*. Santa Cruz, CA: Center for South Pacific Studies, 1977.

Finney, Ben and Karen Ann Watson. *A New Kind of Sugar: Tourism in the Pacific*. Honolulu: East-West Center, 1976.

Gast, Ross H. *Don Francisco de Paula Marin*. Honolulu: Hawaiian Historical Society, 1973.

Gerould, Katharine Fullerton. *Hawaii: Scenes and Impressions*. New York: Scribners, 1916.

Gleason, James Henry. *Beloved Sister: Letters of James Henry Gleason, 1841–1859*. Glendale, CA: A. H. Clark Co., 1978.

Gottdiener, Mark. *The Theming of America: Dreams, Media Fantasies, and Themed Environments*. Boulder, CO: Westview Press, 2001.

Guillemard, Arthur. *Over Land and Sea: A Log of Travel Around the World in 1873–1874*. London: Tinsley Brothers, 1875.

Hawai'i ka 'Oihana Hokele: The History of Hawaii's Hotel Industry, 1840–1990. Honolulu: Trade Publishing Company, 1990.

Hawaii State Planning Office. *Visitor Destination Areas in Hawaii: An Action Program for Development*. Honolulu: Hawaii State Planning Office, 1960.

Hawai'i Tourism Strategic Plan, 2005–2015. Honolulu: Hawaii Tourism Authority, 2004.

Henle, Fritz. *Hawaii*. New York: Hastings House, 1948.

Hibbard, Don J. and David Franzen. *The View from Diamond Head*. Honolulu: Editions Limited, 1986.

Hill, S. S. *Travels in the Sandwich and Society Islands*. London: Chapman & Hall, 1856.

Hitch, Thomas Kemper and Mary Ishii Kuramoto. *Waialae Country Club: The First Half Century*. Honolulu: Waialae Country Club, 1981.

Horvat, William J. *Above the Pacific*. Fallbrook, CA: Aero Publishers, 1966.

Hotel Design: International Portfolio of the Finest Contemporary Designs. Rockport, MA: Rockport Publishers, 1994.

Huffadine, Margaret. *Resort Design, Planning, Architecture and Interiors*. New York: McGraw-Hill, 2000.

Hulbert, Archer Butler. *Pioneer Roads and Experiences of Travelers*. Cleveland: Arthur H. Clark Press, 1904.

Japan-Hawaii Resort Development Workshop. Honolulu: Hawaii State Office of International Relations, 1991.

John Child and Company. *Structure and Growth Potential of Tourism in Hawai'i*. Honolulu: Hawaii State Planning Office, 1960.

Judd, Dennis R. and Susan S. Fainstein. *The Tourist City*. New Haven, CT: Yale University Press, 1999.

Kamakau, Samuel. *Ruling Chiefs of Hawaii*. Honolulu: The Kamehameha Schools Press, 1992.

Ke Kumu: Strategic Direction for Hawai'i's Visitor Industry. Honolulu: Hawaii Tourism Authority, 2002.

King, Pauline. *The Diaries of David Lawrence Gregg: An American Diplomat in Hawaii, 1853–1858*. Honolulu: Hawaiian Historical Society, 1982.

Klein, Norman M. *The Vatican to Las Vegas, A History of Special Effects*. New York: The New Press, 2004.

Kneeland, Dr. Samuel. *Volcanos and Earthquakes*. Boston: D. Lothrop, 1888.

Kohler, Adi and Catherine Tarleton. *Mr. Mauna Kea*. Indian Wells, CA: McKenna Publishing Group, 2003.

Kona Village Resort. Kailua-Kona, HI: Kona Village Resort, 1999.

Kuykendall, R. S. *The Hawaiian Kingdom*. Honolulu: University of Hawaii Press, 1966.

Lasansky, D. Medina and Brian McLaren. *Architecture and Tourism: Perception, Performance and Place*. New York: Berg, 2004.

Limerick, Jeffrey, Nancy Ferguson, and Richard Oliver. *America's Grand Resort Hotels*. New York: Pantheon, 1979.

Lodge, David. *Paradise News*. New York: Viking, 1991.

Lyman, Chester. *Around the Horn to the Sandwich Islands and California, 1845–1850*. Freeport, NY: Books for Libraries Press, 1971. First published 1924 by Yale University Press.

MacCannell, Dean. *The Tourist: A New Theory of the Leisure Class*. New York: Schocken Books, 1976.

Macrae, James. *With Lord Byron at the Sandwich Islands in 1825*. Honolulu, 1922.

McCoy, Esther. *Case Study Houses, 1945–1962*. Los Angeles: Hennessey & Ingalls, 1977.

Nordhoff, Charles. *Northern California, Oregon and the Sandwich Islands*. Berkeley, CA: Ten Speed Press, 1974. First published 1874 by Harper and Brothers.

O'Brien, Eileen. *Here's Hawaii: Pictorial Guide to the Hawaiian Islands*. Honolulu: Tongg Publishing Company, 1964.

Olson, Gunder E. *The Story of the Volcano House*. Hilo, HI: Petroglyph Press, 1974.

Palumbo, Dennis. *Government Participation in the Visitor Industry in Hawaii*. Honolulu: Legislative Reference Bureau, 1962.

Price, A. Grenfell. *The Exploration of Captain James Cook in the Pacific as Told by Selections of His Own Journals, 1768–1779*. New York: Dover Publications, 1971.

Proceedings of the Governor's Tourism Congress December 10 and 11, 1984. Honolulu: Department of Business and Economic Development, 1985.

Riewoldt, Otto. *Hotel Design*. New York: Ginko Press, 1998.

Rothman, Hal. *The Devil's Bargain: Tourism in the Twentieth Century American West*. Lawrence: University Press of Kansas, 1998.

Rutes, Walter A. and Richard H. Penner. *Hotel Planning and Design*. New York: Whitney Library of Design, 1985.

Rutes, Walter A., Richard H. Penner, and Lawrence Adams. *Hotel Design, Planning and Development*. New York: W. W. Norton & Company, 2001.

Schmid, Anne M. and Mary Scoviak-Lerner. *International Hotel and Resort Design*. New York: PBC International, 1988.

Schmitt, Robert C. *Historical Statistics of Hawaii*. Honolulu: The University Press of Hawaii, 1977.

Skogman, Carl. *His Swedish Majesty's Frigate Eugenie at Honolulu, 22 June 1852 2 July*. Honolulu: Loomis House Press, 1954.

Seiden, Allan. *Kalia & the Making of a Legend*. Honolulu: Hawaiian Legacy Archive Press, 2001.

Sheehan, Ed. *The Kahala: The Hotel that Could Only Happen Once*. Honolulu: Kahala Hilton Hotel, 1990.

Simpich, Frederick, Jr. *Anatomy of Hawaii*. Toronto: Coward, McCann & Geoghegan, 1971.

———. *Dynasty in the Pacific*. New York: McGraw-Hill, 1974.

State of Hawaii Data Book. Honolulu: Department of Business and Economic Development and Tourism, 1970–2004.

Stewart, Charles Samuel. *Journal of a Residence in the Sandwich Islands, during the Years 1823, 1824, and 1825*. Honolulu: University of Hawaii Press, 1970. First published 1828 by J. P. Haven.

———. *A Visit to the South Seas in the U.S. Ship Vincennes, during the Years 1829–1830*. 2 vols. New York: Praeger Publishers, 1970. First published 1931 by J. P. Haven.

Stoddard, Charles Warren. *Lazy Letters from Low Latitudes*. Chicago: Neely, 1894.

Thiele, Ray. *Kennedy's Hawaiian Air: Hawaii's Premier Airline*. Kailua, HI: Olomana Publishers, 1994.

Twain, Mark. *Letters from the Sandwich Islands*. New York: Haskell House Publishers, 1972.

———. *Roughing It*. New York: New American Library, 1962. First published 1872 by American Publishing Company.

Vrry, John. *The Tourist Gaze*. London: Sage Publications Ltd., 1990.

Waikiki Special District Design Guidelines. Honolulu: City and County of Honolulu Department of Land Utilization, 1997.

Weisskamp, Herbert. *Hotels: An International Study*. New York: Frederick A. Praeger, 1968.

Whitney, Henry M. *The Hawaiian Guidebook of 1875*. Rutland, VT: Charles E. Tuttle & Company, 1970. First published 1875 by H. M. Whitney.

Williamson, Jefferson. *The American Hotel*. New York: Arno Press, 1975.

Wimberly Allison Tong & Goo. *Wimberly Allison Tong & Goo: Designing the World's Best Resorts*. Mulgrave, Australia: Images Publishing Group, 2001.

Winks, Robin. *Laurance S. Rockefeller: Catalyst for Conservation*. Washington, DC: Island Press, 1997.

Worden, William L. *Cargoes: Matson's First Century in the Pacific*. Honolulu: University Press of Hawaii, 1981.

Yoder, Paton. *Taverns and Travelers*. Indianapolis: University of Indiana Press, 1969.

INDEX